STEPHEN LEACOCK
A BIOGRAPHY

By the same author:

FAIR DINKUM, *an autobiography*

Stephen Leacock in 1939.
Photo taken in the humorist's Montreal home by R. T. Ferguson.

(*Courtesy of Mrs. Seton L. Richardson, Montreal*)

Stephen Leacock

 *A BIOGRAPHY*

by David M. Legate

DOUBLEDAY CANADA LIMITED,
Toronto, Ontario

DOUBLEDAY & COMPANY, INC.,
Garden City, New York

1970

TO
CLASSMATE AND HELPMATE
MARJORIE CECELIA

Grateful acknowledgement is made to McClelland and Stewart, Ltd., Toronto; Dodd, Mead & Company, New York; the Oxford University Press, London; and The Bodley Head, London, for permission to reproduce extracts from Stephen Leacock's books, details of which will be found in Notes on Chapters.

CONTENTS

Contents

Preface

It has long been a strong feeling of mine that before those of us who knew Stephen Leacock actually join him, something should be done. That is the reason for this biography.

Sixteen years ago Dr. Gerhard H. Lomer, one-time librarian of McGill University and a confidant and colleague of Leacock, wrote: "A sympathetic biography of Stephen Leacock by one who knew him personally is a necessity; no one else could do it as it should be done."

On the other hand, Peter McArthur, a friend and mentor of Leacock and a respected humorist in his own right, stated: "As a matter of fact the final biographer of Mr. Leacock will only find it necessary to select from his published works the material for an adequate record of his life."

It is quite true that Leacock poured a great deal of himself into the bulk of his writing and that, consequently, much information about the man may be gleaned from his literary production. But the problem is to know where fact ends and fiction begins. By way of encouraging the present undertaking, Mrs. Donald (Barbara) Nimmo, Leacock's niece, who for ten important years served her uncle as chatelaine and secretary following his wife's death, has written: "Your connection with him at McGill should be of great help as all biographical work done so far has been by people who had never met him, and has been based solely on analysis of his literary work."

In his sixties, Stephen Leacock extended his condolences to any future biographer. He hadn't, he thought, moved about enough to be of much interest to the general public. At that time, of course, he had only visited a mere twenty countries, shaken the world with laughter, and inspired, if not precisely instructed, two generations of college students.

Lack of public interest in him is far from being a problem. The real challenge lies in trying to bring out the curious personality which lurked behind the well-known external trappings of the infectious chuckle, the ready quip, the rollicking essays, the general geniality. For his was not always a blithe spirit. He touched lightly on this when he said: "If a man has a genuine sense of humor he is apt to take a somewhat melancholy, or at least a disillusioned view of life. Humor and disillusionment are twin sisters." Leacock walked hand in hand with those sisters most of his life.

Though one must bear in mind Henry James' exhortation—"Never say you have the last word about any human heart"—the portrait which follows in these pages is drawn with as much accuracy as possible. It has been formed from my personal knowledge and other first-hand sources—the observations of relatives, former colleagues, and of those privileged to sit under him as a teacher.

Because of my conviction that Leacock was indelibly stamped by socio-historical forces even during the tender years before he left his homeland, it seemed essential to visit his birthplace and his childhood haunts in England. At one point, as I motored about the Hampshire countryside in search of clues and "atmosphere," I remarked to my twenty-year-old driver:

"I suppose you are wondering what I'm up to, crawling around churchyards, peeking into old buildings, talking to old people."

He admitted that he was a bit puzzled.

"Well, I'm collecting material for a book. Ever hear of a man called Leacock?"

"Sure," came the quick retort. "He was the fellow who flew the Atlantic fifty years ago with some character named Brown."

Much of Leacock's work is dated. His brand of humor is not to everyone's liking today. He wrote much too much for his own good. Yet in this centennial year of his birth Leacock remains in the world's consciousness. Royalties are still being realized from his books. His name keeps cropping up in unexpected parts of the globe. The U.S.S.R. treasures a native-produced forty-volume edition of his work in English. In 1955 it was announced in the Soviet News Bulletin that, of the thirteen Leacock books then in circulation in the U.S.S.R., his *Funny Pieces* had recently sold in excess of fifty thousand copies. In 1969 his moving little essay "How We Kept Mother's Birthday" was among the pieces set for study in Moscow high schools. More recently, a newspaper in Peking proclaimed the genius of Leacock for the unusual reason that, "like America's Mark Twain, Leacock perceived long ago that United States' imperialism not only wanted to seize the world's material wealth by force, but also sought to take possession of the cultural treasures of all other countries."

A story of entirely different flavor concerns what took place at a UNESCO conference in Paris. A Canadian representative was approached by a delegate of the Federal Malay States who had been a prisoner of the Japanese during World War II. He said he was particularly pleased to meet someone from the land of Stephen Leacock because he owed his sanity to Leacock. He had been able, he went on, to retain among his meagre effects a selection of Leacock's books. By reading and rereading them he and his fellow prisoners had managed to maintain their mental balance.

My own interest in Stephen Leacock spans the period from early adolescence to the present day. My first introduction to him came through my father. He was a rather rare person, who, despite the fact of being a Presbyterian minister, had been blessed with a delightful sense of humor. Since Father was clearly transported by the Leacockian antics and since I respected his judgment, I quickly developed the habit of visiting the local public library every Saturday morning to borrow a Leacock volume. My judgment of my father's judgment was soon confirmed. Here was sparkling fun. But along came a black Saturday. As usual, I had blindly pulled off the shelf a Leacock title and taken it home. What I read dismayed me. It was deadly dull. Leacock had lost his touch, I informed my father, who hastened to point to the title, *Elements of Political Science*.

I questioned then that the same man could be two such distinct men, though the case of Lewis Carroll was known to me. Somehow it bothered me at that age. It bothered me later. It transpires that others have been similarly bothered.

Anyway, at the start of my first year at McGill I managed to waylay my distinguished professor to tell him the story. He enjoyed it hugely, and I had made a friend—at least, until the mid-term exams.

Throughout the undergraduate years and well after, the man himself intrigued me quite as much as his comic confabulations. Inevitably theories began to take shape, some counter to prevailing appraisals. They are presented in this biographical study.

This endeavor owes much to heartwarming co-operation from literally all points of the compass. I hope that I have overlooked no one in the acknowledgements which appear elsewhere in this volume. But this is the place to express special gratitude to two particular people: to Mrs. Nimmo, who knew her uncle as few others did; and to Dr. Ralph Curry, professor of English at Georgetown College, Kentucky, and curator of the Stephen Leacock Memorial Home at Orillia, Ontario. His *Stephen Leacock: Humorist and Humanist* was the first biography.

A final note. This book was written without any assistance from the Canada Council, which refused my application for a grant-in-aid.

D.M.L.

Montreal,
1970.

Stephen Leacock

I

The Hampshire Lad

"It is the wont of biographers," Stephen Leacock complained in his account of the life of Charles Dickens, "to ramble through details of ancestry as tedious as they are remote. Fortunately, nothing of that sort is needed in the case of Dickens. He came of a family on both sides and in all branches as utterly undistinguished as those of all the rest of us."

The facts about Leacock's immediate forbears are neither tedious nor remote. Indeed, examination of those facts is essential to an understanding of the man and his work. Strangely, he always seemed to be anxious to lock within himself his own domestic history. Had he been able to complete his autobiography—he managed only four sketchy chapters—we should not have been any the wiser. "I always feel," he stated airily, "that it is out of place to go into such details."

With typical exaggeration, which, also typically, had a modicum of truth at the heart of it, Stephen Leacock often regaled people with a yarn about his great-great-grandfather John Leacock. Seemingly that worthy retired from his vineyards in Madeira and came to the Isle of Wight with so much money that nobody did any real work for three generations. "The fourth generation, dead broke, started over. Naturally that had to be me."

The Leacocks were certainly well-to-do. Established in their luxurious Oak Hill home on the outskirts of Ryde, they were secure members of an intensely Tory Victorian leisure class. Among the principal playgrounds of that self-sufficient society were the shores and the waters and the leafy glades of the lovely Isle of Wight, nestling in the Channel off England's south coast. It was the setting for Osborne House, Queen Victoria's favorite palace, and for the Cowes regatta, the famous annual social yachting fling. All the while, busy ships from many nations skirted the island bearing riches for Her Majesty's realm. The world was England's oyster.

Even at a time when parental authority was seldom questioned, it still cannot have been easy to keep moneyed youngsters in line. It proved impossible in the case of Peter Leacock, who was to be Stephen's father. Life to Peter was his small blue sailing boat, and the future could take care of itself. His young brother, Edward Philip, or "E.P.," was hardly a model of industry and reliability, but not quite so infected with indolence and purposelessness. He at least became an amusing adventurer and ultimately famous as *My Remarkable Uncle*. In totally diverse ways, both brothers were to exert a considerable influence upon the future economist-humorist.

As a compensating factor to his general uselessness, Peter was a witty talker and he boasted an attractive demeanor not lost on the local young ladies who were prepared to forgive faults in order to keep his company. One of these was a pretty, intelligent girl named Agnes Emma Butler, whose family had enjoyed a long-standing friendship with the Leacocks.

In her middle age, at the behest of her children, Agnes set down an all too brief record of her own heritage and early years. So far as it goes, it is a revealing chart.

Justly proud of her lineage, she drew attention to the impressive line of scholars, academic administrators and clerics. Her father had been an assiduous man of the cloth in the Church of England. Her mother died when Agnes was five; her father, six years later. Relatives conscientiously assumed the responsibility of her upbringing. Her education included private tutoring, attendance at select girls' academies and a spell at a fashionable finishing school near London.

The Butlers were a family of not inconsiderable means. One branch established itself on Canada's west coast. Another thrives today at the pleasant country seat of Bury Lodge in the tidy little village of Hambledon, Hampshire, where Agnes often stayed with her grandmother. The present head of the household there, Brigadier H. D. G. Butler, is naturally pleased with his family's association with the name of Stephen Leacock, although he pointedly says, "His is not my type of humor."

The village's claim to fame is that England's national craze, cricket, is widely believed to have originated there. About this, late in life Stephen Leacock wrote:

> Here, more than anywhere else, began the sacred game—for there is no other adjective that can convey what cricket means to Englishmen than the word "sacred." Here, on the wind-swept open space of Broadhalfpenny Down, was bowled the first ball, the first rushing underhand ball where bowling began. . . . Hambledon, Hants, is to all people who play cricket and love the game as Mecca is to a Mohammedan. . . . The Butler family were intimately concerned with the beginnings of cricket.

By the testimony of others, in young manhood Leacock was a "hit-and-miss" player himself, but he always preferred it to baseball.

From infancy Peter and Agnes had been brought together during the regular holiday months. Despite his aimless ways, his indifferent record at school, and his success at evading responsibility, clearly he exercised a fascination over her. She, on the other hand, was not so distracted as to be unmindful of her studies, her church work and her hobby—painting. Throughout her life she was a proficient watercolorist.

Yet the spell which Peter had cast upon her proved too great. During the summer of 1866 Peter and Agnes became secretly engaged; at night she would creep from the sleeping house to meet him on the little blue yacht. He was just under eighteen—"a minor," to quote the marriage certificate—and she twenty-two when they secretly agreed to hotfoot it to London to take the marital plunge. Thus on New Year's Day in 1867, in the presence of two hastily rounded-up witnesses, they were united in marriage in All Saints Church (long since demolished) in the parish of Paddington by the Rev. J. L. Macdonald, who demanded and received the required licence. Had the worthy Church of England clergyman probed more deeply, he might have felt some qualms. Peter's mother had been a convert to Roman Catholicism and her sons had been herded along accordingly. Peter, however, had wandered away from this, or any other faith.

Agnes had obviously been swept off her feet in classical fashion by the dreamy persuasiveness of her eighteen-year-old swain. Nonetheless, she kept her wits about her to the point that a marriage settlement was carefully drawn up. To the union she brought an inheritance of stocks and annuities amounting to four thousand pounds sterling. It was going to be needed.

Their first child Thomas James (Jim) Leacock was born on July 14, 1867.

Apprised of the marriage, the paternal Leacock—Thomas Murdock—concluded that firm action was indicated. He not only had a shiftless offspring on his hands, but a daughter-in-law, too. Fortunately, there was a ready-made solution at hand, the traditional method resorted to by wealthy English fathers of the Victorian era: pick out an unlikely corner of the Empire, ship off the undesirable (armed with enough wherewithal to keep him away), and hope for the best.

Little time was required to make the necessary arrangements. The spot selected for Peter and his bride was a holding a few miles outside Maritzburg, the capital of the British South African colony of Natal. To prove that there were no hard feelings and to ensure that the long voyage would entail the least possible discomfort, first-class accommodation was provided in a small ship with the very Leacockian name of *S.S. Burton Hatter*.

Agnes kept an informal chronicle of their journey. It soon trails away to nothingness, but not before a glimpse is allowed of the kind of existence the delicate young woman (she had suffered brain concussion in a childhood fall) and her spouse faced. Even with a personal maid to attend to the little chores, the trek inland was exacting. Negotiated by oxcart, with Kaffir bearers carrying the luggage, the journey over rough, sun-baked roads must have been exhausting.

A land agent met them to see that they got settled in a long, low frame home which stood in the centre of some hundred and fifty acres of cornfields, with a couple of paddocks for horses and cattle. Agnes cannot have been overjoyed at the general prospects. She soon became disillusioned about her young husband's ability to handle such a situation. The Natal experiment lasted long enough for Peter to lose his shirt and gain a son. The baby, Thomas James, heralded an eventual brood of eleven brothers and sisters. It is not inconceivable that, as Stephen recounted decades after, locusts were really responsible for destroying the crops and rendering the plantation bankrupt. Peter had apparently made at least a half-hearted effort to work it. Let the locusts share the blame; it was not all theirs.

Stephen wrote in his autobiography:

> Maritzburg in 1867 no doubt appeared singularly quiet, but to those who lived there the whole place, as my mother has told me, was "seething with the Colenso controversy." I imagine few people of today remember the name of Colenso, the Bishop of Natal, the mathematician over whose *Arithmetic* and *Algebra* a generation of English schoolboys groaned and whose mild aspersions on the Pentateuch—I think it means the first five books of the Old Testament—opened the way, like a water leak in a dam, to heresies that swept away the literal interpretation of Scripture. Colenso became a sort of test case, in orthodoxy, and in the law as to the government of the Church of England in the colonies, and locally a test case in the fidelity of the congregation. Some people in Natal would allow their children to be baptised by the bishop and some wouldn't and held them over for the dean any time the bishop was away. My eldest brother got caught up in this controversy and was torn backward and forward before he could be christened.

It was not lack of respect for the heretical Bishop Colenso, but a combination of lack of pluck and money that caused the Leacocks to abandon Natal and take ship back to England.

What transpired when the "bad penny" rolled once again on to the porch of the Isle of Wight mansion can only be deduced by the next station young Peter took up. He became an asphalt contractor and a resident of Swanmore, another Hampshire hamlet. He had presumably been advised that he was expected to fend for himself.

While he was fending he acquired another son, Arthur Murdock (Dick) Leacock in July 1868. Some time later a lustily bawling infant announced himself in the person of Stephen Butler Leacock. The date was December 30, 1869, and the christening took place in the Church of St. Barnabas, which stands today amid ancient headstones at the crest of a rise not far removed from historic Winchester, King Alfred's English capital. (In the records of London's Somerset House the event will be found under the date of January

23, 1870, since the birth was more than three weeks late in being registered.)

For years on end his birth proved confusing to Stephen Leacock. He had been under the impression that his birthplace had been Swanmore on the Isle of Wight. There *was* a Swanmore there, and that is where his grandfather had been born. Two Swanmores within fifty miles of each other ought to be too much for anyone.

The thatched house in which Stephen was born still stands today, after a couple of centuries of constant occupation. Facing the village green (of a now considerably expanded village, of course), it remains pretty much as it always must have been, except for the addition of modern facilities—three rooms on the ground floor and four upstairs, in one of which Stephen's birth occurred. By village standards of the day it was spacious and impressive, and belied the fortunes of the plodding father.

Whether he ran out of enthusiasm for asphalt or ran into debt, Peter left Swanmore to take up temporary residence in Shoreham-by-Sea, not very far away. There he puttered about the undulating countryside talking to and drinking with farmers and cronies. And so, another summons from Leacock Senior, another conference. As a result, the accepted formula would be put to the test again. Since British Empire locusts had allegedly ruined him in a Crown colony, Peter was now to be pointed towards the United States. At the suggestion of an American acquaintance, a determined Thomas Murdock Leacock bought his son a farm in Kansas. This was very much a case of a pig in a poke.

Leaving Agnes pregnant, and now with three toddlers to look after, away went Peter to the Sunflower State, whose motto, *ad astra per aspera*, may have escaped attention in the Isle of Wight. Stephen tried hard to make light of the resulting fiasco ("Simple people, like my father," he once permitted himself). According to him, the total collapse of this American foray was attributable to ravenous grasshoppers.

As his father was ostensibly doing single-handed combat day and night with swarms of leaping insects in the middle of America, the Hampshire lad's fertile imagination was being cultivated by a patient and thorough mother. Her lessons at home were supplemented by formal elementary schooling in a small place called Porchester. The schoolhouse stood on the west side of Portsmouth harbor, looking down on the street where Stephen's beloved Charles Dickens had been born sixty years before, and on Nelson's *Victory*, preserved in dry dock as a symbol of Britain's naval might.

All about the boy there was evidence of history—British history, Roman history, Norman history. In his most parochial of Canadian moods he would never forget that childhood setting.

Instilling a sense of patriotic pride in her boys, Agnes seldom missed an opportunity to explain current events and to expatiate on the background of those events. She linked present military manoeuvres in the Aldershot district with recollections of her own excitement when watching the embarkation of troops at Southampton on their way to the Crimean War, and their return. She told the youngsters about the Victoria Cross her half-brother, Sir Timothy Adair Butler, had won during the Indian Mutiny in 1857. (The medal is still at Bury Lodge.) Memories of great state occasions she had witnessed were called forth and a deep respect for Queen Victoria was engendered. (Seventy years in the future, Leacock would condemn the principle of hereditary rights, the British monarchy being the sole exception.)

By the age of seven Stephen had explored and absorbed information about the ancient (700 B.C.) British stronghold whose earthworks may be seen today outside the sturdy Roman walls of Porchester Castle. In its grounds stands the twelfth-century Priory Church of Saint Mary in the Close. There the boy attended service to hear his "Uncle Charles" (Agnes' uncle) preach each Sunday. The church is itself drenched in history, having once served as a jail for Charles II's Dutch prisoners-of-war. After suffering severe damage by fire, it was restored by Queen Anne.

Nor would he forget, to the extent of talking and writing about it in his maturity, the story of the capture by the British early in the century of the U.S. naval frigate *Chesapeake*. Grandfather Leacock had presented the boy with a "chunk" of wood from the ship (it may be seen still at the Memorial Home in Orillia). Stephen's curiosity was aroused, and this led to research on his part. The vessel had been brought to Portsmouth, where the Admiralty found it to be of not much further use for service in the Atlantic. After the guns had been removed, it was sold to the highest bidder. A portion of the beautiful pitch pine timbers was employed in the construction of houses in the port city, the balance being towed upriver to Wickham—the birth place of William of Wykeham, Stephen was quick to note—for use in the building of a new cattle feed mill. The Chesapeake mill, as it is now called, continues to attract tourists. The present owner admits that if he gets the right price from an American buyer, "he can have it."

Thus local history contributed much to the child's enquiring mind; though when Leacock returned a half-century later, he declared himself "ashamed" of the dwelling that had been his home, with its "little hall and boxes for rooms" and "what my mother had the nerve to call the 'breakfast room.' " On that same visit, he wrote in his memoirs, he visited the old public house, the Crown and Anchor. Either this was a fault of memory, or, more likely, he didn't take the trouble to check. There had never been a pub by that name. It was, rather, The Cormorant, and it flourishes now.

In due course Peter returned from the grasshopper wars of Kansas to find another addition to the family. But his father doggedly presented one more scheme to ensure Peter's absence from the home hearth. It is difficult to understand why, after two abysmal and costly attempts, Leacock the Elder stubbornly insisted on farming as a career for a man who exhibited neither talent for nor interest in agriculture. Yet the newest proposition called for another such effort. The Empire was to be placed on trial again, for this time it was to be Canada. After discussing the matter with the Canadian immigration authorities in London, Thomas Murdock dipped into his well-lined pocket and secured approximately one hundred acres of scrubby woodland.

Somehow Peter still commanded the loyalty of his wife and the admiration of the children. He continued to exude a superficial charm, which at least minimized his less attractive traits. But one can only speculate upon the emotions of the mother when the latest *fait accompli* was made known. She had endured the African experience. She was bearing children, in the face of physical frailty, with breathless regularity. Now she had to pack up everything, lock, stock and barrel, and head for a region well known to be rough on the hardiest.

The site of what was destined to be a permanent home for Agnes lay in the Lake Simcoe area of the recently created province of Ontario, near a hamlet called Egypt, which in turn was near a village called Sutton. Emigrants from Scotland and the Western

Isles were settled all about and were reported to be reasonably happy
in their rugged new home. But they were robust and fearless souls.
Peter and Agnes were of a different, more fragile stock. It was not,
however, for the supine son to reason why. He was sent ahead to
prepare the way.

Agnes also helped to prepare the way. The children were given
a crash course in geography, topped off with fundamental instruction in the far-reaching changes which had occurred in the "colony"
to which they were being sent. With Canadian confederation two
years before Stephen's birth, a British Dominion had been brought
into being. It was not, the mother was at pains to explain, a
"foreign" country to which they were going. The natives would be
friendly. This must have consoled young Stephen as he left his
homeland. But in statements and implied statements he would
cling to the fact that he had been born an Englishman. "Who
wouldn't be?" he once exclaimed.

In his old age he reconstructed briefly the upheaval of 1876—
the mother's tears, the childish excitement. In those days going to
America meant leaving the native heath for good. Certainly, for most
people there was small likelihood of returning. Agnes must have been
only too uncomfortably aware of the fact, yet she appears never to
have raised a voice against the move. It wouldn't have done her any
good: Grandfather Leacock had spleen.

The family embarked at Liverpool in the Canadian Allan Line's
S.S. Sarmatian, a combination steam-sail passenger vessel—"a
great ship, a ship with towering masts and rigging of the grand old
days." Then came the most vivid memory, "saying good-bye to
England as a child."

Writing in the 1940s on "Migration in English Literature,"
Stephen remembered a song the crew sang as the ship slipped down
the Mersey:

Cheer, boys; no more of idle sorrow.
Courage, true hearts, will bear us on our way.
Hope points before and show a bright tomorrow;
Let us forget the darkness of the day.

This was the "up anchor" chant of outgoing ships.

It was all fun for us . . . the wind, the waves, the magnificence of the
"saloon" . . . And then the great sheets of ice until the ship stopped. On

Sunday the clergyman prayed to have it taken away and it went. Then came a morning when someone called down the companionway, "Come and see America" . . . And there it was, a tall, hard coast of trees and rock, clear and bright in the sunshine, not a bit soft, like England.

Not a bit soft, nor likely to become softer, as the Leacocks changed to a riverboat at Montreal and headed for a father and a farm, neither of which was to prove the brightest of prospects.

II

Down to Earth

With conservative corpuscles coursing through a red-white-and-blue bloodstream, six-year-old Stephen Leacock arrived at his new Canadian home in the springtime of the year. At once he encountered a force which was to have a vital effect on his growing-up process: the good earth. In retrospect he would not agree. He frequently spoke and wrote of the harshness of the farming life, the grubby daily chores, the discomforts, the isolation. Unmentioned, though ever present, was the person of Peter. He seems to have been initially earnest in his intentions to found a substantial homestead. But he preferred idleness to industry. Even "Old Tommy," the hired hand, was of little use. A Yorkshireman, he had tried a bush farm of his own and failed. So the burden of the farm work and organization fell ever more heavily on Peter's sons.

The farm itself, long since vacated by its previous tenant, straddled high ground in the township of Georgina in the northeast corner of Ontario's county of York, with a bird's-eye view of Lake Simcoe, where Stephen learned to sail and to fish. Getting to it from the village of Sutton entailed driving over a heavy road through a great cedar swamp a mile through in the centre, all corduroy planking and willows and marsh and water. When the newcomers reached the site on a wind-swept hill space, they came upon a

11

jumble of frame buildings, log barns and outhouses. Years afterwards his mother told Stephen that to her it was a heartbreak. To
Stephen it was "the damnedest place I ever saw."

The first impressions remained with him to the end:

> The house! Someone had built a cedar log house and then covered it
> round with clapboard, and then someone else had added three rooms
> stuck along the front with more clapboard, effectually keeping all the
> sunlight out. Even towards the sunset there were no windows, only the
> half glass top of a side door. A cookhouse and a woodshed were stuck
> on behind. Across a grass yard were the stable, cedar logs plastered up,
> and the barns, cedar logs loose and open, and a cart shed and a henhouse
> and pig sties and all that goes with a farm. To me as a child the farm
> part seemed just one big stink. It does still: the phew! of the stable—not
> so bad as the rest; the unspeakable cowshed, sunk in the dark below a
> barn, beyond all question of light or ventilation, like a mediaeval oubliette;
> the henhouse, never cleaned and looking like a guano-deposit island off
> the coast of Chile, in which the hens lived if they could and froze dead if
> they couldn't; the pig sties, on the simple Upper Canada fashion of a log
> pen and a shelter behind, about three feet high. Guano had nothing on
> them.

Within a year, with the help of local labour, the farmhouse was
extended to accommodate the growing family. The new section was
built of frame lumber only, with lath and plaster and no logs, "thin
as cardboard and cold as a refrigerator." Box stoves—nine of
them—supplied the heating, coal oil lamps and candles, the light-
ing.

Even the nine stoves were no match for the Ontario winter. In
her book *The Man In The Panama Hat* his niece, Elizabeth Kimball, tells of a visit to the old farm with Leacock who remembered
that he and his brothers used to skate on the icy floor of one freez-
ing passage in the farmhouse.

As with other farms in the area, Peter's work involved mixed
farming—wheat and other grains, hay, cattle, a few sheep, pigs
and hens. But, as Stephen wrote looking back, the only thing to sell
was wheat, "the false hope of the Ontario farmer of the seventies,
always lower in the yield than what one calculated (if you calculated low it went lower) and always (except once in a happy year)
lower than what it had to be to make it pay." Little was realized
from the other grains or the cattle, "poor lean things of the pre-
breeding days that survived their awful cowshed."

Yet, in his advanced years, Stephen admitted that "perhaps the old farm wasn't so bad after all." After all, it was to teach him a lesson or two about the ways of Nature and man as they can only be learned far removed from the helter-skelter of city life. He would even profit from the habit of rising before dawn, a habit which remained with him for the rest of his days. And on the farm he would enrich his vocabulary with the addition of some ripe Anglo-Saxon terms that would adorn some of his future offstage performances.

Living in the heart of a snow belt, the Leacocks found the going exceedingly tough. It was hard enough getting to and from the little red-brown building bearing the inscription "School Section No. 3" one mile away, without having to stumble through three feet of snow. And, of course, such conditions brought major farm work to a temporary halt. However, if Peter could produce nothing else, he became expert at siring a family, and this one burgeoned with every passing year.

With a foresight her youngsters soon came to appreciate, Agnes had included in the baggage brought from England not only suitable textbooks but also a supply of good reading for the young mind. The works of Sir Walter Scott were read to the children. *Robinson Crusoe* was on the list. And Mark Twain! A friend in Boston had sent up *Tom Sawyer*, which had just been published, but about which Stephen would say, "Tom Sawyer, I never cared for." Dickens, of course. *Pickwick Papers* made a deep impression on the youngster.

Meanwhile, on his occasional visits to Sutton, reached by an uninviting track through towering hemlocks and birch, he discovered some strangers who whetted his natural curiosity. These had been "rebels" in the rebellion of 1837, which had been put down only forty years or so earlier. The tales they told became part of his store of Canadian history.

"When I was a boy," he told a Montreal audience midway in his professorial career, "history meant to me the story of Greece or Rome, of Achilles in his tall helmet, or at best of Nelson sending up the string of colored signal flags on the bright autumn day of Trafalgar. I never realized that there was history, too, close at hand beside my very own home."

An old grave stood among the brambles at the foot of the farm. "We passed it as we went by at dusk towards the cow pasture in the bush with quaking hearts; in the broad sunlight of day with bold defiance. It recalled a time in the days of early settlement when there was no consecrated graveyard, when each and every one must bury his own dead, and that the grassgrown spot with a rude cedar fence about it that we passed with a shudder or a laugh had been for someone a place of bitter sorrow and unending memory." That, he contended, was "history." As a man he valued no less the great epics of a Macaulay or Gibbon, but he found himself, because of his childhood experiences, drawn more and more to the charm and meaning of the history of little places.

Two years had gone by, two more children graced the domestic scene, when a dimly remembered figure appeared on the farmhouse doorstep. It was Stephen's Uncle E.P. He had talked the Isle of Wight Midas into underwriting a trip to Canada on the flimsy promise that it would ultimately prove a beneficial investment for all parties concerned. Talk—grand talk—and promise were the stock-in-trade of E.P. Without trying he undoubtedly could have sold electric heaters to all the natives of the Fiji Islands. A born salesman, he was his own best customer. As such he understandably mesmerized his nephews, Stephen not least.

Naturally the visit of E.P. could hardly be without some motive. With mouth-watering statistics whomped up at will, he put forward a compelling case. There was, he argued, money to be made— piles of it—out in western Canada. There the first Manitoba boom had already gathered a full head of steam. To get there would, of course, require money. Peter and E.P. put their heads together, with the inevitable outcome that Peter lost his. It was speedily agreed, apparently without protest from Agnes, that certain farm stock and implements (which suddenly had become unnecessary frivolities) would be sacrificed to the cause. A quick auction realized enough funds to set in motion the carelessly laid plans for the westward journey. Everybody seems to have been satisfied with the explanation that any consequent hardship on those left behind would be of a purely temporary nature, since the fortune to be garnered would soon be shipped back from Winnipeg.

Ensuring that his wife was pregnant, according to the now time-honored practice, Peter made ready to redeem himself in the estimation of the entire Leacock clan. The scheme so forcefully promoted by E.P. seemed to be assured of success. The brothers set off for the gold-paved Prairies.

Rid of the encumbrance of their father, the family settled down to keep the farm going as best they could. According to age, the boys divided up the chores equally. Stephen made himself responsible for the market garden.

But although the isolation, the primitive living conditions, and the constant farm chores made life hard for the Leacock children, there were compensations. In the winter there was skating, sledding, snow-shoeing, and even ice-boating on nearby Lake Simcoe. The lake came into its own in those summers when the family rented a cottage at the water's edge. There Stephen and the others could discover the joys of swimming, canoeing, rowing, building rafts and just messing about by the water. Most important of all, Stephen could learn how to sail and to fish, two pastimes which he was to enjoy the rest of his life.

Thanks to his own writings Leacock the fisherman is well-known. Leacock the yachtsman is not so well-known. Yet he was a keen and expert sailor. One of his first independent purchases as a young man was a sailing boat, in which he explored Lake Simcoe tirelessly and skilfully. But sometimes his youthful exuberance led to a spill and a soaking. His friend R. B. Pattison records an attempt by Leacock to perform gymnastic exercises up the mast. When the boat turned over he greeted the event with a laugh and the oft-repeated words, "And the last thing seen of the unfortunate sailors, they were clinging desperately to the torn rigging."

In later life Stephen Leacock was convinced that they had been poor. Certainly, if his recollections about farm revenue were accurate, it would have meant coming close on occasions to bare subsistence level. Yet the family was not entirely dependent upon this income, since Agnes not only received a small income of her own from England but periodic legacies also. How else could they have afforded to rent a summer cottage? Whatever the real circumstances, it speaks much for her that, if anything else suffered, the children's education was the last thing to do so.

Among the "whatever else" must have been some of the Christmases on the farm. Both in his "fiction" and in reminiscential articles Leacock paid more than passing attention to the place which this season of goodwill held in his young life. For example, in "Memories of Christmas" (included in the *My Remarkable Uncle* volume) there is this moving passage:

> My mind conjured up a picture of how I felt, long ago, over sixty years ago, when I opened my stocking one Christmas and found, all wrapped up in boxes and parcels that might have been filled with magic. . . . a little round hard box with a tight lid that might have opened out to be magic music, or goodness knows what—for a child's imagination outstrips reality—but it was only collars. I had hard work to choke back tears. And after that—fat and long and mysterious—was a box that might have held —why, anything! Derringer pistols, Cherokee daggers, anything. . . . But did it? No. It had in it a pair of braces, wheel and all. That broke me down. . . . There is no blame; all parents do it, in such a crowded family as ours was, with a census which went up each year. But at least let me plead for some one present, however trivial, with the true touch in it of the magic of the mysterious. . . .

The foregoing sentiment was much softer than the cynical note that suffused the "Hoodoo McFiggin's Christmas," which appeared in his first book, *Literary Lapses*. By his own confession, Leacock was Hoodoo McFiggin.

Since Stephen was a child given to introspection, complaints that he had been "acting up" at the little red schoolhouse must have seemed strange to Agnes. There had been reports of "showing off" and "wise cracking." This served as a pretext for her to take the action she had been contemplating for some time. She would withdraw the children from school and add pedagogic duties to her numerous other tasks. She had been thinking about such a move because, as her son wrote decades later, "my Mother was haunted with the idea that if we kept on at the school, we might sideslip and cease to be gentlemen." Already the youngsters were beginning to lose their Hampshire accent and were beginning to say "them there" and "who all" and "most always," phrases that "no one can use and grow up a gentleman."

There is more than just a suggestion of class consciousness on the part of his mother in Stephen's statement that the children were only permitted to visit one English family on a nearby farm. "We had hardly any social life. . . . There was a certain queer gentility about it all." The same queer gentility meant that in summer the Leacock children, unlike their friends, were not allowed to go barefoot. It was, he explained, "a question of caste and thistles."

Agnes' best efforts at teaching her brood were of little avail. Her pupils refused to accord her the seriousness a non-relative would have insisted upon. Still determined to keep them at home, she acquired the services of a Mr. Harry Park from the village. The luxury of a private tutor was made possible by financial assistance from Grandfather Leacock in England, specifically earmarked for that purpose. Park, who was preparing himself for university, took some space in the rambling house, made it over into a schoolroom and carried on for a couple of years.

From a business standpoint, however, farm operations continued to prove worrisome. Fluctuating wheat prices were chiefly responsible. Debts rose. Fear and terror stalked the fatherless family in moments of illness. Leacock described one of these moments when, in the 1930s, he paid tribute to Dr. Charles Thompson Noble, then approaching his 101st year. Noble in deed as well as in name, he had spent his entire active career in general practice at Sutton. He had been the Leacocks' physician and father confessor.

One of the boys had been suddenly stricken by an unidentifiable malady. Stephen and another brother, Dick, hitched up their horse on a wild winter's night and drove four miles along the dark, rough road to summon the doctor. They found him playing chess, although the hour was late:

"Doctor," we cried, as we burst in, "hurry and come. Jim's ill—"

"Shut the door, shut the door!" he called. "Come in, boys; here let me brush that snow off you—it's my move, Charlie, remember—now, what the devil's the matter?"

Then we would pant out our hurried exclamations, both together.

"Bah!" he growled, "ill, nothing! Mere belly ache, I guess."

This was his term, his favorite word, for an undiagnosed disease— "belly ache." They call it supergastral aesthesia now. In a city house, it sounds better. Yet how we hung upon the doctor's good old Saxon term, yearning and hoping that it might be that.

But even as he growled the doctor had taken down the lantern from a hook, thrown on a huge, battered fur coat that doubled his size, and was putting medicines—a very shopful it seemed—into a leather case.

"Your horse is done up," he said. "We'll put my mare in. Come and give me a hand, Charlie."

He was his own ostler and stable-man, he and his burly son. Yet how quickly and quietly he moved, the lantern swinging on his arm, as he buckled the straps.

Then, in a moment, as it seemed, out into the wind and snow again, the great figure of the doctor almost filling the seat of the cutter, the two of us crushed in beside him, with responsibility, the unbearable burden, gone from us, and renewed comfort in our hearts. Then as we near the farmhouse and see the light in the sickroom window, fear clutches our hearts again.

"You boys unhitch," says the doctor. "I'll go right in."

Presently, when we enter the house, we learn that he is in the sickroom —the door closed. No word of comfort has come forth. He has sent out for hot blankets. The stoves are to be kept burning. We must sit up. We may be needed. That is all.

And there in that still room through the long night, he fights single-handed against Death. Behind him is no human help, no consultation, no wisdom of the colleges to call on, only his own unaided strength, and his own purpose, and that strange instinct in the fight for a flickering life, that some higher power than that of colleges has planted deep within his soul.

So we watch through the night hours in dull misery and fear, a phantom at the window pane: so must we wait till the slow morning shows dim and pale at the windows. Then he comes out from the room. His face is furrowed with the fatigue of his long vigil. But, as he speaks, the tone of his voice is as that of one who has fought and conquered.

"There—he'll do now. Give him this when he wakes."

Then a great joy sweeps over us as the phantom falls away, and we shudder back to the warm sunshine of life, while the sound of the doctor's retreating sleighbells makes music to our ears.

But, in sickness or in health, in adversity or fleeting prosperity, Agnes set herself an objective from which she would not be budged. Her children's education came first on her list. To this end she called on her reserves of initiative carefully to maintain good relations with her English connections. As the younger members of the family continued to be taught by Mr. Park, with Agnes making herself responsible for religious training, the mother set her sights high for the older boys. In 1881 Jim and Dick were enrolled at Toronto's fashionable boys' school, Upper Canada College. The following year Stephen joined them.

In an essay, "The Struggle to Make Us Gentlemen," Leacock looked back "with that peculiar affection that every one feels for his old school after it has been knocked down and all the masters dead long ago." (The original UCC indeed had been knocked down, but on another site still prospers today.)

According to Stephen, the pupils were told by oratorical visitors that Upper Canada College was founded as "a school for gentlemen." Hence, undoubtedly, Agnes' choice. The boy soon discovered that the teaching staff was to a man hell-bent on stuffing this ideal down youthful throats:

> Personally I got by on a side issue. In those days there was none of the elaborate registration, the card index stuff, that all schools have now. Any information they wanted about us they got *viva voce* on the spot by calling us up in front of the class and asking for it. So there came a day soon after I entered when the principal called me up to be questioned and a junior master wrote down the answers. "What," he asked, "is your father's occupation?" I hesitated quite a while and then I said, "He doesn't do anything." The principal bent over towards the junior master who was writing and said in an impressive voice, "A gentleman." A sort of awe spread round the room at my high status. But really why I had hesitated was because I didn't know what to say. You see, I knew that my father, when in Toronto, was probaby to be found along on King Street having a Tom-and-Jerry in the Dog and Duck, or at Clancy's—but whether to call that an occupation was a nice question.

In between being subjected to a rubric of elegant etiquette, and suffering a spot of scarlatina, Stephen worked hard. His first year report disclosed excellence in Latin, English reading and composition, good results in Scripture, and nothing less than "very fair" in the balance of the curriculum. Give and take a gain here, a slippage there, his marks maintained this very respectable level until in his final year, 1887, he attained the distinction of becoming the school's head boy. (That he nursed this achievement jealously is borne out by a peculiar quirk in his biography of Charles Dickens, who, Leacock felt compelled to remind the world, had never become head boy during *his* schooling.)

In 1883 Agnes decided to move to Toronto to be near her boys. To make this possible she parcelled out the farm to a neighbor for an annual rent of two hundred and fifty dollars, the same amount she had to pay on the mortgage. The younger children (seven by now) were left in the charge of Mr. Park, two domestics and the hired man. According to Leacock, Agnes came to the city "on the strength of a casual legacy." Legacies and remittances seemed always to have materialized at psychological moments. The latest one enabled her to take a comfortable house on John Street, employ two maids and acquire a carriage and pair. Stephen's subsequent repetitive references to a boyhood of poverty just don't make sense.

The sons now became day boys at UCC for a term, living at home on John Street with Mother. In the following year Stephen, the sole family representative then at the school, became a boarder once again. Agnes, having had her costly fling at urban luxury, returned to the Sutton scene, where "the rotten place hung round our family necks for years, unsalable." Jim and Dick went West to seek their fortunes with E.P.

While "living in" anew at Upper Canada, Stephen began to show a tendency "to strut." A faded letter, dated 1887, in possession of the family of one of Stephen's fellow boarders, contains the remark that "we grow tired of hearing about his scholastic triumphs, head boy, etc." Perhaps this was attributable to an attempt to compensate for genuine shyness, or to a clumsy effort to hide a feeling of inferiority in a boy from the backwoods competing with sophisticated and affluent city counterparts. Whatever the reason, in adulthood Leacock the author was to utilize expertly just such psychological conflicts to considerable comic effect.

He was quick to realize the value of living with other boys of varied backgrounds and of being in close contact with the masters under the same roof. With the benefit of hindsight, he remembered the salutary disciplines of Upper Canada's kind of schooling. "It is this new integument—call it, if you like, this new fellowship—that give the peculiar meaning to boarding school friendship, even as the years go by and it all turns into retrospect, to broadening companionship and acquaintance." Patently, the experience proved a godsend to the boy.

Certainly young Stephen had taken full advantage of the opportunities offered at UCC. He had thoroughly justified his position as head boy, both in his studies and in his varied extracurricular activities. He won all of the fifth form prizes: the Classical, the Mathematical, the Modern Languages and, unsurprisingly, the General Proficiency. If he did not manage to make the school's football or cricket teams, he became chairman of the football club and was active in the newly formed literary and debating society.

Clearly his most important work outside the classroom was done on the school's newspaper, *The College Times*, of which he was appointed joint editor and chairman of the Publishing Committee for the 1886–87 year. Through its columns the writer of the future expressed himself on a number of topics, ranging from literature to politics. While the editorials were, of course, unsigned, during his editorship it is not difficult to see Leacock's hand behind a good many of them.

On the national election campaign in 1887 there was, for instance, this comment:

> But it really matters little which of the two great parties holds the reins of power. There is no great issue between them, and the accession of the Grits to power, or the continuance of Conservative rule would probably not affect the country for either better or worse.

But the editorial concern of *The College Times* under Leacock's direction with respect to literature recurred frequently. One comment began:

> Literature as a profession is not very lucrative. Those who depend solely on their pen as their means of subsistence earn but a scanty recompense for their labour; and literary labour, whatever may be said to the contrary, is the severest of all toil.

After continuing in this vein for some time and noting in passing that writing for magazines is the most lucrative branch of writing, the editorial concludes with a ringingly prophetic declaration:

> If literature, the finest of the beaux arts, were not so much neglected, Canada would doubtless be productive of geniuses as great as many of the Old World.

Stephen's first signed piece (over the initials S.B.L.) took the form of a light-hearted prose parody of life at Upper Canada College entitled "The Vision of Mirza." This appeared in the April 7 edition in 1887, and on June 9 it was followed by another parody of school life, this time in the cheerful verse of a pupil just about to leave school.

On graduation and after sitting for his matriculation exams, Stephen went back to the farm to find his father returned from the West. Penniless, needless to say. Peter, the conquered hero, endeavoured to ingratiate himself with the family circle. Sadder, though not one whit wiser, having lost his shirt as a land agent in Winnipeg, Peter returned to his old ways. Domestic conditions deteriorated as Peter's dissolution got worse. Ominous storm clouds piled up about the farm. The mother was reaching the end of her tether. Agnes had tried for a long time to keep her husband's addiction to the bottle concealed from her children. On occasion they must have had an inkling that something was wrong when he lay about the place too tired for work or displayed an uncalled-for crankiness. The mother's powers of endurance had kept the household on a reasonably level keel, even when Peter drove off to the village for a stoking-up session, returning late at night after lights out.

Now the downward slide reached a momentum impossible to reverse. There were whispers of a liaison with the children's nursemaid. Without going into detail Stephen later applied the term "brutality" to his father's treatment of his mother. As the threat of insolvency mounted, so did his father's dependence on liquor.

The crisis arrived one morning in the summer of 1887, when Peter, who had somehow come into possession of an amount of money, put a few belongings together and announced that he was going away again. Neither purpose nor destination was disclosed. He would probably, he allowed, be back in his own good time. There was no concerted rush to encourage him to return sooner rather than later.

Stephen was seventeen when he packed his father into the cutter and drove him to the station. Wordless, they awaited the arrival of the train. Then, just as Peter prepared to climb the steps of the day coach, his son turned on him. Stephen's face was white. His right hand clenched the buggy whip, which he shook at his father, and in low, tense tones said: "If you ever come back, I'll kill you."

Peter never tested the warning. He never came back; nor did Stephen ever see him again.

The Maritime Provinces gobbled up Peter. There he changed his name to Captain Lewis, ultimately taking a common-law wife and settling on Nova Scotia's south shore. In her oddly loyal fashion, Agnes could not abide the term "separation." So far as she was concerned, they simply "lived apart."

The husband outlived his wife by six years, dying at the age of ninety two, less than four years before Stephen himself died in 1944.

A small estate had to be dealt with, remnant of a trust fund established by the long-suffering relatives on the Isle of Wight (where, incidentally, no Leacock lives today). Stephen wrote to a venerable family solicitor in England, stating, "I have not seen my father since 1887," but requesting an accounting of the financial state of affairs. It transpired that there was an inheritance of some eight thousand pounds for Peter's children. Because of wartime monetary restrictions on sterling leaving the country, the children took the only available course and invested their respective legacies in British war bonds.

The sorry chapter of Peter Leacock was closed.

Agnes' capacity for absorbing such physical and spiritual punishment, while continuing to display a semblance of respect for her children's father, speaks volumes for her character. Her sons and daughters were never to forget their indebtedness to her.

With his elder brothers away, the head boy really became head boy now. It was a position in the family that he was to retain until his death. He finally "got rid of the rotten old place on my mother's behalf simply by moving Mother off it and letting it go to the devil —mortgages, creditors, and all. I don't know who finally got it."

The dilemma thus posed must have been doubly painful for him. He stood at an important point along the path to his educational future. On this particular period of his life his sketchy memoirs are as full of gaps as there are pauses in a Pinter play. What text there is has a high proportion of inaccuracies, accountable more to sheer carelessness than to any geriatric condition of mind. Reliable information on this stage of his life is woefully lacking.

Obviously, prime consideration had to be accorded his mother's position. Younger brothers and sisters could not be left in the lurch. On the other hand, Stephen had learned that he had passed his matriculation examinations with flying colors. Under the regulations of the day, by passing these tests he automatically qualified for entrance into the sophomore year of university. As though to clinch the argument, his successful performance carried with it a modest scholarship.

After a lengthy family discussion, agreement was reached that, at all costs, a college career in these conditions could not be turned aside. Accordingly, in November 1887, Leacock was accepted by the University of Toronto. There, in University College, he played the role of a loner. For the most part he shunned extracurricular activities, concentrating on his studies. In consequence he emerged at the end of this first year with brilliant exam results, especially in modern languages.

Once more, however, the family situation called for an appraisal of the young man's plans. Those small legacies were thinning out. The burden of rearing eight youngsters was beginning to take its toll of Agnes. Little aid could be expected from western Canada, where the two oldest boys could spare little, if anything, from their paltry wages. Stephen faced the problem squarely and took the heartbreaking decision to interrupt his college courses.

In these distressing circumstances a job had to be found. He felt he was best fitted for a teaching post. But he would be required to undergo a special three-months' course leading to a high-school teaching diploma. He decided to do so.

To all intents and purposes this implied total abandonment of an advanced education. Since this had been dictated by the urgent demands of the moment, and certainly not by his own wish, drudgery surely was to be his lot. He did not at all like what he glimpsed in the foreseeable future. What he glimpsed was fated to become fact.

III

Progress by Degrees

It is axiomatic that you pays your money and takes your choice. In making available conflicting details about his life Stephen Leacock offered a wide and perplexing choice. His was a malleable memory, manipulated by the mood of the moment. His childhood Christmases, for instance, were either memorable or miserable according to the autobiographical article or fictional sketch the reader happens upon. In the course of a half-century of publication he built up impressive piles of contradictory evidence on all sorts of subjects.

More often than not he sought to convey the impression that his years of teaching school had been a hateful experience. In the final analysis, however, he grudgingly conceded that he had in reality been contented enough. That he inveighed against conditions that obtained in his day is a thing quite apart. Of course his criticisms of indefensible policies were valid. Broadly, the pay was an insult. The atmosphere in which teachers were doomed to exist was an insult. The attitude of boards of management, themselves at best semi-educated, was an insult. Everything was an insult to the sensitive natures of those who were expected to shape and enlighten the nation's youth. Indeed it required too many years to reduce these to half-insults. Dealing in generalities, a specialty of his, Leacock was right; but his bitter portraits of the miseries of the school-teacher's life did not necessarily reflect his own state of mind.

In fact, he found his teacher-in-training course "easy and agree-able and companionable," once he had made up his mind there was no other avenue immediately open to him. It was a situation of rock-bottom necessity. And, he would plaintively add: "My educa-tion has fitted me for nothing except to pass it on to other people."

Once his application had been accepted, Leacock was shipped off, together with a half-dozen other aspirants, to Strathroy Colle-giate Institute in western Ontario. There he was sentenced to three months of instruction on how to instruct.

A story he tells of one incident at the Institute holds significance in more than one respect. He had been watching the principal in action, a very important part of the training program. Without warning he was requested to take over the English lesson in pro-gress. No sooner had he assumed charge than the class was treated to a display of histrionics which was greeted with the unstinting approval of all. The only member of the audience not amused was the principal, whose every intonation and gesture had been accu-rately aped by the nineteen-year-old apprentice.

"I laid it on too thick," Leacock was to admit, an understatement in view of the principal's searing retaliation: "I am afraid I admire your brains more than your manners."

Ever since elementary school, Stephen had been aware of his natural gift for mimicry. It would not by a long shot be the last time the actor in him made its presence felt. The art of the mummer would be increasingly called into play by the pedagogue. He liked an audience.

The episode in which the youthful student-teacher cruelly imi-tated his master clearly worried Leacock later on. It amounted, he said, to a lesson within a lesson. He had not realized how it might affect the person concerned. From that moment he understood "the need for human kindliness as an element of humor." One may be permitted to doubt that such a flash of understanding occurred so swiftly, or that it would exclude other motives from his future prac-tice of humor.

Present in the class that witnessed Leacock's cheeky performance was a schoolboy of twelve. His name was Arthur W. Currie, and he was to become a teacher himself. Of infinitely greater importance, he would command with marked distinction the Canadian Corps in France during World War I, and shortly thereafter, as Sir Arthur, receive the appointment as principal and vice-chancellor of McGill University. At McGill Currie and Leacock were to form an abiding friendship.

In a 1936 issue of *The McGill News* Stephen Leacock recalled this particular teacher-pupil relationship and wrote: "The only close historical parallel to this which I know is that Aristotle taught Alexander the Great; but I like to feel that in the matter of pupils, Aristotle had nothing on me."

The short stretch at Strathroy contributed eventually to the launching of the Leacock literary career. There he was introduced to the sometimes diverting, usually benumbing sensation of boarding house life. Based upon personal experience of such a life, supplemented by that of others elsewhere, a three-hundred-word caricature, "Boarding House Geometry: Definitions and Axioms," would presently be produced by him. Twenty-two years later it would be included in the *Literary Lapses* collection, announcing to the world the arrival of a major humorist.

Among the axioms:

> The landlady can be reduced to her lowest terms by a series of propositions.
> The clothes of a boarding house bed, though produced ever so far both ways, will not meet.
> A bee-line may be made from any boarding house to any other boarding house.

Whatever the real state of his Strathroy boarding house, Leacock's stay had proved pleasant. Scholastically, he had accomplished much and was, on graduation, complimented by the principal. So, armed with a document certifying that he was a specialist in Latin, Greek, French, German and English, and was otherwise competent to be taken on strength of a secondary school establishment, Stephen started looking for a job by the simple process of answering every advertisement in sight. Luck was decidedly on his side. His former tutor, Harry Park, now held the post of principal of Uxbridge High School. There Leacock went as a teacher in modern languages. With a population of about fifteen hundred, Uxbridge was a small agricultural centre only eighteen miles away from his mother's farm. Leacock dubbed it "dull as ditchwater but quite unaware of the fact."

Since he was only nineteen, it occasioned no surprise that some of his pupils were nearly the same age, while one was actually older. However much he was to complain in the distant future (and to get paid for complaining), there is nothing to indicate that this initial venture was at all painful. Out of his $700-a-year income he managed to help his mother with a little money. He felt at home in the town, reassuring himself every so often that it was not to be a lifetime retreat. He could afford "a couple of glasses of beer a day at five cents a glass," not to mention "a plug of 'T and B' once a month at twenty-five cents."

Obviously Leacock had made a mental note in his early reading and had taken to heart Rule No. I of the Harry Wadsworth Club in *Tom Brown's School Days*: "Life isn't all beer and skittles; beer and skittles, or something better of the same sort, must form a good part of every Englishman's education."

What irked him and remained a sore point for a long while was the reaction of the Uxbridge school trustees—"most of them were a poor lot"—when an offer arrived from another institution which represented an increase of two hundred dollars in pay. The trustees told him flatly that he would not be released from his contract. They cared more about their own present than their teacher's future.

On the heels of this disagreeable affair, along came a vastly more enticing opening as junior master at Upper Canada College, his old school. Still the Uxbridge board refused to budge. Leacock readily appreciated what a position at UCC would mean—the chance to carry on simultaneously with his studies at the University of Toronto. This time he dug in his heels and won the day. Not entirely on his own, however. A certain uncle, E.P., hove into view quite fortuitously and smoothed the passage by finding someone to take his nephew's place at Uxbridge.

Ambitious, yet without the glimmer of a notion in which direction he was or wished to be headed, Stephen buckled down to the formidable combination of teaching chores and undergraduate curriculum. The only lectures he ever took at the University of Toronto had to follow his UCC day, where his work ended at three in the afternoon. The university was helpfully indulgent. There was no attendance rule to bother him. In a word, he was proceeding towards a degree on the basis of working overtime in overtime. Fortunately he abjured the advice he cheerfully gave to others: "If at first you don't succeed—quit!"

It has been conjectured that Leacock was always a shy man. This was no more true than that he was an unduly modest man. Along with the geneticists, he was sure that all men are not born equal. Intuitively he felt that there was within him special raw material which the next fellow, including his brothers, lacked. Fulminate as he would against the evils of class distinction, he had an innate feeling of superiority. As he now saw it, his task was to justify that feeling.

He began by getting into student activities at Varsity and by generally becoming a social being. Had he chosen the way of the womanizer, by all accounts Leacock would have been able to rule the roost. Exuding a kind of animal magnetism, he had, it is reputed, "women going crazy about him." While he was later to formulate definite views about the fair sex, in the meantime his manner was far from misogynistic.

In the face of the work load he had saddled on himself, Stephen in his early twenties was not averse to participation in campus parties and other related student frolics. Although the story has apocryphal overtones, Stephen's brother George used to vouch for the truth of one impulsive romantic adventure.

A young Toronto lady of unusually fetching qualities had caught and fixed the Leacock eye. She, however, went off to Colorado with her mother to take treatment for tuberculosis in a sanitorium high on a mountaintop. This establishment was declared off-limits for the lovesick youth. Undismayed, he haunted the vicinity until permission for a visit was forthcoming. Much to his horror, the reunion took the form of a hymn recital (complete with mother) around the piano. Stephen fled, preferring the holier-than-thou air of the Toronto of the nineties.

Student journalism beckoned and Leacock responded, though it is not to be supposed that his dabbling in the weekly newspaper *The Varsity* was a case of coming events casting their shadows before. His contributions were neither better nor worse than any which preceded him or came after him. But in the debating society he did give promise as an unusually lively public speaker for his years.

At long last, in 1891, a well-earned Bachelor of Arts degree was conferred on Leacock. At the same time, appropriately, he received a promotion on the staff of Upper Canada College. There he settled in with the single aim of setting aside enough of his earnings to go in search of further academic honors. It was to prove a long and irritating haul.

Looking back on his dislike of teaching at UCC, Leacock placed half the blame on himself. He had regarded the job as merely a means, a miserable means, to a more desirable end. What that end was had not yet been revealed to him. He was only certain that he wanted to be "above the average," and as sure that he was more than adequately equipped to become so. He had convinced himself, too, that the lot of a teacher was such that it gave no status of any consequence in the community. Yet, when Leacock began to spend his summers at Orillia in the mid-nineties (joining his mother who took a house there in 1895, thus establishing the first Leacock link with Orillia), he must have noticed how the townspeople looked up to a person of his occupation.

Nonetheless, he still held this conviction and it served as a spur to move him to explore other areas. He embarked on two diverse projects, both of which were to have unexpectedly far-reaching results.

First of all, his habit of rising early would be turned to a better purpose. By chance he had become interested in the subject of political economy. He set himself a course of reading, with no one to disturb him at that hour in his comfortable UCC quarters. The experiment helped him to forget what he described as "a job with a blind wall in front of it."

"With all modesty" he liked to think of himself as being akin to John Stuart Mill, who worked by day in the London office of the East India Company and did his literary work in his spare time.

If there was a touch of aimlessness about the self-imposed pre-breakfast economic studies, financial pressure dictated his next decision. His teacher's stipend needed to be augmented. It would have been perfectly adequate for a young master living on the premises; but his mother, brothers and sisters required assistance. He was, in fact, the only son at the time able to offer really substantial financial help.

Leacock had been paddling about in the commercial literary pond on and off for the past two years; a short sketch here, an expanded joke there, a snippet of light verse in between, found acceptance in the humor magazines which then proliferated. Thousands of others were doing the same thing, without a thought of trying to crash the professional ranks. It was the money that mattered, even though the remuneration was piffling. While he had failed to interest editors in his sentimental short stories, some of his material in lighter vein turned out to be salable.

Leacock blamed the trials and tribulations of the classroom for the necessity of this writing sideline. Again, it was to drive dull care away, away from the routine of drilling modern languages into unreceptive minds, away from the rigamarole associated with a teacher-in-residence.

One of Canada's most underrated editors and a satirist himself, B. K. Sandwell had been a pupil of Leacock at UCC. Subsequently they become firm friends. In a 1958 radio interview Sandwell was asked what kind of a schoolteacher Leacock had been.

"Well, a *fairly* good teacher. It was a means to furnish him with enough money to get his Ph.D." But, he went on, common sense underlay all he said. "He always had something good to tell his listeners."

Without warning, one day the staid old institution of Upper Canada College was shaken to its foundations. For some time, however, there had been rumblings of discontent about the administration and the policies of its principal. The faculty was split down the middle on the issues. The board of governors stepped in. Their idea of a solution was to fire the whole kit and caboodle. They did so expeditiously, from the top man to the most junior master. When the dust cleared, the new incumbent faced the task of rehiring and/or confirming dismissals. Leacock was taken on again. He had been saved because he had sensibly remained aloof from pedagogic politics throughout the discontent.

Once in the driver's seat, the new principal, John Parkin, posthaste established his authority, beginning a tradition of leadership which has served UCC well. He liked Leacock. Surprisingly, for the Tartar he was supposed to be, Parkin liked him even more after an incident in which Leacock could have been accused of impudence.

Money continued to be a matter of high priority with Leacock, now twenty-six. He sat down and wrote a letter to the principal on small, notepaper-size stationery, putting the case for an increase in salary.

Towards the end of the first page it read:

. . . unless I am given an increase in salary, I shall be compelled to

and then the next page began

continue in my present capacity at the present salary.

The trick bore enough of a feathery touch to win Leacock a hearing. Shortly afterwards he became senior housemaster with, of course, a boost in emolument.

One day, ruminating about the discipline of the school and the suspected peccadillos of some of the masters, Parkin mentioned to Leacock *en passant*: "I wish I could break this malicious habit of smoking and swearing around the school."

However imaginative a newspaper account of his rejoinder may be, it is in character and is worth recording: "I know it's a difficult habit to break oneself of, Dr. Parkin, but if you will put all your energy into breaking yourself of it, I am sure grace will be given you."

Leacock smoked his pipe like an overloaded chimney. He swore like the farmer he once had been, chewed tobacco vigorously, and he was not above his pint of ale or dram of scotch.

Demanding as his new responsibilities were, the composition of skits and essays was squeezed (a word which would loom larger and larger in his writing routine) into the daily schedule as often as possible. Jokingly he used to say that his matutinal tussles with economics developed in him a sense of humor. So far as economics was concerned, in the end the joke was on him.

During the 1896 term Leacock despatched to *Life*, a New York weekly very different from the magazine which bears that name to-day, an account of a young man's first brush with a bank. Prophetically it carried the title "My Financial Career." Fourteen years later it would lead the contents of *Literary Lapses*, which marked the beginning of a very substantial financial career. In time it deservedly became the most widely read of any of the hundreds of his brief commentaries on human nature. In 1962 Canada's National Film Board was to preserve it on celluloid as an exquisite animated cartoon.

Like everything else, banks have changed radically since Leacock's youth. No longer need a tyro making his initial deposit approach the portals with apprehension. Nowadays he is likely to be herded into a corner by the manager himself and talked into purchasing a yacht or a car with the bank's money. For this reason the present younger generation's reaction to "My Financial Career" may be more muted; but as an example of polished writing skill, the piece remains superb.

Succeeding terms at UCC brought the incessant worker scraps of income from a variety of light-hearted journals in Canada, the U.S.A. and Europe. The money went into a savings account. There wasn't much opportunity to spend it at the rate he was working.

As the century drew to a close two events of singular importance in Leacock's life occurred. He read a book. He met a girl.

The book, which had just been published in 1899, was called *The Theory of the Leisure Class* and had begun to command even popular attention. Its author was a forty-two-year-old college instructor at the newly founded University of Chicago—Thorstein Bunde Veblen—and he was to become known as the founder of institutional economics. One reading caused Leacock to make up his mind overnight; he would like to know more about and from this professor. He set his cap at Chicago.

The girl was Beatrix Hamilton, whose family had been regularly summering near Orillia. Leacock met her during a tennis tournament. It was, to coin a phrase, love at first sight. Those who recall her today speak of her charm, graciousness, buoyant spirits and considerable talent as an amateur actress. She was strikingly handsome rather than the possessor of a chocolate box prettiness. Again Leacock made up his mind overnight and proposed to the lady known as Trix. She accepted.

When in 1899 he precipitately chucked in the towel at UCC in favor of marriage and further studies, Leacock had five hundred dollars in the bank. The bride-to-be would, in the normal course of events, inherit a large amount of money. Her mother was one of the Toronto Pellatts, and her father had amassed a fortune as a stockbroker.

A brief exchange of letters with the new university's registrar not only gained Leacock admission but also a scholarship of modest proportions. To this he added a small bank loan and the die was cast. By dint of determined application he wrapped up course after course and ended his first year with a high standing.

Now Leacock had to pin down Trix to a firm date for the nuptials. Her love affair with the stage transcended that of most theatre-smitten girls. She had undergone training in Boston and eventually contrived to gain a foothold, however slight, on Broadway. Stephen Leacock, the natural actor, thus found further common ground with her.

The final touch was added in the selection of the site for the wedding. New York's Little Church Around The Corner, which had been adopted by the theatrical profession, became the scene of the ceremony that was performed in August 1900. A formal honeymoon had to be dispensed with; it was back to the University of Chicago for the husband's second year.

Along with only five or six others, Leacock got down to work under Veblen. In his 1936 *My Discovery of the West*, Leacock remembered the professor:

> Veblen had a beautiful mind, free from anger and dispute, and heedless of all money motive. As a lecturer he had no manner, but sat mumbling into his lap, scarcely intelligible. But the words which thus fell into his lap were priceless. . . . His writings, brilliant though they are, are too abstruse for popular reading, and not abstruse enough to be unintelligible and rank as gospel, like the Social Credit of Major Douglas.

It is difficult to comprehend what in Veblen's then controversial theories appealed to the essentially conservative nature of the Canadian. Perhaps it was just the Veblen vogue which acted as the magnet, initially. The American had been enjoying the companionship and stimulation of such national figures as the philosopher John Dewey and the physiologist Jacques Loeb.

Veblen has been described as a visionary rather than an economist or sociologist, though certainly modern social sciences owe much to him. There was about his teachings the tone of a socialist and even, at times, an anarchist, with his belief in the hopelessness of either capitalism or state control providing solutions for modern society. Leacock's thirty-year-old mind, stuffed full of self-taught nineteenth-century orthodox theories, must have been awhirl.

Leacock and his wife, living in comfortable rooms and making friends effortlessly, found Chicago to their liking. But, somehow, he had to fatten an all too slender income and there was little time to give any thought to humorous compositions. Before entering his third year at Chicago he managed to make an arrangement with

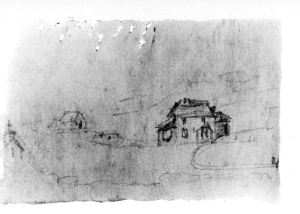

(1) A sketch by Stephen Leacock's mother of the cottage in Swanmore, Hants., where he was born on December 30, 1869. At far left is the church where he was baptized. *(Courtesy of Mr. Vincent Green)*

(2) On the reverse side of the sketch Agnes Leacock wrote "Cottage (& church) at Swanmore, Hants., England – where Stephen was born. 1870" *(Courtesy of Mr. Vincent Green)*

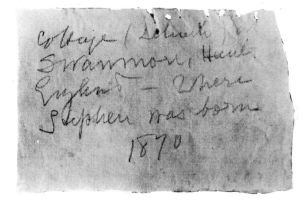

(3) The cottage as it looks today. *(Courtesy of Mr. Vincent Green.)*

(4) The Leacock family in the Isle of Wight about 1870. Left to right: Grandfather Thomas Murdock Leacock, Edward Philip Leacock ("My Remarkable Uncle"), Walter Peter Leacock, Jim, Dick, Agnes and a very young Stephen Leacock. (*Courtesy of the Public Archives of Canada*)

(5) Stephen Leacock in appropriately nautical attire at Ryde, Isle of Wight, about 1875. (*Courtesy of the Public Archives of Canada*)

(6) The Leacock family outside the farmhouse at Sutton, Ontario, in 1887. Left to right: Teddy and Gyp, Charlie, Stephen, Dot, Carrie, Agnes, Daisy, Maymee, Jim, Missie and George. (*Courtesy of the Public Archives of Canada*)

(7) Upper Canada College, Toronto, as Leacock knew it as pupil and teacher. The circular top floor window on the right marks the room he occupied as a master before the school moved in 1892. (*Courtesy of the Upper Canada College Archives*)

College Times.

Vol. VI.   TORONTO, NOVEMBER 4, 1886.   No. 1.

The College Times.

Joint Editors:

S. B. LEACOCK; F. J. DAVIDSON.

Sub-Editors:

B. M. JONES; H. G. CROCKER.

Publishing Committee:

S. B. LEACOCK, *Chairman*, H. G. CROCKER.
F. J. DAVIDSON,   D. J. ARMOUR, *Treasurer*.
B. M. JONES,   O. P. EDGAR, *Secretary*.

All literary contributions should be addressed to the Editors, with the writers' signatures appended.

All communications of a business character should be addressed to the Secretary.

The College Times is issued every alternate Thursday during the Collegiate year.

Yearly subscription fee, $1.00; single copies, 10 cents.

FANFARE.

From the depths of dimly-remembered days, bursting the shackles of inaction which have bound it in later years, the literary genius of Upper Canada College appears once more, and THE COLLEGE TIMES, phœnix-like, has re-arisen from its ashes.

ration evince literary tastes; and, when it is considered that many of the prominent men of Canada to-day, of those who take a most active interest in the promotion of literature, were once students of this College, no one will be sorry to see the boys of the present following in their footsteps.

To those who have spent their boyhood's days here, in this time-honoured temple of learning, THE COLLEGE TIMES will return like an echo of the past, which, reverberating through the chambers of memory, arouses reminiscences of long-forgotten, yet familiar, experiences of younger days.

To those who have more recently said farewell to the College, it will be a tie, binding them more closely to the old associations which they treasure in connection with the school they have left.

And, among the boys of to-day, it will, we trust, meet with a popularity which we shall endeavour to make it merit; and, on the whole, with a success at least as great as that of its predecessor.

(8) Leacock's distinguished record at Upper Canada College was marked by his editorship of *The College Times*.

And men, not boys, are now at her feet,
   And yet—do you think I'm a fool?
Why! I don't give a rip for the maiden sweet,
   And the Tam's worn while carrying coal.

D. F.

THE VISION OF MIRZA.

(New Edition.)

*   *   *   *   *

The genius then led me to the top of a lofty building, situated within pleasing gardens, and surmounted with a turret on which waved an antique flag. On examining its waving folds I saw there cabalistic writing, executed in dull green, upon the surface of the flag. The writing appeared to be Arabic, for I was able to distinctly

is Mark-us Furius Demerit-us. His," said the genius mournfully, "has been a *tragical* life. But look not on them more," he added, nervously, methought. "Nay, tell me," said I, "why they appear so joyous?" "They have been to the bursar's," hastily answered the genius. While I was yet pondering on this mystic answer one of the Romans down below looked upwards. "Come off the roof, you duffer!" he called to the genius, and we adjourned.   *   *   *

S. B. L.

P.S.—I have since made inquiries as to who my friend the genius was. I only succeeded, however, in finding that he is in the sixth form; but as there are so many geniuses in the sixth, the information has not enabled me to discover his identity. I have heard that a price of ten demerits has been set on his head.

(9, 10) It was in *The College Times* edition of April 7, 1887, that "The Vision of Mirza" appeared. This was the first published article signed by Leacock. *(Illustrations courtesy of the Upper Canada College Archives)*

(11) University College, the University or Toronto, in Leacock's day. His interrupted course there spanned the period from 1887 to 1891. *(Photograph from the University of Toronto Archives)*

Stephen B. Leacock.

Upper Canada College,

— May. 7. 1886.

— Oct. 9. 1886.

— Dec. 18. 1886.

Handy Classical Dictionary.

Jan. 15. 1887,

May 6 1887

Stephen B Leacock

Uxbridge

April 9

1889

(12) On the flyleaf of his dictionary Leacock recorded some of his movements, including his sojourn as a teacher at Uxbridge. *(By courtesy of Mr. Howard F. A. Lacey, Upper Canada College)*

The Varsity

PUBLISHED EVERY TUESDAY MORNING DURING THE ACADEMIC YEAR, IN THE UNIVERSITY OF TORONTO

BY

THE LITERARY AND SCIENTIFIC SOCIETY

The Annual Subscription is $2.00 a year, payable strictly in advance. Single copies, 10 cents.

All literary contributions and items of College news should be addressed to THE EDITOR, University College, Toronto.

All communications of a business nature should be addressed to THE BUSINESS MANAGER. Advertising rates can be had on application.

The office of THE VARSITY is at the corner of Spadina avenue and College street, rooms 3 and 5, Bank of Commerce Building.

Anonymous contributions will be published if approved by the Editor.

The Editorial Staff.

EDITOR-IN-CHIEF	- - -	WALTER S. McLAY, '91.
BUSINESS MANAGER	- -	G. HOWARD FERGUSON, '91.
TREASURER	- - -	WILLIAM H. BUNTING, '92.

ASSOCIATE EDITORS.

C. A. STUART, '91.   J. S. SCOTT, '91.
S. B. LEACOCK, '91.   A. P. NORTHWOOD, '91.
A. M. STEWART, '91.   H. W. BROWN, '92.
S. J. ROBERTSON, '92.

Medical representatives on the staff have not yet been appointed.

The Directorate.

C. A. STUART, '91, Chairman.   W. H. KNOX, '93.
J. McNICOL, '91.   W. C. CLARK, '93.
A. T. KIRKPATRICK, '91.   F. H. MOSS, School of Medicine.
J. A. McLEAN, '92   J. B. LOCKHART, '92.
J. W. ODELL, '92, Secretary.

OCTOBER 7, 1890.

The Sanctum Philosopher.

THE Sanctum Philosopher will be glad to receive any contributions that may be produced by those philosophically inclined among his readers. Short comments upon University matters, notices of books recently published, literary curiosities and the discussion of current events in the literary world will be gladly inserted. Caustic sarcasm of an impersonal nature and cynical reflections on the vanity of human life will be especially welcomed.

* * *

The following quaint pun has been forwarded to me, accompanied, I am proud to say, by two dollars: Two Frenchmen were one day observing a passing funeral. The horse, whose office it was to draw the hearse, appeared restive, and, at length, frightened at the dulcet strains of a hand organ, took madly to its heels, "rider and hearse in one sad burial blent." "Ah, comme c'est drôle," remarked monsieur to his companion, "il a pris le mors entre ses dents."

* * *

Alas! how often are we wounded in our *armour propre!* How often do the tenderest feelings of our nature excite the mockery of the ignorant! It was my lot last week to carry to the Sanctum a bundle of papers bearing on the title page the classic inscription, THE VARSITY. Feeling within my bosom the conscious pride of authorship, I was gazing fondly at the literary babe that nestled in my arms. When about to cross the threshold of the door that leads to Parnassus, I met a horde of urchins pouring from a neighbouring day school. "Say, mister," cried one of the foremost *gamins*, as they surrounded me, "Will you gim'me one of them *handbills*." Oh, ye gods, HANDBILLS!

* * *

Many are the interesting souvenirs that have been made from portions of the débris of our great alas. The

---

(13, 14) At the University of Toronto, Leacock became involved in editorial work on *The Varsity* newspaper. He also contributed a column under the nom de plume of "The Sanctum Philosopher." (*Photographs from the University of Toronto Archives*)

(15) The staff of *The Varsity,* 1891. Leacock, at right, wearing mortarboard, was later very proud of this picture, and hung it in his study at Old Brewery Bay. (*Courtesy of the Public Archives of Canada*)

(16) Leacock taught at Upper Canada College from 1889 till 1899. In this classroom photo of the Class of '97 Leacock is seventh from the left. *(Courtesy of the Upper Canada College Archives)*

McGill University in Montreal to act as a special lecturer in history and political science, shuttling to and from the Windy City until he acquired his doctorate.

To those who have been critical down the years of Leacock's qualifications as an economist—and they are legion—it must be pointed out that much of his work at Chicago occurred in the political science department, although the subject of his thesis dealt with laissez-faire. As a prominent American educator (and a former student of Leacock) has noted: "I do not recall that there was anyone in the Chicago economics department of the time who had the competence to give good training."

In his affectionate account of Leacock's life, Dr. Curry recites from the record of work at the University of Chicago an incident which marked the oral portion of Leacock's Ph.D. examination in May of 1903. He had been directed by the committee's chairman to discuss the tax system of the state of Illinois, to which came the frank and firm reply: "Gentlemen, let me say that I know nothing of the tax system of the state of Illinois, but, if you will allow me, I will speak on the theory of values." He spoke for hours, with his adjudicators taking turns to listen to him. He passed.

Like the head boy distinction of yore, Leacock treasured his Ph.D. for ever after. It represented the fruit of much hard work and financial strain on his part and he didn't propose to let people forget it. As a pose, he spoofed the accomplishment, and in all likelihood there was a particle of truth in the amusing tale he told of how he decided to take his Ph.D. to Europe with him. The only way to do this, of course, was to sign himself on the ship's passenger list as Doctor Leacock.

> I was just settling down in my cabin when the steward rapped, opened the door, and announced: "Dr. Leacock? The Captain's compliments, doctor, will you please come and have a look at the second stewardess' knee?" I was off like a shot. But it was no use. Another fellow got there ahead of me. He was a Doctor of Divinity.

In a moment of false modesty he had something else to say about the acquisition of a doctorate of philosophy when he stated: "The meaning of this degree is that the recipient of instruction is examined for the last time in his life, and is pronounced completely full. After this, no new ideas can be imparted to him."

Yet he had every reason to be proud and overjoyed. He had entered the twentieth century with a bride, a doctorate and at least a clear idea of what he wanted to do—become a university professor. The only problem was, where?

IV ❧❧

"Leaky Steamcock"

It was not to be a hit-and-miss business. Leacock wanted to select a university as a man would pick a home—the intention being to bed down for an indefinite, perhaps a permanent stay. In his innocence Leacock hoped for an appointment at the University of Toronto. This recommended itself on the grounds that he had already broken the social ice there, Trix would be in familiar surroundings, he was an alumnus, and he would be within shouting distance of the northland lakes and woods he knew so well. McGill had been helpful when he had needed help. But there were, it seemed to him, more advantages on the Toronto scene.

A fellow teacher at Upper Canada College, Pelham Edgar, had noted and admired Leacock's self-imposed early morning economic studies program. In those UCC days Edgar had introduced Leacock to Professor James Mavor of the University of Toronto in the hope that the latter would encourage Leacock to the point of guiding him in his reading. It soon became evident that Mavor didn't like the young teacher, and he pointedly refused to co-operate. Whether this was a purely personal animus or an honest belief that Leacock was not cut out to be an economist never became clear. The unpleasant fact is that Mavor's attitude had hardened by the time that Leacock sought a job at the university eight years later. Mavor, as head of the department, remained adamant, and by this action was responsible for Leacock's going to Montreal.

When, as a second choice, McGill was approached, the way had already been paved. Not only had Leacock, as a special lecturer, given the first course in political science in the faculty's history, but Dr. William Peterson (later Sir William), the principal and vice-chancellor, had cause to remember the fact.

Members of the class of Arts '02 liked the lecturer's method of teaching and were not hesitant to talk about him. They finally decided to take the unprecedented step of formally informing the head of the university of these feelings. A committee of the class waited upon Principal Peterson to tell him what a good teacher Leacock was. It was not in the nature of Peterson to wax enthusiastic over any student opinions on any subject, and he said so. There the matter rested.

Leacock knew nothing about this incident, nor would he learn of it until 1935, when an Old McGillian told him. He was gratified, however, by the expeditious manner in which his application for a staff appointment was approved. In 1903 he became a full-time member of the recently created department of economics and political science.

The university which the thirty-three-year-old Leacock was joining had already, under Sir William Dawson, established an international reputation in medicine and the sciences. Peterson, who had succeeded Dawson in 1893, believed that the Faculty of Arts needed to be and should be nurtured and expanded. He tried to furnish the incentive. A man in his middle years, with airs of aloofness and unconscious condescension, Peterson was often in conflict with the staff, the student body and even the people of the metropolis. But Leacock, some twenty years his junior, had few complaints about the principal. Both were from the old country, both were dyed-in-the-wool imperialists, both were humanists, and they shared a classical background. Peterson was not to evince an intimate concern in the younger man's progress, but Leacock was to benefit greatly from their kindred interests.

The Montreal in which the Leacocks settled (they had taken a small flat near the college) had long ago become the commercial and cultural centre of the country. Its population then had reached 380,000, compared to the very much more provincial Toronto's

120,000. Yet the James McGill farmstead, on which the university had been built, continued to have the aura of a sylvan retreat, set in the midst of a residential district which bore the marks of much wealth. It was only at the turn of the century that businessmen thought of moving their operations from the downtown port section to the comparatively peaceful environs of St. Catherine Street. The line of demarcation between the English-speaking and French-speaking area was still unmistakably drawn. Leacock showed no inclination to stray across it. He was not anti-French, just very pro-Anglo-Saxon, and always would be.

Once established in their new home, the Leacocks were now able to execute a plan which had been in the making for a year. There had never been time for a proper honeymoon three years previously. The opportunity now presented itself prior to undertaking the McGill duties in the autumn. They went to Europe for a few weeks in the summer, travelling in England and France.

He returned to an Arts faculty where the enrolment of male students numbered only one hundred and fifty-six. The majority of these were not disposed to dedicate themselves to the cause of economics and political science. That it was a select undergraduate body he was certain. He made the point years later in his history of Montreal. A state university, such as the University of Toronto, "has to teach everybody. McGill doesn't have to teach anybody. In Medicine, McGill from the richness of its soil, restricts its crops as they restrict coffee in Brazil and hogs in Missouri."

The nights of extramural humorous writing appeared to have been dismissed as a passing phase, "when an industrious man of my genius, if he worked hard and kept clear of stimulants and bad company, could earn as much as eight dollars a month with his pen." The two dollars here (which, in fact, was what he received from a Toronto newspaper for his first funny effort) and five dollars there were no longer essential. He did not propose to fritter away more substantial talents.

The wit remained in evidence, however. A student of that era, the late Murray G. Brooks, of Easthampton, Massachusetts (who helped to compose the McGill anthem, "Hail, Alma Mater"), kept a journal of his campus days:

When we entered the classroom for political science, we were all agog with curiosity. Up to the professor's desk shuffled an untidy, dishevelled figure, apparently just risen from a night on a park bench, none other than Stephen Leacock, known to us students as "Leaky Steamcock." Before he said a word, we all wanted to laugh. Sometimes brilliant and scintillating; often, perhaps after a bad night, serious and deadly dull, his flow of words was as tangled as his mussy hair. Occasionally his humor would break through and he would have the class in a roar. A born actor, at his best he could hold the class spellbound. No one ever skipped one of his lectures. The risk of missing one of his bright days was too great. A tricky examiner, he never gave as high marks as one hoped for.

It was in Brook's class that two young men, who always chose to sit in the back row, used to indulge surreptitiously in a game of tic-tac-toe whenever monotony set in, as it sometimes did. One day one of the young men was absent. Before starting his lecture, Leacock turned to another student in the front row and said: "Mr. Jones, would you please go to the back row and play tic-tac-toe with Mr. Smith; he has no one to play with him today."

The weariness of the rigid schoolroom had given way to the freshness and informality of the lecture room. He was making it his own. The performer in him gradually began to show itself. Moreover, Leacock had formulated a theory about teaching. He did not believe in chasing students "over a prescribed ground at a prescribed pace like a flock of sheep." That system contained in it the seeds of destruction. Reluctantly he adhered to the rules which insisted upon tests and recitations and marks and attendance sheets. He abided by the regulations, though they were more often than not perfunctorily observed.

As he was to say many times in his writings, Leacock held in contempt any literal application of the principle of written examinations. There were other ways of evaluating young minds. A striking example of this has been provided by George S. Currie, of Montreal, a noted McGill alumnus of the professor's early stewardship.

Currie and two fellow students were walking home from college after having just written an economics paper. Several blocks from the university they encountered "Leaky Steamcock," who was en route to the campus. He stopped to greet the boys and then volunteered:

> I've just passed all three of you in your exam. You (pointing at one of the three) have come first. There's not much difference between you two (indicating Currie and his friend), so I've tied you both for second.

Leacock had not, of course, yet seen the exam papers. With supreme confidence in his judgment of people, he knew what he'd find in them. The results, when posted, were as predicted.

Let it be said that this was by no means a common practice—yet Leacock always had the measure of his students.

Meanwhile, besides making their students write examinations, professors were also expected to write books, to justify their existence. In the middle of the 1903 session Leacock addressed himself to just such a task. His topic, of course, was political science. He spent three years on his *Elements of Political Science.* When it was published the word spread that here was a no-nonsense, crystal-clear survey of the fundamentals of the subject. Although he went beyond those fundamentals to grapple with contemporary and temporary conditions which eventually rendered the treatise passé, the book eventually earned more royalties than the best of Leacock's best-selling fiction of the future. In short order it became required reading in three dozen American universities, was translated into eighteen languages (including Urdu), was reissued seven years later, and was revised in 1921.

This publishing success brought him added stature at McGill. Invitations for outside speaking engagements were beginning to come his way. Public bodies found the combination of academician and entertainer irresistible. He had not written a line of humor for eight years. The speaker's platform, however, served as a proving ground for his histrionics and his humor.

Leacock's abilities had come to the attention of Martha Carey Thomas, organizer and president of Bryn Mawr College from the staff of which the professor of economics had recently resigned. She wrote to Leacock asking him if he would like to consider taking on the position. Leacock carefully explained his feelings on the matter in a letter to Principal Peterson:

"The position she is offering only carries with it a salary of $2000 and, as the cost of living at Bryn Mawr is very high, it has no material advantages over the position I now occupy. . . . I wrote to her and declined to apply. I thought it better to let you know of this in order that, in the event of Martha Thomas writing to you, you should not suppose that the matter was of my seeking."

After a decent interval Principal Peterson received another and much longer letter from Leacock which began, "I wish to ask for an increase of five hundred dollars in salary", and which required six and a half pages to explain why he wanted the raise. He outlined his achievements to date, including the financially successful book on political science, but quickly added: ". . . my private life has been an uninterrupted succession of overdue accounts, protested notes and legal proceedings for debt." In conclusion he pointed out: "It is not however because I am in debt that I am asking for an increase in pay. It is because I think I am worth it."

Peterson concurred in this self-assessment of worth and granted the $500 raise.

In 1905 Leacock was granted leave of absence by the board of governors for a series of six lectures on the British Empire under the auspices of the May Court Club in the nation's capital. A year later he was appointed associate professor of political science and history. Then, in 1907, he published another work, *Baldwin, Lafontaine, Hincks: Responsible Government.* This was a historical study of Canada's early political affairs. It was included in the extensive *Makers of Canada* series, but otherwise caused little stir.

In the classroom he had been primarily identified as a political scientist and a historian, filling both roles admirably. But Leacock, his Ph.D. in economics ever in mind, nursed an ambition to make a reputation as an economist and he let this be known to the university administration.

He let it be known in a manner which could only raise the hackles of his senior colleagues. The newcomer's bumptiousness had not smoothed his path at the university. Now he dreamed up new courses and managed to get them into the curriculum without the prior approval of his immediate boss, Dr. A. W. Flux, the departmental head.

Flux initiated a considerable correspondence with Dr. Peterson over Leacock's personality and methods. He went further, writing to Veblen at the University of Chicago to ask him point blank if he considered that Leacock had the necessary competence to undertake lecturing in economics. Flux reported to Peterson that he found in Veblen's reply "a hesitancy to praise" and that any enthusiasm had been couched in "curiously vague terms."

"For the sake of peace" Flux let Leacock have his way. And Leacock doggedly pursued it.

On the campus he was surrounded by distinguished colleagues, notably the great physicist Dr. Ernest (later Baron) Rutherford, who pioneered the nuclear research which led to the atom bomb. On one occasion Leacock's mother had been brought to town to be shown the sights. At a reception Agnes was introduced to Rutherford. She had been warned that he was a famous scientist. That was quite enough for her to jump to conclusions. He must therefore, she decided, automatically be an agnostic. Summoning every theological argument at her command, she proceeded to dress down the professor as though he were a celebrated infidel. Leacock, describing the scene afterwards, said: "I admired Mother but my heart went out to Rutherford."

Leacock himself showed more interest in what he called the eccentric confrères of his own Arts faculty. One of these was "Pat" Johnson, professor of mathematics and dean of Arts:

> His specialty was exactitude, the full rigor of the rules. He looked on the rules of the Arts faculty, as formulated in the calendar, as comparable to the propositions of Euclid. I remember he once reprimanded the professors on the ground that "various blanks" had been removed from the calendar and he wanted them put back. As to what he meant,—ask Euclid, who was suffering something of the same treatment at that very time.
>
> I came in for a reprimand from the Dean before I had been a month at McGill. I had invited a distinguished American visitor, an authority on immigration (the topic of the hour) to come and talk to my class. As a matter of academic interest and common sense, I got permission beforehand from Principal Peterson. The lecture was a great success. But the next Monday Dean Johnson sent for me. "You had a stranger in your classroom on Thursday?" he said. I admitted it. "He gave a lecture," said the Dean, "and don't you know that no person is permitted to give a lecture in a McGill classroom without the consent of the Corporation?" "It was all right," I said, "I got leave from Dr. Peterson." "Hoot!" said Pat, "and what would he know about the rules? and him only here seven years." That was the back kick he wanted, so he let me go, kindly enough.
>
> At the time I thought this "seven years" very funny. Later I came to share his opinion entirely, and to feel that no opinion at McGill should be taken except from people there at least twenty years on the spot.

But the anecdote of McGill—every word of it true—that will never die concerned a friend and colleague of Leacock, who called it "The Story of the Professor, the Gold Fish and the Policeman":

> One of our professors of physiology was out visiting one winter night,

and the people at the house showed him a gold-fish that had died because the water that it was in had frozen. The professor looked at the fish and said, "Let me take it home and I think that tomorrow I can treat it in the laboratory and revive it."

So when he started for home they wrapped the gold-fish in a bit of tissue paper and the professor put it in his overcoat pocket. It was a cold night, very late and with lots of deep snow along the street. On the way home he put his hand into his coat pocket and accidentally flipped out the gold-fish and it fell into the snow.

The professor knelt down to pick it up, but he couldn't find it and stayed there on his knees groping for it. Just then a policeman came along on his beat, stopped and said, "What are you doing there?"

Professors hate to be questioned. He just looked over his shoulder and said, "I am trying to find a gold-fish."

The policeman then understood that he was dealing with a mental case, and he said, coaxingly, "Now you just come along with me and I'll take you to a place where we've a whole lot of gold-fish—all you want!"

"All right," the professor said, "only just help me to get this one first."

To humor him the policeman knelt down and began groping in the snow and, first thing he knew, out came a gold-fish! He was absolutely flabbergasted. "Great heavens!" he said. "Are there any more?" "Maybe a whole lot," said the professor. As he started off for home again, the policeman was still on his knees looking for gold-fish.

This yarn was not embellished; in fact, it lacked a few of the actual facts. There had been an eye-witness to the episode—Stephen Leacock, who had been out on the town with the professor of physiology.

In the Spring of 1907 Canada's relatively new Governor-General, Earl Grey, proved to be Stephen Leacock's latest and most important personal conquest. He had heard Leacock speak in Ottawa on the topic of Empire unity. He was impressed. At the same time he was aware that the Cecil Rhodes Trust was looking for someone to visit the outposts of Empire to speak in the Imperial cause.

Earl Grey lost no time in summoning the professor to Government House in the nation's capital and sought his reaction to the idea of a tour to include South Africa, Australia and New Zealand. The Governor-General reminded Leacock that his friend Dr. Parkin, of Upper Canada College, had made a similar tour twenty years before on behalf of the Imperial Federation League with eminently impressive results. Leacock replied that he would give the question prompt and profound consideration.

A few days later, on March 26, Earl Grey received a four-page memorandum from Leacock setting forth in detail how such an undertaking should be conducted, complete with a general title for the lectures to be delivered—"Imperial Development and Organization." Nor did Leacock overlook the matter of the lecturer's emolument—a suggested five hundred pounds per annum.

Thereupon the Governor-General did not miss a trick. He speedily enlisted the active approval of Dr. Parkin, who was now a trustee of the Cecil Rhodes' bequest. More important he wrote to Peterson at McGill, inviting him to Government House "to discuss with you a plan I have very much at heart, namely, that of turning Dr. Leacock loose on to Australia and Canada, as an Imperial missionary. . . . Will you spare him? He might, at the end of two years, return to you. . . . I think you will be doing a service to Canada and the Empire if you can see your way to allow him to do this work, for which he is by nature so admirably fitted."

In the end McGill's board of governors granted their new associate professor of political science and history one year's leave of absence. Moreover the university was to pay all expenses, with the Rhodes' Trust making a cash contribution. For his part, Earl Grey went on record that if the final costs exceeded the money available "I will guarantee the difference."

Leacock was 37 when he and Trix sailed from Halifax in May on the Allan liner *Victorian* for England. Shortly after his arrival he opened his series of talks at the Royal Colonial Institute, which promptly made him a member, and at the Victoria League in London. At Oxford he addressed a group of Rhodes Scholars and was a dinner guest at All Souls.

Canada's Governor-General had paved the way well. Leacock spent the week-end with Rudyard Kipling at his country house, Bateman's in Sussex. He lunched with Arthur J. Balfour, lately Prime Minister of the United Kingdom. And he saw much of Fleet Street's notables, particularly the editors of *The Times* and *The Morning Post*, and wrote an article for the latter.

After spending a few days in Paris "for my wife's shopping," the Leacocks set sail for the Antipodes from Marseilles on the *Macedonia*. From the purely mechanical standpoint, it was an awkwardly arranged itinerary, for though they arrived in Australia, the first speeches were to be delivered in New Zealand. After both these countries came South Africa and then the Leacocks had to double back to catch a ship for Canada.

But there can be no doubt about the triumphant progress of the humorist-to-be. He was lionized everywhere he went, one of his greatest successes being at the University of Cape Town. After landing on Canada's West Coast in due course Leacock continued his speech-making in all the major Canadian cities from Vancouver to Montreal.

"When I state that these lectures," he wrote in a biographical note for a publication called *Canada,* "were followed almost immediately by the Union of South Africa, the Banana Riots in Trinidad, and the Turko-Italian war, I think you can form some idea of their importance."

The applauding audiences, the glittering dinners and receptions, the virtual hero-worship of one who could make arid topics palatable by the injection of diverting digressions were exciting enough. At the same time, Leacock had been thinking of things of quite a different order. A new note was struck in a missive the acclaimed traveller wrote to his sister Daisy before a third of his world-encircling venture had been accomplished.

To her Stephen Leacock expressed the hope that by next Spring (it was then September, 1907) he would be able to purchase "a small place on Lake Couchiching." He was prepared, he said, to live in a tent or a shack until he could afford to build on the property. He knew what he wanted—a garden, a small orchard, a ten-acre farm, hens, and a cow and possibly a horse. In a later letter from "down under" he stuck to the subject as though it were an obsession:

When I build my house, I shall make it very plain but at the same time very large. I mean to plant a good avenue of trees leading up to it. In a few years with hard work it will begin to look fine. After it has been up two or three years, I shall brick it with white brick and put in lattice windows in place of the original ones and tile instead of shingles on the roof. Then, by adding a sun dial, a nook and three wall-flowers, it will become a charming English place—I'm tired of cities and people—it's a case of Good-bye proud world, I'm going home.

For a man who had begun to climb with authority the foothills of a lofty profession, the bald admission of a desire to get away from the mainstream of activity must have struck his intimates as odd. To make it more puzzling, he did not seem to have any alternative occupation in mind. Nor was this desire for a place in the country a passing fancy engendered by the rough and tumble of travel in strange parts. His mother was presently to receive a letter in which the son even talked of retiring at or before the age of fifty-five.

The news which awaited his return to duty must have tempered any rash move to cut himself off from the active world. He was greeted with the announcement of his appointment as professor of political economy. His salary rose to thirty-five hundred dollars. Shortly after this welcome development, the board of governors passed a curious resolution. Leacock was to be given a seat on the Faculty of Arts; in addition the principal was instructed "to ask" Dr. Leacock "to take charge" of the department of political economy "until the Board is ready to proceed to the appointment of a professor."

Leacock "took charge," with a thousand-dollar increase for his trouble.

A month before Leacock set out on his Empire travels, he was one of a dozen men—university staff and local graduates—who met with a view to discussing the advisability and feasibility of setting up a club for college people in the city. The twelve decided to go ahead with the project. In the spring of 1908 the University Club of Montreal opened its doors a few blocks along Dorchester Street from the veteran St. James's Club.

In this connection an erroneous idea that has gained wide currency needs to be corrected. Neither of these social institutions was the object of Leacock's barbs when he created what he called the Mausoleum Club in *Arcadian Adventures with the Idle Rich* and subsequent sketches. Plainly what Leacock had in mind was the recently organized (1906) Mount Royal Club on Sherbrooke Street (Plutoria Avenue in some of his satires)—the expensive and exclusive home away from home for cautious conviviality on the part of Montreal's affluent set. While Leacock often consorted with the latter, this did not mean that they enjoyed his stamp of approval.

As for the University Club, this was to mean a great deal in the life of Leacock. Its jealously guarded masculine atmosphere served as an escape from the flightier affairs of home and town and gown.

Although hardly a celibate, Leacock was beginning to form some views about the place of woman in man's scheme of things. Emphatically women were out of place in a man's club, and soon he would grieve openly over their infiltration of institutions of higher learning. There were other club amenities, too, which were vital to him. He could, to his heart's content, concentrate on two favorite pastimes—whisky drinking and billiards playing. He was adept at both.

In the summer of 1908 the longing for country life which he had expressed in family correspondence from the Antipodes took concrete shape. He started surveying his old stamping ground in the Orillia region. One of Lake Couchiching's sheltered bays appealed to him and he decided that he had found what he was after. On the property he purchased, a brewery had once operated. What was to become a famous address—Old Brewery Bay—came into being. ("I have known that name, Old Brewery Bay, to make people thirsty by correspondence as far away as Nevada.") Throughout his life Leacock was a useful carpenter. So with brother Charlie's help, temporary shelter was soon erected. The original building, named the "cook house," was to become the nucleus of a dwelling that grew in all directions, adding rooms and wings as the need arose.

As stubborn as he was gifted, the scholar who wanted to put the dust of urban living behind him, even to renounce the "proud world," had made a start. He had invested his savings in what he hoped would ultimately become "a charming English place." He was thirty-nine when his love for the rural existence caused him to sink down roots, just as he had consolidated himself in the academic world.

Miss Eleanor Cruickshank, of Maple, Ontario, took most of Leacock's courses at McGill from 1906 to 1910. She recalls an incident relating to the professor's new-found joy at Orillia. At the end of the 1909 session he announced to his students that he was turning down an invitation to give a series of ten lectures in the Maritime Provinces at one hundred dollars a lecture. The reason? The farm at Orillia was going to take all his time and he had to go and plant his vegetables. Being an economist, he knew that if he could market his produce without the benefit of a middleman, he would make more money.

Stephen wrote his brother George in Kirkland Lake to contact the local merchant and quoted such low prices that the retailer, with visions of supplying the fresh-vegetable-hungry market of the whole northland, said he would take a carload each week.

Time passed and no carload. At last George wrote again to Stephen. The next week a six-quart basket with a few radishes, carrots and beets arrived with a note: "Expectation greater than realization."

With all his hankering after the peace of the countryside, Leacock was enough of a practical economist to know where his bread and butter were coming from. And he wanted more bread and more butter and a lot more whisky. One of his Montreal cronies at this time was B. K. Sandwell, a former pupil of Leacock at UCC. Sandwell was currently the drama editor of *The Herald*. In the near future he would become associate editor of Montreal's *Financial Times* before joining Leacock as an associate professor of economics for four years. Thereafter he was to go on to Queen's University to head the English department before assuming the editorship of *Saturday Night*, which he retained for nineteen years. Leacock and Sandwell clearly had a lot in common. In 1909 they failed to see eye to eye on one issue.

Leacock had been glancing through what it pleased him to call his "literary files." These consisted of manuscripts, clippings and copies of magazines—the results of his nocturnal humorous labors of the 1890s. It seemed to him that a selection of these efforts put together in book form might produce some revenue, thus refurbishing a bank account depleted by his recent real estate acquisition.

What did Sandwell think about the possibility? Unhesitatingly Sandwell advised against such folly, arguing that a collection of this kind could only do harm to Leacock's substantial professional reputation.

This advice was ignored. Leacock packed up the material and sent it off to Houghton Mifflin, who had published *Elements of Political Science*. He invited their opinion about the humorous pieces. They regretted to say that they were not interested, chiefly because "the humor was too uncertain."

Sandwell's stand seemed to have been vindicated. But Leacock refused to be discouraged, as most neophytes would have been. When brother George (who was said to have been even wittier than Stephen) showed up one evening, he was persuaded to look over the old pieces that had appeared in print between 1891 and 1897. He pronounced them still good. He was ready to back his belief by seeing a local printer about the costs of the proposed undertaking.

Consulting the Gazette Printing Company, George learned that a modest book, retailing at thirty-five cents, would give the author a profit of seven cents. The two brothers decided to have a go, with George paying the printers fifty dollars on account. A proper division of the profits, it was agreed, would guarantee five cents per copy to George as publisher, the balance of two cents to Stephen.

The bargain was to be short-lived. On reflection—whether because of his genuine concern about risk, or a sixth sense that he really might "have something" in this endeavor—Stephen reimbursed his brother and assumed full responsibility.

The exchange of letters between Leacock and the Gazette people revealed the former as a hard-headed businessman, with sound ideas on copyright, distribution and the like. He even assumed the mantle of his own promotion manager, preparing posters and seeing that they were properly displayed by the newsdealers who had undertaken to handle his little book. Future publishers were to come up against this "know-how," occasionally to their dismay.

Leacock's inordinate love of alliteration—he could never shake it—produced a title, and *Literary Lapses* was gobbled up in no time, all three thousand copies and all in the Montreal area alone.

As this was happening, John Lane, the well-known British publisher, arrived in Montreal on one of his annual visits to Canada. He always had two purposes in mind when he came to the city—to promote his own firm's books and to search for rare steel engravings, of which he was an avid collector. In the process of browsing he picked up a copy of *Literary Lapses* for shipboard reading. Enraptured by the stylish nonsense, immediately on his arrival in London Lane cabled Leacock an offer to publish an English edition. Leacock replied, "I accept with thanks!"

While the book was in the works during 1910, a trip to England was indicated in order to meet Lane, sign a contract and feel the publishing pulse generally. He would draw on the proceeds (about two thousand dollars) of his locally produced book, banking, too, on what might be forthcoming from the professional British publication. He was not, however, going to miss any tricks in the meantime. On one of the rare occasions Leacock resorted to a typewriter, he pecked out a letter to C. Harold Hale, editor of the Orillia newspaper, the *Packet Times*:

> I am going over to Europe this summer and shall not be able to come to Orillia, and would like to rent my little place there. . . . As you know it has a shanty on it with furniture and cooking things etc. . . . The shanty is, of course, no good; I say it in all humility, but at any rate it should make a first class camping place, and the point itself is delightful. I was wondering whether you would care to find me a tenant for it. I will rent the place for the summer for $40, and if you rent it for me I will give you $5 commission on doing so. Advertising in the *Packet* would not cost you anything and might find a tenant. . . .

There was another thirty-five dollars to go towards the English visit!

For John Lane and his Bodley Head house this was the beginning of a long and profitable association. For Leacock it was not only to be an expansion of his present world, but a whole new world. If he was not exactly, as the Bodley Head shouted from the rooftops, "The Canadian Mark Twain" (Clemens had just died), the generally favorable critical reception and the widespread sale of *Literary Lapses* set him on a totally unanticipated course.

The tenor of the reviews in both England and the United States placed emphasis on the American character of the humor. In this connection it is worth noting that an American publisher had first rejected the work before Lane's English house, in very quick time, accepted it without reservations.

In London the *Pall Mall Gazette* hailed the little book as "sketches that are worthy of comparison with the best in American humor." A similar, if slightly more qualifying note was sounded by the New York *Herald*: "A good example of the humor of American journalism."

American in large part, yes, in its use of blunderbuss exaggeration; yet uniquely English in its keen sense of the ridiculous. Certainly the tentative tomfoolery was journalistic with a vengeance; quite understandably so, since it had been written in a school or university atmosphere, with all the collegiate influences which that conveys. Moreover, it had been originally tailored for the popular funny weeklies of the day.

Admittedly "My Financial Career" has been Leacock's most reprinted short piece; "Boarding House Geometry," contrived as it is, evokes the essence of the landlady stereotype and the domain she dominates; and "Hoodoo McFiggin's Christmas" is literally autobiographical and, as such, significant; otherwise the judgment of Houghton, Mifflin was not wide of the mark. The contents were part ingenious, part infelicitous, part all thumbs. The reason for the great and immediate impact it had on its readers lay in its fresh simplicity. To proclaim as a masterpiece this bundle of bright little bits—as has been done by otherwise responsible critics—is to make a travesty of literary values.

The market was quick to react to the book's success. Led by the editor of *Harper's*, newspapers and magazines of all kinds rushed in with requests for contributions from this refreshingly comic and, in the main, kindly satirist of the human condition.

Literary Lapses went into edition after edition after edition. As it snowballed, its author found himself at a crossroads, with three possible roads open to him. He was on record as stating that he wanted to get away from the madding crowds. He was a figure of growing importance in university circles. His name was now on countless tongues as a facile master of the absurd.

With three choices at hand, would it be foolhardy to try to combine them? He would try.

After all, 1910 was also the year of the comet—Halley's. Its appearance, however, had been predictable.

V

Riding Off In All Directions

"I did not permanently get started writing, except for a few odd pieces, until I was forty years old." Leacock interposed this bit of encouragement in some advice to aspiring authors many years later. He might have added that life for him had really begun at forty. The reception of *Literary Lapses* had opened up many new vistas for him. A man of many sides had now to choose sides.

The pleasant situation in which he found himself in 1910 did not so much detract—as Sandwell had warned—from his position as an economic theorist as it distracted attention from the fact that he actually was not properly qualified as an economist at all.

Dr. Jacob Viner, of Princeton, a distinguished economist who served as one of President Roosevelt's "Brains-Trusters" during the New Deal period, studied under Leacock. "His teaching," says Viner, "of what he thought advanced economics was a farce, and I'm afraid some of us gave him a rough time, until the girls in the class, out of pity for him, asked us to lay off." Indeed, a fellow student has said that Viner knew more about economics than did his mentor.

Viner, however, was "much more respectful of Leacock as a teacher of political science. His junior year course covered a wide range of matter, and was well presented. He kept his biases well under control, and he gave his students full opportunity to state their views."

A noted Montreal lawyer, A. Sydney Bruneau, Q.C., supports the latter statement. He recalls an occasion when he had the temerity to run counter to Leacock's pet ideas on political science. An exam paper called for an essay on Imperial Federation, one of Leacock's favorite schemes. Bruneau set himself to combat the professor's thesis, treating it as a relic of the past, and submitting that the tide had already turned in the direction of Canadian nationality. For his trouble, Bruneau received 98 marks. Some time after, the student thanked Leacock and apologized for opposing his views.

"Tut, tut. I don't expect my students to agree with me. I like them to give me their honest views, and I really enjoyed your paper. I had hard work to refrain from giving you perfect marks. Though, mind you, you didn't convince me!"

The dishevelled appearance of the lecturer failed to improve. The tattered gown gained more frayed edges. The unruly hair became even more mutinous. An old safety pin continued to do service for a missing link in the gold waistcoat watch chain. But in his lecturing style there was a change of tactics. Leacock had apparently made up his mind to draw a strict line of demarcation between the classroom and his new dimension as a humorous writer. Two men who sat under him in those days cannot recall a single occasion on which Leacock did or said anything which would remind his students that, as a moonlighter, he was also a professional humorist. He was still preoccupied with John Stuart Mill, Adam Smith and Malthus, and it was work all the way for his young charges.

Leacock's new-found vocation required equal attention. He had published a few articles in professional journals to keep up his academic end. But he was persuaded to capitalize as speedily as possible on the amazing success of *Literary Lapses*.

During the vacation months of 1910 Leacock had been putting what were supposed to be the finishing touches to his modest summer house at Old Brewery Bay. At the same time he was working on some sketches that he had contracted to write for the Toronto literary weekly *Saturday Night*. This was a series he called *Novels in Nutshells*. As these parodies began to appear, the author concluded that the quickest way to his second humorous book would be to reproduce the series, amended and expanded, in a single volume. It was at once a convenient and profitable practice, which, for the most part, he was to follow for the remainder of his life.

And so there came into being the following year a book entitled *Nonsense Novels*. The book enjoyed unexpected promotion from exalted quarters in the United States. In a political speech Theodore Roosevelt cited a phrase from one of the stories, at the same time acknowledging the source. The quotation came from "Gertrude the Governess," a mildly amusing take-off on the Victorian romantic novel, in which the lovelorn Lord Ronald "flung himself from the room, flung himself upon his horse and rode madly off in all directions." The statement has become part of the English language. Presidential endorsement is evidently potent, as witness the vogue for Ian Fleming's spy stories that was set in motion when John F. Kennedy let it be known that James Bond was one of his favorite fictional characters.

The New York *Evening Sun* considered that the chief virtue of *Nonsense Novels* was that it allowed a busy reader "to become familiar with the work of our most popular novelists in one sitting. What is more, and what differentiates the volume before us from the volumes it mirrors, he will have some fun."

In London *The Star* rated the book as more humorous than *Literary Lapses*, "that is to say, it is the most humorous book we have had since Mr. Dooley swam into our ken. Its humor is so rich that it places Mr. Leacock beside Mark Twain." (Martin Dooley, the hero of Finley Peter Dunne's sketches, was a philosophic Chicago bartender who reviewed the events of the world with a wit and wisdom his era found irresistible.)

In recent times extravagant claims have been made on behalf of *Nonsense Novels*, such as that it is one of Leacock's best efforts. It was certainly topical burlesque then, with an adroit piling-up of exaggeration. The desanctification of faddist fiction had been brilliantly effected by Bret Harte in his *Condensed Novels* (first in 1867, again in 1902). Leacock had obviously been influenced by Harte's work, though the mimicry was much broader. In the novelette "Hannah of the Highlands," Leacock lampooned Walter Scott's historical romances with a vengeance—the personal feuds of the clans, the beauty of the glens, the religious differences. "Shamus

McShamus, an embittered Calvinist, half crazed perhaps with liquor, had maintained that damnation could be achieved only by faith. Whimper McWhinus had held that damnation could be achieved also by good works." The fight was on. The feud lasted for six generations.

Chivalric romance came in for some expert manhandling in "Guido the Gimlet of Ghent," which opened with these words: "It was in the flood-tide of chivalry. Knighthood was in the pod." The case of mistaken identity in the end, with the consequent grief, revealed Leacock's sure touch for the ridiculous.

Undoubtedly Leacock had H. G. Wells in mind when he composed "The Man in Asbestos: An Allegory of the Future." Here in the year 3000 unimaginable things had been achieved, such as "surgical education," which was "the simple system of opening the side of the skull and engrafting into it a piece of prepared brain."

This kind of parody was beloved of Leacock. He would return to it time and again.

Towards the end of his life Leacock was in correspondence with Professor Alexander Cowie, of Wesleyan University, Middletown, Conn. The latter had published a book on the subject of sentimentalists in fiction and the "social life novel," as Leacock would have it. He wrote to Cowie bewailing the "awful formulas" resorted to in current literature:

> . . . the 300 pages of swearing called an historical novel . . . or the 300 pages of subsistence farming that shows the life of the crackerjacks of the Back Ozarks. . . . I begin to think that literature is like women's fashions and based on the idea that people like "something else." . . .

He went on to damn

> the exaggerated outgrowth of humanitarianism (what a hell of a word, but it looks correct) that went into the eighteenth century anti-slavery pity-the-poor etc. . . . the kind of thing that gave us Sambo the faithful nigger, the little match girl, the chimney sweep stuck in the chimney, etc. . . . I've often wanted to collect a lot of that stuff and write about it. . . . You may have seen such poetry as—
> *Little Annie and her mother were walking one day*
> *In London's fair city so wide. . . .*
> An aristocratic "barouche" comes barouching past. Little Annie gets peeved with envy. But her mother points out a little boy whose bare feet stick out of his boots in the snow. . . . This, you see, levels Annie up to

the average. . . . Some of this stuff was meant, I think, to keep the poor from waking up.

But if Leacock was averse to formula fiction, he was not above developing formulae of his own, and sticking to them, willy-nilly.

Nonsense Novels, first published in 1911, went into forty printings in the following three decades. Its immediate success served to instil confidence in an author who had not yet got over his flattering experience with *Literary Lapses*.

With everything pointing to further success, Leacock was emboldened to purchase a house. This was a new, commodious residence of three storeys, built on the lower slopes of Mount Royal at the top of Cote des Neiges Road. Mrs. Leacock made herself responsible for the furnishing and tasteful decoration of the house, making sure that her husband had a spacious study for himself. He made sure that the large covered verandah would contain a couch. He had suddenly decided that, come snow or rain, he would sleep outdoors. Unfailingly he slept in this fashion, sometimes, when the temperature neared zero, covering himself additionally with his coonskin coat. The arrangement was a good one. Rising at his usual five or five-thirty hour, he was able to get to his study without disturbing anyone. Immediately before breakfast, after two hours of pen and ink work, he would go for a short walk on the mountain. In fact on most days Leacock walked to the university. His daily routine there had been conveniently arranged to fit his purpose, with his first lecture scheduled late in the morning.

The professor was heading east one morning along Pine Avenue, college-bound, when he met a student who had a disconsolate look about him. They continued together towards McGill. The ensuing conversation elicited the fact that the boy was broke. This was soon remedied. The professor proffered a ten-dollar bill, which was, needless to say, eagerly accepted on a loan basis.

In a day or two the same student came seeking advice. Leacock was as free with his advice as with his money when the cause appealed to him. The boy's name was W. E. Gladstone Murray, of whom Canada would hear a great deal, particularly as chairman of the infant Canadian Broadcasting Corportion in the thirties. Young Murray had been editor of a weekly campus publication called *The Martlet* (the heraldic bird on the university crest). He explained to Leacock that he wanted to start a daily college newspaper. Leacock's practical advice proved invaluable and *The McGill Daily*, with Murray as editor, came into being. It remains today the oldest student daily newspaper in the Commonwealth.

Despite the disparity in their ages, Leacock and Murray became fast friends. They found a common bond in the game of billiards. As a result the professor submitted the undergraduate "to periodic humiliation with his superior skill," and, as Murray further reported:

> In 1911, after a game one evening, Dr. Leacock remarked that he was tired of these "unrelated and insignificant encounters." Whereupon he challenged me to 20,000-up, which he estimated we could finish in 20 years. . . . The games took place in widely varying environments—clubs, private homes, grand hotels, but mostly in good old down-to-earth pubs. Actually the game ran for thirty years and was never finished, the final score being 18,975 for Dr. Leacock and 17,793 for me.

One of these contests on the green baize took place in the Oxford and Cambridge Club in London in 1921 during Leacock's lecture tour of England. G. K. Chesterton happened to be on the premises. As soon as he heard that Leacock was playing billiards, the famous man joined the interested gallery. Unfortunately no details have been preserved of the meeting of minds which followed the game. Later, however, Leacock told Murray that his chat in the club with the celebrated English writer had "helped to crystallize my conception of humor as, perhaps, the highest product of civilization." He was to paraphrase the experience a number of times, but particularly at the end of his *Humor and Humanity*.

Leacock was well on the way up the literary ladder. He was also entrenched at McGill "in charge" of his department, "one of the prizes of my profession."

Of his academic estate in 1911, he indulged in odious comparison:

> I am able to regard myself as singularly fortunate. The emolument is so high as to place me distinctly above the policeman, the postman, streetcar conductors, and other salaried officials of the neighborhood, while I am able to mix with the poorer of the businessmen of the city on terms of something like equality. In point of leisure, I enjoy more in the four corners of a single year than a businessman knows in his whole life. I thus have, what the businessman can never enjoy, an ability to think, and, what is still better, to stop thinking altogether for months at a time.

Of time to think, let alone stop thinking, there was little. He was proceeding at an increasing pace in several directions at once. One of the new directions was an exploratory mission into the world of politics. In 1911 he had been invited to be a member of the Fleming Electoral Reform Commission of Quebec. No sooner had he begun to complete his responsibilities on this commission than things started to stir politically in Canada as well as below the border.

In the same year President Taft had, with congressional approval, reopened the door to a reciprocal trade agreement with Canada. Wilfrid Laurier, Canada's Liberal Prime Minister, jumped at this opportunity which many of his countrymen had been seeking. The previous reciprocity treaty had come to an end in 1866. Laurier called a general election and in no time Leacock became involved on the side of the Conservatives. He was in the fight with both feet, not as a standard-bearer, but as an active supporter of candidates in a Montreal constituency and in his home riding at Orillia. Into the bargain he had been persuaded by a rising political star, R. B. Bennett, to lend a hand in national propaganda.

Instilled in him from his earliest years, Leacock's Tory loyalties got the better of his previous economic advocacy. In his teaching he had been strongly opposed to the protective system in Canada. Now he had publicly committed himself to condemning reciprocity with the U.S.A.

This position of his in the campaign recalls one of the most biting comments ever made about Leacock's ability in his chosen profession. Dr. J. C. Hemmeon, an economist of the first rank and a colleague of Leacock, had made the statement in the classroom that "all economists are free-traders."

"But," objected a student, "Dr. Leacock is a protectionist."

"I repeat," retorted Hemmeon acidly, "all economists are free-traders."

Economist or not, the professor's drawing power on the hustings proved as potent as it also did in the back rooms where election propaganda was being churned out. Somehow Leacock had dredged up a character from Fleet Street who had been roaming the city looking for a job. Although he was not the most abstemious of souls, he commanded a brilliant turn of phrase and a sound knowledge of newspaper techniques. Both of these had been sharpened by his association in England with the rabble-rousing W. T. Stead of the Westminster *Gazette*.

Sober or otherwise, between them the pair drew up telling full-page advertisements, which were "matted" and shipped across the country. The tenor of the Conservative message was to the effect that the Liberals were selling out to the United States. With his imperial prejudices, Leacock was in his element.

In very acceptable French Leacock spoke tirelessly in Montreal; back home, both in language and in fact, he barnstormed the territory around Orillia. One eyewitness was Leslie M. Frost, a future premier of the province of Ontario, who recalls:

> Concerning the reciprocity address, I was present in the Orillia Opera House when this was delivered in 1911. Actually Stephen made a very devastating attack on the whole reciprocity idea. In the judgment of Orillians, assessed years afterwards, it was counted that Stephen's address had considerable to do with the election of an anti-reciprocity Conservative.

Laurier's party was decisively beaten. So impressed was R. B. Bennett by the Leacock contribution that he tried to persuade him to take a continuing interest in politics. It is doubtful, however, that as rumor later had it when Bennett became the country's Prime Minister in 1930, he offered Leacock a cabinet post. Frost dismisses the thought. "I think that Leacock's entry into the Cabinet would have been altogether too imaginative for R. B. Bennett. Conversely, Leacock would never have been a good member of a cabinet 'team.' " He believes Leacock did have an aptitude for politics but would never have fitted into a riding situation. "He was too unusual and too eccentric." In retrospect Frost thinks that Leacock's humor was very much more important than his politics—"It would seem to me that Leacock was, in many ways, out of tune with reality."

On the other hand, a former student and colleague, who rose to national prominence in the field of Canadian economics, thinks differently. Eugene Forsey regards Leacock as "one of the most brilliant men I have ever known." He considers that the professor-humorist could have had a successful career in politics "and might easily have become Prime Minister."

Tongue in cheek, Leacock thought he had perhaps missed the boat:

> I failed entirely in Canadian politics, never having received a contract to build a bridge, or to make a wharf, nor to construct even the smallest

section of the Transcontinental Railway. This, however, is a form of national ingratitude to which one becomes accustomed in this Dominion.

There is more irony than meets the eye in this ostensible jest. Naïve as it may seem for a man of his years, Leacock on a number of occasions voiced his disillusionment about the lack of honesty in the political arena. In so saying, he gave a pretty clear indication that he knew he was not cut out for such a role and that he would not have anything to do with it in person. This did not prevent him from stating and restating his views on the platform or through the press at the drop of the proverbial hat.

Leacock's humorous output had been immensely salable to date. B. K. Sandwell, who had tried to restrain his friend at first, now realized his editorial instinct had been wrong in this particular case. He was now about to serve as a vital link in the next step of the Leacock literary progress.

Sandwell had a friend on *The Montreal Star*. He was the paper's managing editor, Edward Beck, who was interested in persuading the professor to do some special work for *The Star*. Beck approached the proprietor and publisher, Sir Hugh Graham (raised to the peerage in 1917). Graham was that rare specimen of newspaper owner—a journalist from the ground up. He thought the project sound and urged Beck to begin negotiations.

Acting as intermediary, Sandwell brought Leacock and Beck together. Between the three agreement was reached on a serial-type contribution which would have a distinctive Canadian setting. Out of that conference was born *Sunshine Sketches of a Little Town*. "It was," said Sandwell, "the only really large-scale commission ever received for a fictional job to be done for a purely Canadian audience . . . after all, he had a wealth of material not too suitable for his American buyers."

As instalment followed instalment in *The Star*, readers were kept guessing whether the sketches were outright fiction or not. Orillians did not need to guess. They knew. Leacock had been so ingenuous as to pinpoint living people by using real names, not to mention magnifying their faults.

He was extremely lucky to escape libel actions. In a letter to a friend late in life, Leacock disclosed:

A lawyer friend of mine, Mel Tudhope, of Orillia, now Judge Tudhope, wrote me a mock letter threatening to sue me for libel against these people. It was only fun, but it led the publisher to think it wiser to alter the names so in the book edition they are changed.

Sandwell has described how the sketches evolved. "The stories were shaped out at the dinner table in the Leacock home on Cote des Neiges Road . . . it was a fascinating business to watch them developing in the telling." Typically, Leacock acted them with appropriate gestures, great gusto and evident self-appreciation. Here was the raconteur in action. Guests at the frequent dinner parties, over which Trix presided as a gracious hostess, remember how the host's chair was placed well back from the end of the table so that he could rise at any moment to walk up and down while making a point, as though he were in the classroom.

In fact, this was the test to which he subjected most of his short bits and pieces. He would read them aloud in his study or in the dining room to whatever audience he could assemble. At Old Brewery Bay his favourite audience was his brother George, who was a well-known wit himself and the source of some of Stephen's material. The two of them would go over the material, tossing ideas back and forth, laughing all the while, until Stephen felt that they had hit on the best possible form. Thus, in effect, the articles became conversation pieces in print, which accounts for Leacock's constant use of the first person singular. In essence, his were oral compositions, and *Sunshine Sketches* is the supreme example of his chosen form.

Neither an originator nor an innovator, Leacock was, rather, an acute observer of the passing scene, and especially of character. He looked about him, kept abreast of the news of the day, recorded what he saw and heard and then molded it as he saw fit. Such was the case with *Sunshine Sketches*. He did not even coin the name Mariposa, which was Orillia in disguise, though some learned gentlemen have seen in it an exquisite creation of the Leacock imagination. The author simply took the name of a little-known settlement, a stone's throw from Orillia, which had existed before he had come to Canada as a child.

In the preface Leacock made the patently false claim that he had not done "anything so ridiculously easy as writing about a real place and real people." He could not have done otherwise. He was mis-

takenly convinced that he had the power to create lifelike characters. At the same time he admitted that "I have no notion as to how
to make things happen." What he did have was an abundant ability
to transfer the genuine article from life to the printed page in compressed form. This, and a plenitude of other evidence, should have
put paid long ago to that periodic exercise in futility, the discussion
of the question "Could Leacock have become a novelist?" He may, as
his son has said, have dreamed of becoming "the great Canadian
novelist." If so, it remained a dream, for he knew his limitations. He
had neither the time nor the talent to tackle the major task of the
novelist. He couldn't or wouldn't try to sustain the necessary narrative, quite apart from character delineation.

Leaving theory aside, what did actually happen was that he acci-
dentally unearthed a market for brisk and slightly irreverent skits.
These guaranteed quick returns. That is what he was interested in.
He told his friend Sandwell so. This time Sandwell agreed.

Although widely read elsewhere and still a favorite in Canada,
Sunshine Sketches never reached the circulation of his other collections, earlier or later. Although the sketches were based upon and
aimed at specific townspeople, it is probably true, as Leacock insisted, that they could be applied to "about seventy or eighty" other
towns in the country or, for that matter, in the U.S.A. As a whole
it was fundamentally a parochial treatment of parochialism. As
such its appeal was restricted.

This was not the opinion of a young student at the University of
Toronto. He was Douglas Bush, who was destined for a career of
distinction as an outstanding authority on English literature at
Harvard University, among other appointments.

Dr. Bush, now retired in Cambridge, Massachusetts, writes:

> When I was an undergraduate at Victoria College, Toronto, I wrote a
> piece in praise of Leacock (especially in praise of *Sunshine Sketches*,
> which is a finely authentic picture of a small town in Ontario, with all its
> exaggeration—I grew up in one). It may have been Professor Pelham
> Edgar who got the piece into the Toronto *Star*; at any rate I didn't send
> it in. I had declared that Leacock was better than Mark Twain. His agent,
> I suppose, sent it to him and he wrote a note to repudiate such an opinion,
> and, by way of confirmation, sent me a copy of *Huckleberry Finn*, in-
> scribed "with Stephen Leacock's best wishes, McGill University, Nov. 23.
> 1915."

Although Leacock gave the characters in the book fictitious names, a large portion of the Orillia community did not cool down for some time. The local barber who had unwittingly supplied Leacock with titbits of information, apologized to his other customers in sorrow and in anger: "How in hell was I to know he would put these things in a book." Certainly it must have required courage for the author to run the gauntlet of outraged civic pride as he continued to spend summers at Old Brewery Bay.

The man whose little Orillia studio filled Leacock's photographic needs for many years has described an incident which occurred in the year *Sunshine Sketches* raised local hackles.

Herbert Stewart was a youngster then. He had become ill with diphtheria in the family quarters over the shop. The attending physician pointed out that, in view of the acutely infectious nature of the disease, the patient must be moved elsewhere or the business would have to be quarantined. There was no hospital. Nobody lifted a hand to help. In desperation a tent was set up in a field on the outskirts of the town. But the owner of the tract of land objected, as did his neighbours. The sick boy, his mother and a nurse were forced to move on to another isolated site on the shores of Lake Couchiching. There were further howls of protest. Orillia's police chief went to arrest the elder Stewart for allowing his family to move without prior permission. Several citizens threatened to petition the county council.

Word of the family's plight reached Leacock's ears. He acted promptly. Visiting the distraught father, he said: "Bring the lad over to my place on the bay, Frank. They can stay there for the rest of the summer. There'll be no neighbours except me, and I'm damned sure they won't catch neighbouritis from me."

This was done. The child was nursed back to health and to a future of happy business associations with the man who had mirrored Mariposa.

In Montreal McGill's Principal Peterson had been focussing his attention on strengthening and expanding the Faculty of Arts. Encouraged by this trend, Leacock asked for and obtained permission to shore up the staff of his economics and political science department. While he had no intention of letting external commitments interfere with the exercise of his academic responsibilities, the going was hard. There were increasing demands upon him for public speaking engagements. He had produced three books in three years and was always busy trying to satisfy requests from magazine editors in both America and England.

Leacock went to New York to consult the U.S. branch of his English publisher, John Lane, on future strategy. While he was there he received an invitation from the Lotus Club to attend a dinner in honor of Philip Gibbs, a prominent British journalist. At the coffee stage of the proceedings there was no sign of Gibbs. He had warned the chairman in advance that another pressing engagement might detain him. But unless he turned up very soon the dinner seemed bound to be a fiasco.

As the program of preliminary speeches came to an end, there was still no guest of honor. In desperation the chairman turned to Leacock and pressed him into making some remarks.

It was a new public Leacock who filled the gap. His reputation had preceded him. He was among friends. The actor dipped into his bag of tricks. Unabashed, he introduced the "business" of appearing to enjoy his own jokes even before he had finished them. This tactic had been tried before, but in limited doses and with some doubts as to its effectiveness. The torso began to shake with merriment, while the granite face broke into a wide grin. Here the effect was devastatingly contagious. The Manhattan reception led him to conclude that the theatrical device was worth nurturing.

At intervals during the continual hilarity he would stop, listening like an Indian or a trapper for the footfall of Gibbs. But Gibbs never materialized, and nobody cared. The speech was a tour de force of impromptu wit.

As he was assembling funny book number four in 1913, the time arrived for the University Club to move into its brand-new building on Mansfield Street, where it stands today. On the eve of the operation Leacock carefully contemplated his specific duties. He was in charge of the vitally important task of moving the bar. With a characteristic eye for detail where money was concerned, he had totted up the moving expenses. Not only would it be costly to shift the bar's contents, but hazardous—all those bottles! On that final evening he submitted to his fellow members of the club's council what he thought was a bright solution: "Let's save on expense by drinking all the liquor right here and now." He was voted down.

The new premises on Mansfield Street became almost as much a part of Leacock as Old Brewery Bay. In an atmosphere of tasteful elegance he ceased to be the actor. It was enough to sit and sip, play billiards and enjoy good companionship. To this day the area around the chair he consistently occupied, where the posthumous Richard Jack portrait now hangs, is known as the Leacock corner.

A decision to undertake annual book publication was made at this time. His new compilation derived its title, *Behind the Beyond,* from its leading piece, "a modern problem play in three acts." It neatly tore apart the "society" dramas which then monopolized the stages of Broadway and London's West End. The book's contents constituted a combination of the even and uneven, the strained and the inspired. There were four sketches dealing with an American's first visit to Paris, where he searched without avail for "something wicked" or even "real wicked."

Possibly Leacock was at his happiest in satirizing the fraternity of classical scholars, to which he himself undoubtedly belonged. In "Homer and Humbug," for example, he wrote:

> I know there are solid arguments advanced in favor of the classics. I often hear them from my colleagues. My friend the professor of Greek tells me that he truly believes the classics have made him what he is. This is a very grave statement, if well founded. Indeed, I have heard the same argument from a great many Latin and Greek scholars. They all claim, with some heat, that Latin and Greek have practically made them what they are. This damaging charge against the classics should not be too readily accepted. In my opinion some of these men would have been what they are, no matter what they were.

For the most part, however, Leacock's interest lay in the common or garden variety of human beings. Life's frustrations, large or small, as they pressed on the barely identifiable little man, were the stuff of Leacock's humor. He was no longer one of that breed. To his own satisfaction he had elevated himself much above the average. Personal unsureness was a thing of the past, except, possibly, in the case of his tenuous standing as an economist. He was all for the little man—as so many writers have been and continue to be— because it was overwhelmingly good business for a humorist. (His literary revenue had now tripled his college stipend of forty-five hundred dollars.) But he himself had once been downtrodden. From his farming and schoolteaching days he knew what the feeling was, and expressed it on behalf of those who found themselves battering their collective head against the stone wall of authority, pomposity and injustice.

Leacock had now achieved the freedom that accompanies success. He was ostensibly happy, even though complete contentment continued to repose only in the surroundings of Old Brewery Bay. There he would head virtually as soon as the last student had left the classroom at the end of the spring term. He was so eager to be off that he hardly ever waited for the Convocation ceremony.

But a distant cloud caused him growing concern. For the past three years he had been closely following developments in Europe, which stirred memories of his postgraduate experiences in Chicago. There in 1901 it had been his habit, in order to brush up on the language, to fraternize with the German colony in the city. He remembered how his German friends used to annoy him with their militant talk of *"Der Tag."* Ever since, he had had an uneasy feeling about the aggressive spirit of the Fatherland. Now he was sure of a coming international eruption and kept telling his students that war with Germany was inevitable. His students didn't pay much attention to his warnings, of course. Leacock was just being funny.

VI

War and Pieces

Stephen Leacock took the year 1914 in his stride from the outset, though it was destined to be no laughing matter for a great many people. Even if he knew that war lay just over the horizon, as the chancelleries of Europe certainly did, the professor and the McGill campus were at peace with themselves. McGill's Officers Training Corps may have been the first such organization on the American continent when it was founded in 1912. But in 1914 it was still less interested in shooting than in competing for honors in the city's indoor softball league.

In the previous year Leacock had founded the Political Economy Club, with the help of his departmental associate, Dr. J. C. Hemmeon. A spare figure, with a detectably cynical outlook on life, Hemmeon had been thoroughly grounded in economics at Harvard University. An air of amused tolerance characterized his attitude towards his now celebrated chief. The pair complemented one another, however, in their common interest. In organizing the club, they worked together amicably, though perhaps not to the extent of blissful brotherhood in general departmental affairs.

The genial senior partner chose his friends carefully. The quality Leacock sought above all others was joviality. He found this in good measure in a dapper young professor in the department of romance languages. Ten years Leacock's junior, René du Roure came from a Parisian family with a distinguished record in the service of the republic. A slight, perky, impeccably groomed person, du Roure had arrived in Canada in 1909 to take a post at the French Canadian University of Laval. Within three years he transferred to the staff of McGill. Gradually a friendship began to blossom between the ebullient Gallic dandy and the rough-hewn, sloppily attired Englishman. A fondness for conviviality, a keen sense of humor, and a love of history provided the strong bonds in what was to be one of the most important relationships in Stephen Leacock's life.

Had Leacock chosen to follow his historical inclination there is small doubt that he would have excelled in that field. His natural bent for putting virtually everything into an historical context informed his college lectures and a good deal of his writing. Having opted otherwise, he still managed to work occasionally along such lines. At this particular time he had completed a three-volume contribution to a new series called *The Chronicles of Canada*. However insubstantial these works may seem today, it was a remarkable achievement to turn out *The Dawn of Canadian History, Adventures of the Far North* and *The Mariner of St. Malo* while faced with heavy demands in his humorous output.

Even as this trio of popular histories came on the market, Leacock had put the finishing touches to what, in a very real sense, was a book rather than an assortment of diverting essays. In method and in motive *Arcadian Adventures with the Idle Rich* revealed its author in a fresh light. The broad caricature of *Sunshine Sketches* suddenly gave way to a new and determined incisiveness. He could no longer plead an inviolable marriage with kindly humor and only kindly humor. Having disposed of small-time foibles in the *Sketches,* Leacock took aim at the big city—which was clearly recognizable as Montreal, despite an awkward effort to play to the U.S. market by pretending that the setting was an American metropolis.

It could have been said of *Arcadian Adventures*, as George Bernard Shaw said of Mark Twain, that Leacock had to "put things in such a way as to make people who would otherwise hang him believe he is joking."

As has already been pointed out, the Mausoleum Club of *Arcadian Adventures* could only be the plush Mount Royal Club and not his own University Club. Alongside the dwellings of Montreal's aristocracy, the Mount Royal Club stood on Sherbrooke Street, which in the book became Plutoria Avenue:

> Here you may see a little toddling princess in a rabbit suit who owns fifty distilleries in her own right. There, in a lacquered perambulator, sails past a little hooded head that controls from its cradle an entire New Jersey corporation. Nearby is a child of four, in a khaki suit, who represents the merger of two trunk-line railways. You may meet in the flickered sunlight any number of little princes and princesses far more real than the poor survivals of Europe. Incalculable infants wave their fifty-dollar ivory rattles in an inarticulate greeting to one another. A million dollars of preferred stock laughs merrily in recognition of a majority control going past in a go-cart drawn by an imported nurse.

Traditionally the begowned men and women of academe hold the materialistic world in disdain. Leacock was no exception. He knew enough about political economy to understand how some of the rich had become rich. Yet, if and when they sought him out, he was not averse to their company. Only half-jokingly he noted in *Literary Lapses*:

> I mix a good deal with millionaires. I like the way they live. I like the things they eat. The more we mix together, the better I like the things we mix.

But he reserved judgment about their character. Scorn-tinged satire crept into all his commentary on the rich, in this work as well as in numerous later references to a sealed-off, well-heeled citizenry. He bewailed the prewar accumulation and concentration of wealth in Montreal. "The rich in Montreal enjoyed a prestige in that era that not even the rich deserve," he wrote three decades afterwards. Where money was concerned, the green-eyed monster kept rearing its head in Leacock, to the point that he became petty. The "super-rich" in the Montreal of those days, he scoffed, collected paintings. "It is the simplest and easiest of all collecting hobbies: the price tells you exactly what you are getting; you have only to look on the back of the picture to appreciate it."

It was as obvious as the safety pin on his watch chain that Leacock's Plutoria University resembled the Royal Institution which employed him. When *Arcadian Adventures* appeared the undergraduates were quick to see the point. *The McGill Daily* generally recommended the book, adding significantly that his Plutoria University "is supposed to be a thousand miles away, but it reads like it is awfully close to home."

The spoof—to put it mildly—on the two churches of St. Asaph and St. Osoph was inspired by current events. In 1914 negotiations had been put in train between two of Montreal's leading Presbyterian churches with a view to their uniting beneath a single roof. Convenience, rather than any suggestion of ecumenicity, dictated the idea. Leacock latched on to this project and made it his own in the chapter, "The Rival Churches," with the truth thinly veiled. His strict upbringing in the Anglican faith having run its course, he had few inhibitions in dealing with the mores of organized urban religion.

Leacock's hypercritical mood spared no one in *Arcadian Adventures*, dispelling the argument of his idolators that his pen never recorded an unkind word. The biting tomfoolery in "The Yahi-Bahi Oriental Society," for instance, must have given hurt to a small coterie of his fellow citizens who represented a branch of a Middle East religious sect. The orthodox Leacock's impatience with radical departures from the conventional sometimes pushed him into overstatements which ceased to have risible results.

"When a thing is funny, search for the hidden truth." Once more, a Shavian aphorism. For Montrealers—and perhaps Chicagoans, New Yorkers and San Franciscans shared the guilt—the search was not difficult in "The Great Fight for Clean Government," which brought *Arcadian Adventures* to a close.

Unlike Mark Twain, Stephen Leacock was not a militant reformer. He simply could not be bothered. He saved his proselytizing efforts for the British Empire. His humor was strictly commercial.

St. John Adcock Brown, a British critic, may well have had *Arcadian Adventures* in mind when he discussed Leacock's humor in *The Glory That Was Grub Street*: "Under all the burlesque it is a drastic criticism of life as some of us really live it. Leacock translated his philosophy into laughter, but it is a philosophy nonetheless. His irrepressible feeling for the ridiculous keeps him from treating absurdities as if they were not absurd."

Perhaps in "The Great Fight" they were rather more tragic than absurd. As an historian, years in the future, Leacock set down straightforwardly the facts he had joked about earlier. "The age of expansion threw upon the city a larger and larger need for public works and a greater and greater opportunity for public theft." He added that the struggle "for clean government had been going on ever since the city had been a city; but so had the struggle for dirty government."

Flagrantly dishonest aldermen, aided and abetted by a favored criminal element, precipitated in 1909 a demand for a clean-up campaign in Montreal. An angry citizen's association came into being. There is no indication of Leacock's having identified himself with this group of incensed burghers. The final pages of *Arcadian Adventures* constituted his contribution to the cause, and he let it go at that. For all the author's talk about Congress and the U. S. Senate and state legislatures, the Canadian metropolis knew beyond a doubt that it was Leacock's target.

For once he had discarded feathery nonsense, openly embracing scathing sarcasm, and come as close as he ever would to creating a unified literary structure, complete with some three-dimensional characters—e.g., the Rev. Uttermust Dumfarthing, President Boomer of Plutoria University, and Lucullus Fyshe, president of the People's Traction and Suburban Co., the Republican Soda and Siphon Co-operative, and chief director of the People's District Loan and Savings.

While this book was receiving critical acclaim (though it was not to become widely popular), Canada, along with the rest of the Empire, had come to the side of Britain in "the war to end war." It was not a unanimous gesture on the part of the Dominion. Divisions of opinion existed and these would continue to bedevil the country. His own patriotism easily fired, Leacock assured his students that nothing draws the members of a family together like disaster. He predicted that Empire solidarity would emerge from the European conflict. He was not always a flawless prophet.

Like the downtown press, the columns of *The McGill Daily* increasingly gave themselves over to war news and the university's own participation. The name of Stephen Leacock appeared frequently as he spoke and wrote about the causes of the armed confrontation and its likely consequences. He numbered among his happier memories the times when he helped to train cadets at Upper Canada College. His pride in McGill's effort—especially in the volunteers from his own classes—knew no bounds. At forty-four he himself reckoned his talents could be put to better use on the Canadian scene rather than in uniform in Europe.

One note of personal regret marked those days. Prof. René du Roure—the embodiment of Parisian culture, charm, wit and courtesy—had unhesitatingly returned to his native land to join the French forces. Severely wounded in his first battle, du Roure served three years as a prisoner-of-war in one German hospital after another. Typically, the enthusiastic young academic established a school for French language instruction during his internment

In a city which would become the focal point of French Canadian dissension over Canada's involvement, McGill's graduates and undergraduates flocked to the colors. A McGill regiment was the initial aim. Over the long haul, however, the goal set and attained included six separate infantry companies for the Princess Patricia's Canadian Light Infantry, a siege battery, and a 500-bed army general hospital recruited from the Medical School. (One of the staff members of this unit was Dr. John McCrae, the author of *In Flanders Fields*.)

A special war contingent supplement prepared by *The McGill Daily* contained a contribution from Stephen Leacock, who took delight in an anti-German propaganda piece entitled "Side Lights on the Superman: An Interview with General Bernhardi." The general was depicted as visiting Leacock at McGill. The professor wanted to know how the intruder had managed to get by the university's janitor, to which the German replied, "I killed him."

"We Prussians," said Bernhardi, "when we wish an immediate access anywhere, always kill the janitor. It is quicker; and it makes for efficiency. It impresses them with a sense of our *Furchtbarkeit*. You have no word for that in English, I believe?"

"Not outside of a livery stable," the professor replied.

Leacock made a point of keeping in touch with his soldier-students overseas. Two such—Paul S. Clark and W. C. Nicholson of Montreal—would normally have graduated in the spring of 1915. Instead, they enlisted in February and soon saw action. The professor replied to a letter from Clark, congratulating the men on their knight errantry, and further stating that the best thing he could do for them would be to recommend, on their return, that they be appointed to the Canadian Senate, "where they would never have to work or think any more." Clark never returned.

On the home front there were great expectations of an impending event in the Leacock household on Cote des Neiges. After fifteen years of married life, Trix was pregnant. Husband and wife—now forty-five and thirty-six respectively—had long given up hope of raising a family. The news, confirmed in January 1915, exhilarated both.

With this additional responsibility to spur him on, Leacock piled work upon work. Superimposed on his university schedule and on several magazine commitments was a plan for another book collection. But everything had to be put aside in the face of a government request that he embark on a tour of several cities in both Canada and the U.S. to raise money on behalf of the Belgian Relief Fund. Instead of prepared lectures, he settled for readings from his own writings. These engagements continued, at first with some intensity, later spasmodically, well on towards the end of hostilities.

Most of the money realized by these efforts was directed to assist Belgian refugees quartered in Nantes. Curiously, twenty years later, in *My Discovery of the West*, Leacock would make cruel fun of the mayor of Nantes for his entirely understandable ignorance of Canadian geography.

An unidentified town in Vermont also left a scar on his memory. The chairman of the meeting arrived late, forgot to mention the Belgian Relief Fund and got Leacock's name wrong. He tried to make amends at the end of the meeting, as Leacock acidly described:

> "Just a minute, please, ladies and gentlemen, just a minute. I have just found out—I should have known it sooner, but I was late in coming to this meeting—that the speaker who has just addressed you has done so in behalf of the Belgian Relief Fund. I understand that he is a well-known Canadian humorist (ha! ha!) and I am sure that we all have been immensely amused (ha! ha!). He is giving his delightful talks (ha! ha!)—though I didn't know this until just this minute—for the Belgian Relief Fund, and he is giving his services for nothing. I am sure when we realize this, we shall all feel that it has been well worth while to come."

In the evening of his life Leacock spoke a good deal about the vagaries of speechmaking and how he had hated it, much as Mark Twain had claimed before him. He was perhaps only recalling the tiresome occasions, such as the Vermont meeting. He really revelled in talking in public when the audience was large and responsive, the chairman on time and alert, and a little envelope containing his fee was handed to him at the conclusion of the gathering. The only fee-less appearances he thoroughly enjoyed were when he talked to students or rampaged up and down the country damning prohibition in the United States.

The Leacocks' 1915 summer vacation at Old Brewery Bay had to be cut short. The time for Mrs. Leacock's confinement was drawing near. Almost immediately on their return to Montreal an unexpectedly quick trip to the hospital had to be arranged. Then on August 19, 1915, a son was born.

The letter that the ecstatic new father mailed to his mother in Ontario that same afternoon contained a mixture of elation and foreboding:

My Dear Mother—

Young Stephen was born at a quarter to three this afternoon. He is a fine big boy, in fact a regular corker, and weighs eight and a quarter pounds. Beatrix had made an error about the date of his birth, but thank Heaven, we left Orillia in time or the journey might have been too much for her. He had a close run for his life as he had decided to throw himself into the world wrong end first. We had the three best men in Montreal and four nurses. Peters told me that without those *seven* people working at it, there would have been no chance. Beatrix was taken ill at 6 this morning and I drove her over to the maternity hospital. She had a bad time but it is over now & she is resting & doing fine. The baby looks just like Barbara and little Stephen and me and all the rest. Beatrix was awfully well right up to the end except that she had a bad fall two days ago. But Peters says the baby is not a premature baby being if anything over developed. Beatrix will have to stay where she is for some time, I don't know how long, two weeks I should think. How soon can you come down? We must take up the arrangements for the christening right away. I want my friend Mr. Symonds the rector of the cathedral to do it.

I need hardly say that your journey down is of course to be at my expense. If you haven't the ready money wire or write me & I'll send it.

I gave the telegraph company a dollar to take the message from Sutton to the Grange. So don't let them charge you for it. . . . I never yet saw a baby that looked so complete, so all there, so little like a red monkey as Stephen does: indeed he seems to me a most remarkable child. . . . Be sure to let me know right away how soon you can come, and come as soon as you can.

Your loving son
(Old) Stephen Leacock

P.S. Tomorrow I am going to make my will and appoint trustees, guardians, and a staff of godfathers, godmothers, proxies, and assistants. We have decided that from the boy's birth there shall be no extravagance on him. We got from Eaton's a plain basket for him to sleep in,—there— I guess this is as much as it is fair to inflict in one dose.

Although it was not immediately apparent, trying times lay ahead. In the letter to his mother Leacock seemed to have some vague premonition of them, despite the assurances of the physicians.

Here was a turning point, with completely new responsibilities being visited upon parents who were no longer young. To all intents and purposes the marriage had been a happy one, in large part due to Trix's great adaptability to her husband's Victorian nature. That he adored her is a matter of accurate record. But, like any upper-middle-class Victorian, Leacock had an instinctual inclination for male companionship, for the life of clubdom. This must have had its effect on domestic circumstances from time to time. Mrs. Leacock, raised in the colonial atmosphere of Toronto, had married a man of the world even before he had been catapulted into popularity.

In any case, Trix with much good sense cut her cloth accordingly. She was now the partner of a famous man whose waking hours were crammed full of activities, all of which commanded public attention. As a public figure he was often required to be away from home. As a writer he quite properly insisted upon a certain amount of solitude. His friends were men friends for the most part. But Trix was armed with tact. Her interests—largely of a social and sporting nature—were not his; his, not hers particularly. Aside from the drama, she had little interest in literature. Yet she dutifully listened to the readings of her husband's work when she formed his one-woman audience at home, and in general played the perfect hostess.

About womankind Stephen Leacock harbored some reservations, thereby betraying a posture common to his class in nineteenth-century England. It was not that he believed woman's place to be in the kitchen entirely, far from it; but he would often give voice to the proposition that she should never be too far from it.

VII

The Sexes, The Stage, The "Squeeze"

The early stages of World War I witnessed a marked increase in the enrolment of female students at Canadian universities. In the autumn of 1915 a hundred and fifty-one women registered in McGill's Faculty of Arts and Sciences. Either out of curiosity or serious intent, a number of these found their way into Stephen Leacock's lectures. The professor was not amused.

Leacock was not a misogynist, but he entertained a reluctance to recognize parity between the sexes. Undoubtedly this attitude owed something to an inherited Victorian male arrogance. At any rate, he could hardly have been unaware that his idol, John Stuart Mill, had preached feminine emancipation as far back as 1867, or that, in the year of Leacock's birth, Mill had published his controversial thesis *The Subjection of Women*. Leacock had earlier seen for himself in England the militant suffragettes in action.

Despairingly he would write: "Women have taken over half of man's world, and kept the whole of their own. Man's sense of humor—his distinctive attribute—has to survive as best it can in this necessary circumstance."

Leacock took no detectable stand on women's suffrage, but he was to return frequently to his argument that a firm line should be drawn in point of their participation in higher education. Co-education disturbed him, and this gave rise to some generalizations which stamped him as old-fashioned even in the first quarter of the twentieth century. He once envisaged the dreadful possibility of all-female college enrolment, with the last male student committing suicide.

It meant little to him that twenty-five years previously Oxford had bowed to the inevitable, that now it harbored four women's colleges. It was not his wish to bar the other sex from tasting the delights of knowledge for knowledge's sake. And he was willing to concede that, especially in the New World, certain young women were confronted with the problem of preparing themselves to earn a living. But do not, he pleaded, clutter up the professions with women who eventually would get married, thus having wasted their time at university. In a word, he thought women could best exercise their considerable influence in the home itself.

> There is no use pretending about it. It may sound an awful thing to say, but the women are going to be married. That is, and always has been, their career; and, what is more, they know it; and even at college, while they are studying algebra and political economy, they have their eyes on it sideways all the time. The plain fact is that, after a girl has spent four years of her time and a great deal of her parents' money in equipping herself for a career that she is never going to have, the wretched creature goes and gets married, and in a few years she has forgotten which is the hypotenuse of a right-angled triangle, and she doesn't care. She has much better things to think of.

As though to keep them away from the ivy halls at all costs, Leacock recommended more practical alternatives; nursing, as a very odd example:

> There is more education and character-making in that than in a whole bucketful of algebra. . . . But no, the woman insists on snatching her share of an education designed by Erasmus or William of Wykeham or William of Occam for the creation of scholars and lawyers; and when later on in her home there is a sudden sickness or accident, and the life or death of those nearest to her hangs upon the skill and knowledge and a trained fortitude in emergency, she must needs send in all haste for a hired woman to fill the place that she herself has never learned to occupy.

This fixation prevailed until the end of his days. In his seventies he persisted in the belief that "college education for girls, it seems to me, has been greatly overdone." A woman's role was "home and mother."

Demonstrably, Leacock took his cue from Charles Dickens, the writer he worshipped (though roundly denouncing his personal conduct). Dickens' women, Leacock wrote, were "either angels or freaks—the latter being the real women of the novels." Additionally Leacock had persuaded himself that "women are not humorous, except by exception." Possibly this was another way of satisfying himself that their company, by and large, was dull compared to the René du Roures of this world, who could better appreciate the pungency of Leacock's off-duty language.

Yet one could never discern in his day-to-day behavior the faintest glimmer of uncourtliness.

Indubitably he did not share George Meredith's sentiment that "a witty woman is a treasure; a witty beauty is a power." A vague Victorian spirit of exalted superiority pervaded the posthumously published *Last Leaves* when he addressed himself to, and emphatically answered the question: "Are witty women attractive to men?" No, he thought, "the truth is that the ideal of ordinary men is not a witty woman but a *sweet woman*." The italics are his.

As for, in his phrase, this "sex stuff," Leacock had yet to learn that Victorian morality was not synonymous with virtue undefiled. Forgetting (or not having read) English fiction of earlier epochs— Henry Fielding, for instance—he guilelessly considered that "the wholesome days of the Eighties and Nineties" had been replaced by a brand-new invention of the twentieth century—filthy books. "Many of our so-called best-sellers merely sell because they contain every here and there a patch of dirt. The readers gather just as horse-flies do along a road where a well-fed horse has passed."

He ventured an explanation of this "noxious atmosphere":

It may very likely be that this outbreak of sex-obsession came as one of the unforeseen by-products of the emancipation of women. In the old Victorian days, now passing out of memory, women had quite a different place from what they have now. The men did everything and ran everything, and women represented the ornamental side of life and the household side. They were given a sort of general commission as angels, fairies, grandmothers and such, and with that the men kept them pretty well excluded. They never got out without a chaperone and a book of rules. It wasn't quite as complete as the Turkish system but it was nearly as good.

While the man's thinking on this specific theme moved along on such fuzzy lines, life in the Leacock household on Cote des Neiges Road hardly patterned itself on the Haworth parsonage of the Brontes. The commodious home, complete with smartly-uniformed French-speaking maids, regularly welcomed visitors, including Leacock's students. The comfortably furnished dining room fitted his insistence on dressing for dinner. What he considered to be an agreeable way of life included the dutiful observance of such dying niceties as the ladies' departure for coffee in the drawing room while the men dawdled over the port and their cigars.

The study remained the strict male preserve. It was unmistakably his territory. The orderliness of the occupant's mind bore no relation to the clutter of books, magazines, papers and manuscripts strewn about him. Like his academic gown the Leacock den became a stranger to immaculacy. And so it was with his workroom at Old Brewery Bay.

A few months prior to the arrival of Stephen, Jr. Leacock had been in correspondence with a Basil Macdonald Hastings, an Englishman who had asked permission to dramatize "Q: A Psychic Pstory of the Psupernatural," which had appeared in *Nonsense Novels*. This mocking of spiritualism—which was experiencing an understandable wartime vogue—revealed in part Leacock's contempt for the subject and for the people who pretended to practise it. At one gathering in New York he devoted his entire lecture to a condemnation of spiritualism, declaring the best way to attack it was to "laugh it out of existence." He laughed it out in "Q."

Since the adaptation was simply to take the form of a one-act play, Leacock agreed with Hastings on a fifty-fifty split of the royalties, based on one guinea in toto per performance. Two prominent actors—Charles Hawtrey and Miles Malleson—headed the cast when "Q" was produced at the London Coliseum on November 29, 1915.

In its review the British theatrical weekly *The Stage* observed: "Under different circumstances the sketch might be written off as talky and lacking in action, but the neatness of the lines and the work of Hawtrey and Malleson stifle all such suggestions. It is wittily written." *The Daily Telegraph* settled for: "Professor Leacock's amusing little tale."

The streak of theatricality in Leacock's work, if not in himself, had not escaped the notice of others. Already the editor of the Century Publishing Company in New York had admired the little burlesque which gave its title to the *Behind the Beyond* miscellany. In a letter to the author, he expressed the conviction that this ought to be acted. From England the manager of the London Theatre Company, which produced plays both in the West End and on Broadway, wrote to say that "everyone has the potentiality of one book in him—why not a play?" He went on to urge Leacock to try his hand at one. But the professor's interest had by now been totally captured by a proven profitable formula. He couldn't be enticed away from it. As an afterthought, however, Leacock instructed his American agent to make sure to include in future contracts protection against dramatic rights "should I propose to do a play."

If Leacock was not equipped for a novelist's role, he held distinct possibilities as a playwright. His love of the stage was strong, and he had talent both as a mimic and as a writer. Facility for crisp dialogue, coupled with a good feeling for a dramatic situation spasmodically brought from his pen diverting playlets for private production in the home or at university functions.

A decade later he would actually earn a little money from the theatre, again in his native land. In the mid-twenties he received a letter from a history don of Jesus College, Cambridge. The correspondent, V. C. Clinton-Baddeley, wanted Leacock to know about an undergraduate revue, the highlight of which was a sketch derived from *Behind the Beyond*. He sought Leacock's blessing for an attempt at a commercial production in London. The Canadian approved.

After attracting capacity audiences for several months at the St. Martin's Theatre, the play *Berkeley Square* had begun to suffer box-office malaise. Some kind of shot in the arm was indicated, and Clinton-Baddeley saw his chance. He proposed *Behind the Beyond* as a possible curtain raiser. The offer was accepted, with Valerie Taylor and Roland Culver—once more, leading artists—as the principals.

The playlet had its premiere on the last night of 1925. On New Year's Day, 1926, the comment in *The Times* ran:

> An admirable burlesque, part of the recent Christmas revue presented at Cambridge.

In three acts, which take only about a quarter of an hour, it is a pleasant adaptation from a parody by Mr. Stephen Leacock of "society" drama.

The story is not much more ridiculous than that of many London plays, but the absurdities, usually so mercifully disguised, are here underlined. The result is extremely amusing.

Less restrained, the critic of *The Daily Telegraph* reported:

The fall of the curtain was greeted with an amount of enthusiasm which is seldom given to a curtain raiser. A terrific tabloid society drama, gorgeously funny. This would emphatically be a thing to be seen, even if it did not precede a play so charming as *Berkeley Square*.

From time to time the humorist toyed with the idea of tackling the commercial theatre on his own hook. But he never did. It was too time-consuming to plot a play of conventional length. Besides, the toil of revising, before and during rehearsals, under exacting procedures and directors was too terrible to contemplate. But his subsequent association with Clinton-Baddeley, who adapted several of Leacock's short pieces, turned out to be moderately remunerative.

Leacock a dramatist? The possibilities were there. Yet it would have been a risky venture because of the notorious uncertainty of playgoers' tastes, which caused even established professional dramatists to halt in their tracks occasionally. Montreal could furnish samples of those fickle tastes which may well have deterred Leacock. However, the city was to become one of the liveliest theatre centres on the continent, and would remain so until the onset of the Great Depression. As a town for tryouts prior to Broadway openings, it was second only to Boston. It boasted three busy legitimate houses, and a better-than-average stock company, not to mention a superior Community Players group and three vaudeville theatres.

In 1915 Leacock paid little more than passing attention to the minor fortunes of "Q." He had another book on the market. It rejoiced in the inspired title *Moonbeams from the Larger Lunacy*. It contained a revealing preface. Shamelessly Leacock told his public:

The prudent husbandman, after having taken from his field all the straw that is there, rakes it over with a wooden rake and gets as much again. The wise child, after the lemonade jug is empty, takes the lemons from the bottom of it and squeezes them into a still brew. So does the sagacious author, after having sold his material to magazines and been paid for it, clap it into book-covers and give it another squeeze.

The contents of *Moonbeams* embraced a casual selection of the year's contributions to a dozen or so American publications. He even threw in "Side Lights on the Superman," which had been tossed off for *The McGill Daily*'s war supplement in March. It met only *McGill Daily* standards. Whether or not he really believed it, world peace could not be long delayed according to one other sketch. "In the Good Times after the War" envisaged a rapturous postbellum moment in the British House of Commons in 1916.

"Squeeze" as he would and did, guilty of repetitiousness in subject and phrase as he was, encouragement arrived from all quarters. Such was the demand that it seldom occurred to him—or if it did, he shrugged off the idea—to rewrite or to polish the original pieces before reissuing them in book form. He may well have been right not to do so, rather to allow the diamonds in the rough to go forth again, counting heavily on the quality of spontaneity. Even such inflated concoctions in *Moonbeams* as the bit about "Ram Spudd: The New World Singer" evoked the plaudits of critics and book-buyers alike. The mood of the marketplace cried out for the kind of fun he was able to offer, the further removed from reality the better.

But Leacock himself kept in touch with reality. He was constantly in correspondence with friends and former students who were in the firing line, and took personal interest in one particular career. A boy who had been his pupil in the old and detested collegiate teaching days had gone to France as a lieutenant-colonel. By 1916 he had become Major-General Arthur W. Currie. And Leacock's long-distance billiards opponent, Gladstone Murray, had proved to be a plucky pilot at the front.

The slaughter in France cast a shadow everywhere. Canada was now on a full war footing, despite political bickering concerning overseas service. Leacock's bright brand of banter filled a need. In this year his *Further Foolishness* spared none of his favorite targets, including the female of the species and the wealthy. Regarding the latter he was moved to wonder considerably if the rich are ever happy:

A friend of mine who has ten thousand dollars a year told me the other day with a sigh that he found it quite impossible to keep up with the rich. On his income he couldn't do it. A family that I know who have twenty thousand a year have told me the same thing. They can't keep up with the rich. There is no use trying. A man I respect very much who has an income of fifty thousand dollars a year from his law practice has told me with the greatest frankness that he finds it absolutely impossible to keep up with the rich. He says that it is better to face the brutal fact of being poor. He says he can only give me a plain meal, what he calls a home dinner—it takes three men and two women to serve it—and he begs me to put up with it.

As far as I remember, I have never met Mr. Carnegie. But I know that if I did he would tell me that he found it quite impossible to keep up with Mr. Rockefeller. No doubt Mr. Rockefeller has the same feeling.

This, of course, teasingly discussed the problem of relative values. Yet Leacock's fascination with the *idea* of the rich ran deeper than the average man's simple covetousness. He had paid lip service to the idea of egalitarianism. At the same time, as an ambitious man, Leacock knew what George Orwell was to state later—that some people are more equal than others. Money was a major means of getting above the average, and, as such, Leacock pursued it relentlessly.

The well-heeled Americans were not yet involved in World War I. But this did not prevent the professor from firing a few pointed shafts in the general direction of Washington. All but naming President Wilson, "The White House from Without In" must have sounded daring at a time when Canadians were hoping for a radical change in U.S. foreign policy which would lead to active support of the Allied cause.

Further Foolishness also proclaimed all over again the author's professed belief that a primary condition of humor must be harmlessness and the absence of spleen and rancor. At this stage he really was protesting too much.

The year was not allowed to pass with only an annual book of humor. He wrote several articles; in one of which, "Let Us Learn Russian," Leacock permitted himself a prediction. This was based on his intuitive feeling (and fear) that Marxist philosophy was a growing challenge to mankind: "The Russian Empire and the Russian people are destined to play a great part in the world in the century that is opening."

To the columns of *The New Republic* he contributed his views on O. Henry, who had died in 1910. Since that time the critics had been baying at his ghost like a pack of mad hounds. Leacock had been indebted to O. Henry for certain fiction techniques—indeed, for ideas, too, as is shown by a comparison between Leacock's "The Errors of Santa Claus" and O. Henry's "The Gift of the Magi." The two were extraordinarily similar in theme and treatment. But his defence of O. Henry's reputation was sadly oversimplified. Leacock jumped off the deep end by extolling the American's humor well above and at the expense of his acknowledged mastery of the surprise short story form as a whole. O. Henry's humor was purely secondary.

After six short, starry years Stephen Leacock now exhibited signs of growing seriousness about his art and himself. In the latter part of 1916 he brought out *Essays and Literary Studies*. These meditations were the culmination of some brooding by a professor who had to mingle with professors. The latter, in varying degrees, either envied their celebrated colleague or, like Dr. Hemmeon, tolerated him. At least one of his scholarly confreres held the Leacock wit in a certain amount of disdain. He was Professor Paul Lafleur of the English department. The two managed to offend each other and a frothy feud bubbled up.

The humorist, in an honest effort, endeavored to extend the hand of friendship one day by suggesting a bury-the-hatchet dinner at the University Club. The invitation fell on deaf ears.

"Very well," said Leacock, "you can go to hell."

"*That* I would infinitely prefer."

It was not said lightly.

From time to time Leacock had fretted about the trivial nature of some of the things he had been manufacturing. If his fellow professors did not say so in as many words, brother George did criticise such triviality. It had been George who had lent the necessary impetus to the original publication of *Literary Lapses*. It was George who had been the source of some of the stories which Stephen had put into print, and a useful audience for many others. It was a genial George who followed his brother's progress with a prideful yet critical eye. In the back of his mind Stephen also stored B. K. Sandwell's strictures of yore. For reassurance he recalled the impression conveyed to him in London by G. K. Chesterton—that humor represented the highest form of civilization. So, in defending himself, he resorted in *Further Foolishness* to such whopping plaintive statements as:

. . . ordinary people, quite unconsciously, rate humor very low: I mean they underestimate the difficulty of "making humor." It would never occur to them that the thing is hard, meritorious and dignified. Because the result is gay and light, they think the process must be. Few people would realise that it is much harder to write one of Owen Seaman's "funny" poems in *Punch* than to write one of the Archbishop of Canterbury's sermons. Mark Twain's *Huckleberry Finn* is a greater work than Kant's *Critique of Pure Reason*, and Charles Dickens' creation of Mr. Pickwick did more for the elevation of the human race—I say it in all seriousness —than Cardinal Newman's *Lead, Kindly Light, Amid the Encircling Gloom.* Newman only cried out for light on the gloom of a sad world. Dickens gave it.

But the deep background that lies behind and beyond what we call humor is revealed only to the few who, by instinct or by effort, have given thought to it.

And so, as one of "the few" and in sombre frame of mind, Leacock examined a number of topics in *Essays and Literary Studies.* In the course of the ruminations he hit upon the essential difference between American and British humor:

A large part of American humor lacks profundity, and wants that stimu- lating aid of the art of expression which can be found only among a literary people. . . . The British people, essentially a people of exceptions, produce a light form of humorous literature because of their literary spirit, and in spite of the fact that their general standard of humorous perception is lower. In the one case humor forces literature. In the other literature forces humor.

Uncomfortably, Leacock knew where he stood—in the American zone for the most part. More often than not his British heritage and classical training showed through his material. The more senti- mental moments were filled with a Dickensian flavor, as witness his several excursions into the theme of Christmas. Otherwise the style and the attack, consciously or unconsciously modelled on Mark Twain, bore the marks of the New World, and were sharp- ened accordingly for pecuniary gain. Yet doubtless due to his Eng- lish background and his academic training, he always seemed to be ill at ease in handling the American idiom. With all due respect to J. B. Priestley, Leacock may hardly be credited with giving voice to an indigenous Canadian humor. There is no such thing. The deadly serious Canadian disposition has so far given birth to little more than a sort of stilted comic allusiveness which falls far short of even Stephen Leacock's evaluation of humor.

Towards the end of 1916 a professional friend in Toronto asked Leacock for his opinion about establishing a Canadian humorous magazine along the lines of *Punch*. Leacock spoke of the difficulty of reproducing in Canada the tone of *Punch*—"kindly, never partisan, never bitter." He added that "our public would have to be educated to it, and our writers have to learn the art of it."

Possibly his playful response to an English critic at this time found Leacock in a moment of exact self-appraisal. A British reviewer patronizingly dismissed the Leacockian recipe as merely "a rather ingenious mixture of hyperbole and myosis.

Chastising him with his own tools, Leacock turned on his adversary:

> The man was right. How he stumbled upon this trade secret I do not know. But I am willing to admit, since the truth is out, that it has long been my custom in preparing an article to go down to the cellar and mix up half a gallon of myosis with a pint of hyperbole. If I want to give the article a decidedly literary character, I find it well to put in about half a pint of paresis. The whole thing is amazingly simple.

What's more, the whole thing was amazingly apposite.

VIII

Whisky Galore

The metaphorical supply of myosis, hyperbole and paresis in the Leacock cellar did not dry up during 1917. Like its brewmaster, it simply languished. For the professor it was a melancholy year. For the first time since 1910 no new book emerged bearing his name.

Important events during this period ought to have cheered him. In April the United States declared war on Germany. In the same month Canadian troops, with matchless courage and skill, won the battle of Vimy Ridge—"the greatest British victory of the war up to that time." It was also in 1917 that Major-General Arthur W. Currie, Leacock's former school pupil, was promoted to lieutenant-general and took command of the Canadian Corps.

With plenty of others to keep him company, the professor had envisaged a short, if violent war. Instead, it was now into its fourth year. Despite all the propaganda predictions, the Western front held promise of little better than a stalemate. A disconsolate humorist was in no mood to ply his trade.

Only a few months earlier, in *Further Foolishness*, Leacock had rung the changes on a Dickens story:

George Grossmith, the famous comedian, was once badly run down and went to consult a doctor. It happened that the doctor, though, like everybody else, he had often seen Grossmith on the stage, had never seen him without his make-up and did not know him by sight. He examined his patient, looked at his tongue, felt his pulse and tapped his lungs. Then he shook his head. "There's nothing wrong with you, sir," he said, "I expect you're run down from overwork and worry. You need rest and amusement. Take a night off and go and see George Grossmith at the Savoy." "Thank you," said the patient, "I *am* George Grossmith."

Charles Dickens had used the great clown Grimaldi to make his point. Other writers have played upon the same theme. The occasional fit of dejection is their common lot and Leacock had more than his share. Elizabeth Kimball was told by Leacock's son that his father did have a wide range of moods: "A man who is given to high spirits and great elations naturally experiences the reverse. Just as he was way up when he was up, so he was away down when he was down." With a large measure of success he strove to mask the fact. Like Dr. Samuel Johnson, Leacock could at times shout defiance at his anxieties in tremendous roars of laughter.

Recent developments on the Canadian home front were sufficient to cause concern to all but the most apathetic. French Canadian nationalism, with the fiery Henri Bourassa, founder and editor of *Le Devoir*, as its mouthpiece, had been on the warpath long before the outbreak of war. Ever since his arrival in Montreal, the Anglo-Saxon Leacock, although he was a fluent French speaker, had paid sparse attention to the arguments being flung about. He merely thought that the British since 1759 had exhibited the utmost consideration for the French in Canada—their traditions, culture and language. *En passant* he would tell his students that in 1763 the Treaty of Paris was the occasion when the French language "was fastened on to Canada." The outpourings of the likes of Bourassa only baffled him.

Yet in 1917 matters came to a head. The events which followed were to leave their stamp on the country's future. Leacock the historian was able to sense the portents, but he would not be dragged into contemporary public controversy.

In Ottawa the Conservative government's alarm over the man-power shortage in the actual theatre of operations led to a bold move in June—the Military Service Act, or conscription. Immediately, this act precipitated serious dissension within the ranks of the Liberal party. Worse, it led to vitriolic speeches at meeting after meeting in Montreal and to street riots and gunfire in Quebec City. That August the bedroom wing of the country house of Lord Atholstan (the former Sir Hugh Graham and a friend of Leacock), publisher of *The Montreal Star*, was blown up. Fortunately a last-minute business engagement had kept the newspaper proprietor in town that night. Atholstan had defiantly plumped for conscription as the only way out of the nation's problems.

A general election in December returned Prime Minister Borden and his party. A coalition government was promptly formed to ensure that the business of the war would be carried on in orderly fashion. Canada continued to play a major part in the war; but the cleavage between Quebec and the rest of the country caused wounds which remain unhealed to this day.

In this atmosphere of national hullabaloo Leacock stuck closely and wisely to his college work, obdurately refusing requests by his Tory friends to join the fray. The professor was deeply distressed by what he ventured to say in his classes would prove to be an irreparable rift in confederation.

Meantime his pen had not been altogether idle. He continued to emphasize the strains that the mechanics of humorous writing imposed on its creator. Nothing infuriated him so much as to hear somebody say, "It must be great fun writing the things you do." Yet he contradicted himself. To one audience he admitted that such work was not really so difficult: "You just jot down ideas as they occur to you. The jotting is simplicity itself—it is the occuring which is difficult."

The "occurring" in the 1917–18 period had been infrequent; enough, however, had "occurred" to encourage him to plan another volume of pieces. This carried the title *Frenzied Fiction*, a farrago that understandably dealt with various aspects of the war.

Up to this point Leacock had kept his own counsel on the subject of American participation. One of his few outspoken comments found expression in the new book—a brief essay he called "Father Knickerbocker: A Fantasy". This took to task hedonistic Manhattanites for lounging "in the foul atmosphere of luxury" while the fate of the world hung in the balance over Europe. And he drew a comparison with the old days in New York, pointedly referring to the time when citizens walked "with their wives, their own wives on the greensward." This contrasted with the prevalent philosophy

of wine, women and song. Leacock was not exactly antipathetic to
that same philosophy, but in his present moralistic mood he didn't
even try to be funny.

He was, however, back in his best burlesque manner with "My
Revelations as a Spy." This piece played amusingly on the mania
for espionage scares on both sides of the Atlantic. It should have
shamed the many people given to this kind of thing, but they were
probably too busy laughing to note the lesson. Equally expert,
"Back from the Land" recounted the ridiculous experiences of "a
grimly determined set of men" who went out from the city to the
land in an effort to solve the food shortage crisis. Hilariously they
accomplished a minimum with a maximum of patriotic fervor. This
left Leacock to meditate upon the whole question of gardening:

> It appears that the right time to begin gardening is last year. For many
> things it is well to begin the year before last. For good results one must
> begin even sooner. Here, for example, are the directions, as I interpret
> them, for growing asparagus. Having secured a suitable piece of ground,
> preferably a deep friable loam rich in nitrogen, go out three years ago
> and plough or dig deeply. Remain a year inactive, thinking. Two years
> ago pulverize the soil thoroughly. Wait a year. As soon as last year comes
> set out the young shoots. Then spend a quiet winter doing nothing. The
> asparagus will then be ready to work at *this* year.

It is worth noting that in fact Leacock was himself a devoted
and skilled gardener. He loved his English roses. And he always
took great pride in pointing out how many of the vegetables and
fruits served at Old Brewery Bay were "home grown."

The same book contained some simple solutions for the practical
farmer:

> If a farmer would only realize that the contents of a circle represent the
> maximum of space enclosable in a given perimeter, and that a circle is
> merely a function of its own radius, what a lot of time we would save.

Another searing satire on the bogus aspects of spiritualism found
its way into *Frenzied Fiction*. His "Personal Adventures in the
Spirit World" first presented the author as a sceptic, then a confirmed believer. Via mediums and seances, he experienced encounters with people of the past. His great-grandfather was among
them:

"Where are you, great-grandfather?"
"Here," he answered, "beyond."
"Beyond what?"
"Here on the other side."
"Side of which?" I asked.
"Of the great vastness," he answered. "The other end of the Illimitable."
"Oh, I see," I said, "That's where you are."

It must have been a calculated risk to guy this sort of theme while wholesale sacrifices were being made and while millions of sorrowing realtives were turning to anything for spiritual succor. Nonetheless, Leacock doggedly pursued his announced aim to laugh spiritualism out of existence.

For obvious reasons prohibition was another *bête noire*. Leacock was leading from prejudice here. He touched on the subject twice in *Frenzied Fiction*. In an introductory statement to "In Dry Toronto" he noted that those of his readers "who live in Equatorial Africa, may read this under the title *In Dry Timbuctoo*; those who live in Central America will kindly call it *In Dry Tehauntepec*." Of course, the universality of interest was there, but "In Dry Toronto" was quintessentially the Toronto of that day.

In Leacock's gallery of saints there was no room for puritans, prigs, meddlers or hypocrites. All these, and more, were in evidence in the world which was emerging from World War I. In "This Strenuous Age" he shuddered at the thought of "total prohibition," when the joys of the body and soul would be banished forever. He would listen to and *almost* agree with warnings that alcohol rots the gut, destroys the brain cells, reduces working power, muddles thought, and so on:

> Very dreadful, not a doubt. Alcohol is doomed; it is going, it is gone. Yet, when I think of a hot Scotch on a winter evening, or a Tom Collins on a summer morning, or a gin rickey beside a tennis-court, or a stein of beer on a bench beside a bowling-green—I wish somehow we could prohibit the use of alcohol and merely drink beer and whisky and gin as we used to.

So great was his self-discipline (not to mention his tremendous tolerance) that none of these beverages ever interfered with Leacock's work, though they held pride of place in his program of relaxation. Nor could he ever be properly accused of seeking to conceal his delight in such indulgences. The occasions were not rare when a class could spot that the previous evening had been a rough one for the lecturer. By the same token, if one of his students turned up obviously a bit the worse for wear, a bond of sympathy became evident.

One young man staggered into the classroom for a morning bout with political economy, doing his level best to indicate an awareness of his surroundings and an appreciation of the discussion in hand. With a knowing air which caused the student's head to throb the more, Leacock worked the economic discussion round to the beer trade, extolling by the way the brands available at the Pig and Whistle (in the gone but not forgotten Prince of Wales Hotel on McGill College Avenue). "I expect," he added, looking everywhere but at the person concerned, "some of you gentlemen have good reason to know about this." They all knew, and each must have wondered if he were the target of the professor's cautionary remark.

When Leacock was about to embark on a lecture tour, his flask led the list of items to be packed. According to one chronicler, Leacock passed up an invitation to accompany Vilhjalmur Stefansson, the famous Canadian-born Arctic explorer, on a polar expedition. He had learned that whisky would not be allowed on the voyage. Even on his own much less ambitious voyages at Old Brewery Bay, while black bass were the official attraction, liquid refreshment was a more predictable constant feature.

After the majority of Canadian provinces in 1918 misguidedly decided to follow in the wake of the U.S. Volstead Act and bring prohibition to Canada, Leacock became a "wet" crusader with a vengeance. Pernickety he may have been about payment for most of his public appearances, but he made it a principle not to accept fees for anti-prohibition speeches.

Canadians put up with the intolerable governance for nine years. At the end of this time a number of municipalities exercised local option to retain their "dry" status. Leacock regarded it as a personal insult when Orillia did this. He had to send some distance down the line for his supplies, an inconvenience that the author of *Sunshine Sketches* looked upon with oft-remarked resentment.

On his Old Brewery Bay estate the "farm" equipment included an old truck which, through a combination of eccentric original design and neglected upkeep, was instrumental in bringing its owner into the clutches of the law. The city of Brockville police charged Leacock with failing to equip his vehicle "with flares and clearance lights." Accordingly, he was fined nineteen dollars (in absentia). Accompanying his cheque were his answers to the court's queries concerning his personal habits: "I read fairly well, but need spectacles; I write quite nicely, with many volumes to prove it. I drink every day."

At the war's end in November, Leacock and his wife began to implement plans to make their summer home more habitable. Heretofore they had been content with what Leacock had called "a shack." The time had arrived to make room on the property for a more comfortable cottage. As far as Leacock was concerned the erection of a boathouse was every bit as important. Not only was a boathouse needed for all the normal aquatic activities of holiday living, the sailing and the fishing that he loved: Leacock had a further requirement that a new boathouse could fulfil perfectly. He wanted an adequate room well removed from the domestic routine where he could spread his books and papers and work uninterruptedly.

Thus when the boathouse was built, it sported an upper story which served him for years as a working hideaway, no less untidy than his Cote des Neiges study. The frame house itself had ample space for visiting friends or relatives and stood back from the water a hundred yards or so, commanding a fine view of the lake.

As usual, Leacock turned the experience to good purpose. He produced a short story, "How My Wife and I Built Our Home for $4.90," "related in the manner of the Best Models in the magazines." Describing the feverish anticipation and the exciting preparations, he acknowledged his disappointment at the slow pace of realization: "Owing perhaps to my inexperience, it took me the whole of the morning to dig out a cellar forty feet long and twenty feet wide." And the impatience of the wife! She had only managed during the same morning to clean up the lot, stack the lumber, lift away the stones and plant fifty yards of hedge.

But in the Leacock household as 1919 dawned there was increasing uneasiness. To all intents and purposes Stephen, Jr., had maintained a healthy progress. Yet it appeared to the parents and their Montreal pediatrician that the child was not maintaining normal growth. The father could not shake off the memory of the day of the boy's birth, when he had felt an ill-defined premonition (implicit in the letter to his mother at the time) that all was not well. The son's condition, as yet far from clearly diagnosed, would plainly continue to be a source of anxiety.

Leacock's domestic worries were in part alleviated by the return to McGill of that romantic bachelor René du Roure. He had been released by the Germans in 1918 and for the remainder of the hostilities had served as an aide on the French general staff. The spirited thirty-nine-year-old Frenchman lost no time in renewing with his tousled forty-nine-year-old partner a series of billiards battles calculated to divert members of the University Club for two decades.

One story is told by the lady who was then the secretary of the French department. Professor du Roure entered his Arts building office one day wearing a worried look. After mumbling to himself for a while, he eventually confided in the secretary that he was suspicious of Leacock.

"It always happens," he said with a puzzled expression.

"What always happens, sir?"

"Well, when Dr. Leacock and I are playing billiards it seems I am always called to the telephone. Then, when I return, I could swear that the position of the billiard balls has been altered. Moreover—but, no . . ."

"But, what Professor du Roure?"

"I don't like to say it. I hardly like to think it. But do you suppose Dr. Leacock arranges those telephone calls?"

When he was ultimately confronted with this accusation, Dr. Leacock flatly denied it. But the phone calls ceased forthwith.

On a Sunday in January 1919, tragedy struck on the campus. Principal Peterson—now, with a wartime knighthood, Sir William —had a special engagement with Sir Harry Lauder in a downtown church. The two Scotsmen were to co-chair a meeting at which money was to be raised on behalf of the families of Scottish servicemen killed or disabled in the war. The program had barely begun when Sir William fell from his chair. He had suffered a stroke from which he was never fully to recover. In consequence he submitted his resignation to the university, which, in his individualistic fashion, he had served well.

Leacock's distress over the plight of Peterson was considerably

(17) Leacock studied economics under Thorstein Veblen at the University of Chicago from 1899 until he received his doctorate in 1903. This photograph of the campus was taken in 1907. *(Courtesy of the University of Chicago Archives)*

(18) Early in his academic career Leacock wrote his first book. It was a sober, serious textbook, yet it was a best seller.

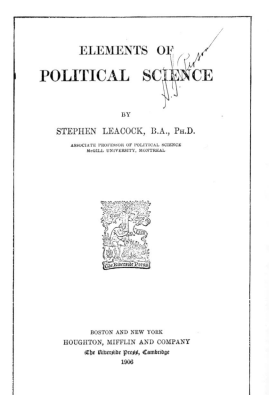

ELEMENTS OF

POLITICAL SCIENCE

BY

STEPHEN LEACOCK, B.A., Ph.D.

ASSOCIATE PROFESSOR OF POLITICAL SCIENCE
McGILL UNIVERSITY, MONTREAL

The Riverside Press

BOSTON AND NEW YORK
HOUGHTON, MIFFLIN AND COMPANY
The Riverside Press, Cambridge
1906

(19) Leacock married Beatrix Hamilton of Toronto in August, 1900. Since "Trix" was appearing at the time in a small Broadway part, the wedding took place in New York's Little Church Around The Corner. *(Courtesy of the Stephen Leacock Memorial Home)*

(20) In 1908 Leacock bought property at Old Brewery Bay near Orillia, Ontario, and built a temporary hut. Here (in wheelbarrow) he relaxes from his labors, in mixed company. *(Courtesy of the Public Archives of Canada)*

(21) Here Leacock (top row, second from left) relaxes in the strictly masculine company of cricketers. *(Courtesy of the Public Archives of Canada)*

(22) The Mariposa Band, as sketched by A. G. Racey when *Sunshine Sketches of a Little Town* first appeared serially in *The Montreal Star* in 1912. (Courtesy of *The Montreal Star*)

MISSISSAGA ST. LOOKING WEST, ORILLIA, ONT.

(23) The *Sunshine Sketches* were written about a real town. Here is the "Little Town," Orillia, Ontario, in 1910, only two years before the sketches were published. (Courtesy of Orillia Public Library)

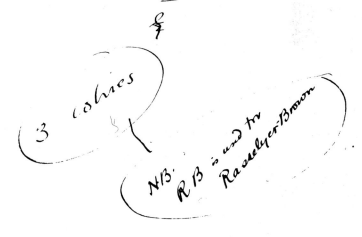

Arcadian Adventures with
The Idle Rich

&

Stephen Leacock

Chap. IV.

the Yahi-Bahi Oriental Society

of Mrs Rasselyer=Brown

&

3 copies

NB. R B is used for Rasselyer=Brown

(24) The title page, in Leacock's handwriting, for Chapter 4 of *Arcadian Adventures with the Idle Rich*, which was published in 1914. The original manuscript is in the Leacock Room, McLennan Library, McGill University. *(Courtesy of the McLennan Library of McGill University)*

(25) William Notman photo of Leacock taken in 1914. *(Courtesy of the McCord Museum of McGill University)*

(26) Stephen and Beatrix Leacock with Stephen Leacock, Jr.,
outside their Cote des Neiges
home in Montreal in 1916.
*(Courtesy of the Public Archives
of Canada)*

(27) Leacock and son at Old
Brewery Bay in 1916. *(Courtesy
of the Public Archives of
Canada)*

(28) Beatrix with Stephen, Jr., on the dock at Old Brewery Bay about 1917. *(Courtesy of the Public Archives of Canada)*

(29) *(Below)* Tea at Leacock's Old Brewery Bay home about 1920. Left to right: Leacock, Freddie Pellatt (brother-in-law), Beatrix, Stephen, Jr., and Mrs. H. T. Shaw. *(Courtesy of the Public Archives of Canada)*

relieved by the speedy action of the board of governors in securing another Scotsman, whose Celtic sense of humor had appealed to the professor when they were both members of the University Club. In 1913 this Dr. Auckland Geddes had become professor of anatomy on McGill's medical faculty. He had brought from the old country an enviable reputation in his specialties of surgery and research.

At the outbreak of war Geddes returned to his homeland, enlisted, served in the trenches, was severely wounded, and became Minister of National Service in the Lloyd George government. He later was appointed Minister of Reconstruction, received a knighthood and accepted the principalship of McGill.

Leacock was looking forward to renewing an old friendship until No. 10 Downing Street intervened. Strong representations were made to Sir Robert Borden, the Canadian Prime Minister, by David Lloyd George. As a result, Geddes' services were retained by the imperial government. Without ever taking office, Sir Auckland resigned from McGill and went to Washington as British ambassador.

McGill's governors now had another hunt on their hands. They wasted no time in making what they must have known would be a controversial appointment. General Sir Arthur Currie had returned from the war a national hero. Indeed, he had acquitted himself so well that, at one stage of the conflict, Lloyd George and Field Marshal Jan Smuts had seriously considered Currie as a possible substitute for the arrogant Field Marshal Haig.

Despite his pride in the accomplishments of the man whom he had taught as a boy, Leacock shared the scepticism of many newspaper editors who received the news with wonder and, in some cases, disapproval. Currie's academic shortcomings were cited. True, at one time he had been a schoolteacher. But that brush with pedagogy had been followed by a spell as a real estate agent out West.

Leacock's misgivings about Currie soon melted away. This imposing figure, heavy of jowl, with a tendency to "brass hat" portliness, had the heart of a great human being. He swiftly won the support of the professoriate and the student body alike. Quite apart from his earlier association with Currie, Leacock admired the general for having passed the Leacock test—by getting above the average from a very humble start in life. This was yet another reminder to Leacock that all men are not born equal.

One of Sir Arthur's many strengths rested in his realization of his own limitations in the rarefied atmosphere of academe. Gradually but surely, one of the men on whom the celebrated soldier came to lean for advice was Stephen Leacock, whose increasing visits to the administrative wing were marked by an easy informality.

Currie faced an enormous challenge in preparing McGill to absorb the returning veterans. Leacock, too, faced problems, what with increasing registration in his department. Because his literary reputation was now at its peak Leacock had to contend with students who put down their names in economics and political science as much for the man as for the subjects. One student remembers his first sight of the professor in those days:

> It was in the inside entrance corridor to the old Arts building. Ahead of me I saw a burly man; his left arm was through the left sleeve of his gown and clutching an armful of dog-eared files. The right side of the gown stretched along the floor behind him when it caught on a splinter. With one swoop he gathered it in and strode into the classroom with me behind him.

In the passage of years that gown had become a trademark. At one time it did not seem like an affectation, rather just carelessness. Now he himself was conscious of its symbolic comical character. He played it for all it was worth.

Early in the fall of 1919 Leacock went to New York to deliver a lecture at Columbia University. An eyewitness of that event writes:

> I don't remember the subject, but as a topic he got on to *Gowns*. He talked of various kinds of gowns, and said he himself often wore one that suggested more than it revealed—a nightgown. On the way out I heard an elderly matron say to another: "Isn't it awful that Columbia University should allow a man like that to lecture in its halls?"

Although the war was over and the Kaiser tucked away in exile at Doorn, Leacock still had something to say about both. In his customary fashion, he gathered these observations into a book called *The Hohenzollerns in America*. Sardonic touches characterized most of the contents, which ranged from the ways of war correspondents, to a club's disastrous efforts to raise funds for Belgian Relief, to a dinner party at which a returned soldier reveals what war is about and what it has done to him and others. This particular section, "The Boy Who Came Back," found Leacock in an embittered frame of mind and not backward in admitting it. Again pulling no punches, in "The War Sacrifices of Mr. Spugg" the author let fly at his favorite target of the plutocracy and the power of money. Mr. Spugg was the kind of Croesus whose noble nature risked tremendous personal hardship by doing without the services of his valet and two chauffeurs so that they might enlist. When it became a matter of his son being drafted, his patriotism dictated that his son should not go to war, for the family business could not possibly dispense with his talents.

Echoes of "Hang the Kaiser" had not yet died away. Leacock pulled out all the stops in the title sketch to lambaste the deposed emperor and his entourage. From the standpoint of popular satire, this was one of his best pieces. The Crown Prince Willie, in Leacock's imagination, had been discovered in unexplained possession of a quantity of table silverware, goblets and arms. A nephew of the Kaiser complains about Cousin Willie's offensive conduct in a hospitable foreign land. To this the once mighty Hohenzollern retorts that his son

> might very well be collecting souvenirs as memorials of his residence in America; all the Hohenzollerns collected souvenirs; some of our most beautiful art things at Potsdam and San Souci were souvenirs collected by our ancestors in France fifty years ago.

The ex-Kaiser went on to say that, if the Great War had turned out as it should and if his soldiers had not betrayed him by getting killed, "We should have had more souvenirs than ever."

After this book had been well launched, Leacock then tackled an assignment for the *New York Times*—a six-part series on social justice. In addition he wrote two articles on the evils of prohibition. He might have been forgiven if he had coasted a bit, but he was not yet through with 1919. In that year he helped to found *The McGill News*, the organ of the Graduates' Society of McGill University (which celebrated its golden anniversary in 1969). Leacock became the first chairman of its editorial board and contributed original pieces spasmodically for the rest of his days.

Not least among his fond memories of the closing year was the correspondence which had suddenly burgeoned between himself and Robert Benchley, whose broad impishness was not unlike the distinctive productions of Leacock's own genie. Years later Benchley, in a tribute printed in the *Laugh with Leacock* anthology, boyishly stated:

> I have just returned from abroad, and I hope that it is not too late for me to say that I have enjoyed Leacock's works so much that I have written everything he ever wrote—anywhere from one to five years after him. In case the proof-reader thinks that I meant "I have *read* everything he ever wrote," please tell him that I really meant "written."

So, with renewed vigor, Stephen Leacock could (and no doubt did) drink to the New Year. On the eve of his fiftieth birthday he was ready for what history would eventually designate the Roaring Twenties.

IX

Debut of a Decade

On January 10, 1920, the League of Nations came into being. Its two principal objectives were the preservation of peace and the improvement of human welfare. Its limitations, however, were clearly marked from the beginning, when, despite having sixty-three nations as members, the organization failed to persuade the United States to join. Nonetheless, hopeful speculation about its future was rife in the ivory towers of academe. As a point of departure for argument, the League provided a field day for economists and political scientists.

Leacock, who tried to be an optimist (on the surface, at any rate), tended to express misgivings in the classroom about the widely acclaimed new world order that would result from the ostensible spirit of co-operation. He suspected—and he was right—that after the holocaust of World War I governments would have their hands full coping with problems on their own front doorsteps; any kind of planning on a global scale would have to wait for a considerable while.

A lachrymose missive, which he included in "Letters to the New Rulers of the World," commended the League's idealistic goals. But the letterwriter pointed out with regret that the League was not doing anything in particular for his own little town. "Your

League is all right, but somehow the gate receipts of it seem to go in the wrong direction." The insular mind never failed to intrigue Leacock.

For all its pride in the modicum of international status Canada acquired as a member of the League, its internal troubles were enough to turn the country inward. The task of moving the young nation into the paths of peace appeared to be insuperable. Post-war unrest taxed the talents of the legislators, federal and provincial, who were on the receiving end of endless doses of gratuitous advice from all sectors of the population.

One of Leacock's pronounced virtues as a university teacher was his habit of applying theory directly to events in the workaday world. So the contemporary scene entered into his lectures, serving to capture students' attention. For example, there had been a general strike in the city of Winnipeg the year before. This economic weapon, employed for the first time in Canadian history, had threatened to paralyze the heart of the western part of the country. The repressive actions taken by the authorities to cope with the situation were very controversial. But they were supported by the conservative Leacock. He advocated social justice; but at the same time he dreaded the socialistic lengths to which it might be stretched.

As the new decade opened Canada began to experience an economic depression. Agrarian unrest assumed major proportions in the West. With the resignation of Sir Robert Borden as Prime Minister on grounds of ill health, the shrewd Arthur Meighen took over the reins at Ottawa. Naturally, as an arch-protectionist, Meighen enjoyed Leacock's approval.

The professor always admitted that anyone studying economics in his classes, with a view to turning it into Conservative politics, would find it "a thing easily done under my regime."

In the general circumstances of universal readjustment, Leacock's original publishers reckoned that the time was ripe for a reissue of *Elements of Political Science*, which had so speedily taken root as a standard college text in 1906. As a moneymaker it had yet to be outdistanced by any one of the humorous works, profitable as these continued to be. Leacock did not revise *Elements* to any appreciable extent, but the new edition soon proved it had been worth the effort. Now long since outdated, the book in its day served a real purpose as an introductory manual.

The war, which even now was proving to have been the great watershed in modern society, had made an impact on Leacock's thinking. Still a Tory, he was at least examining various theories being put forward as solutions for social and political ills. The previous year had seen a half-dozen of his articles published in the *New York Times*. Slightly expanded, these were now brought between the cover of a book, *The Unsolved Riddle of Social Justice*. Although they were elementary in character, they could not hide the author's dilemma. He had begun to sense, with an easily imagined reluctance, that hard-line conservatism must give way to more liberal processes in the economic sphere. "Everybody," he said, "who has ever tried to study the political economy of our times— everybody with a brain not ossified by wealth or debilitated by birth—knows that we live in an unjust world."

At the final page the riddle of the title remained unresolved. But the burden of the presentation revealed a change in Leacock's outlook. He insisted that the shortening of the hours of work should be among the primary aims of social reform. Public opinion, he argued, required to be reshaped on the subject of work in relation to human character and development. These were not new ideas, even for the 1920s, but they represented an easing of Leacock's previous rigidity.

Conceding that "the details are indistinct," Leacock ventured to suggest the need for "a progressive movement of social control, alleviating the misery which it cannot obliterate." By his definition, however, "progressive" had its limits. The movement should stop well short of any form of socialism, a philosophy that was anathema to him:

> With perfect citizens any government is good. In a population of angels a socialistic commonwealth would work to perfection.

There were contradictions in his attitude, a not uncommon occurence in Leacock's case. On the one hand he saw the necessity for the reform of the system of landownership, "so as to eliminate the haphazard gains of the speculator and the unearned increment of wealth created by the efforts of others." On the other hand he proclaimed, in a ringing generalization, that "the private ownership of land is one of the greatest incentives to human effort that the world has ever known."

Indirectly, his political stance had already been given away in *The Hohenzollerns in America*:

> To avoid all error as to the point of view, let me say in commencing that I am a Liberal Conservative, or, if you will, a Conservative Liberal with a strong dash of sympathy with the Socialist idea, a friend of Labour, and a believer in Progressive Radicalism. I believe there are ever so many people of exactly the same way of thinking.

Sometimes Leacock's logic could be unfathomable. Perhaps it would be more accurate to say that he often distinguished between logic and "horse-sense." In a moment of jocularity he described an actual incident in one of his classes. On an examination paper he had set the question: "What do you know about the Treaty of Utrecht?" A student took the professor at his word. He answered: "Absolutely nothing."

"I had to give him full marks," Leacock explained. "It was a perfectly logical situation."

In his extra-curricular work in 1920 Leacock met with unexpected trouble. He had no intention of abandoning his habit of turning out one funny book per year. Thus he gathered together an assortment of magazine creations, which he had modelled along the lines of his immensely successful *Nonsense Novels*. This collection he labelled *Winsome Winnie*, after the lead-off story, and despatched it confidently to his publisher, whose reception of it proved to be less than ecstatic. It appeared that the publisher was concerned about decreasing Leacock sales. Indeed, the firm was losing money on him.

Taken aback, Leacock promptly shot off a letter to the managing editor:

> I was sorry to learn from your telegram that you had refused my offer. Your publishing at a loss will, of course, be a disastrous thing for me as your interest and mine will be exactly opposed, and you will have no incentive to advertise or to push my book. In other words, it bids fair to be strangled in its cradle, whereas I am quite convinced that it is the best book I have done since *Nonsense Novels*, and that with energetic and enterprising handling it could have been a great success.

Indeed this was the first rebuff Leacock had experienced since Houghton Mifflin had rejected his *Literary Lapses* a decade before.

With a mixture of cajolery, huffing and puffing, and an ultimate readiness to accept a reduced royalty deal for this one occasion, Leacock persuaded Dodd, Mead to undertake publication of *Winsome Winnie*.

As Sir Compton Mackenzie has so rightly observed in his marathon autobiography: "Of all the tastes one should argue about, taste in humor is the least arguable of all." Leacock's view of *Winsome Winnie* was soon substantiated. It was so marketable that it eventually went into eight editions. And the quality could be equated with some of the *Nonsense Novels*.

When the book appeared in England, James Douglas' review in *The Sunday Express* made an interesting point:

> The moment I cross the frontier into Leacockland, I see life from a different angle—the angle of impudence.

This very flippancy made one of the burlesques, "The Split in the Cabinet, or The Fate of England," an example of the humorist at the top of his spoofing spirit. Superficially idiotic in plot and characterization, this parody of an old-fashioned political novel got at the core of Westminster hanky-panky. It may be read today with relish.

Another sheer flight of fancy, written with his feet firmly anchored, "Buggam Grange: A Good Old Ghost Story" dealt unmercifully with writers of the haunted-house genre. Again Leacock flourished in dealing with the supernatural. In this instance, however, craftsmanship was not permitted to suffer. In fact, read a half-century after its first appearance, "Buggam Grange" stands as an impeccably fashioned simulation of a whole range of Gothic romances.

Couched in his more familiar style of broad attack, "Who Do You Think? or The Mixed-Up Murder Mystery" dealt amusingly with the whodunit tribe, readers as well as authors.

Thus his waggish nature refused to be downed by the vexatious conditions in the country at large, or by his nagging anxiety over his five-year-old boy. The latter's health continued to remain good; but the slowness of the child's growth preyed on the parents' minds, since the Leacocks' pediatric adviser himself could offer no solution.

As usual, the summer of 1920 found the family at Old Brewery Bay ("It's also a distillery," Leacock assured an impending visitor). He complained about expenses. But boating, fishing, tennis and golf figured prominently on the agenda. As host in Montreal Leacock had built an enviable reputation for gracious formal hospitality. Those who were privileged to be his guests on the shores of Lake Couchiching saw an almost entirely different man. Relaxed, loving the smell of the soil, basking in the sun and fresh air and, above all, in the complete absence of formality in dress and conduct, here he was in his natural habitat. The rumpled tweedy clothes, the tangled tie, remained exactly the same, even in the garden or on the lake. But the professor shed his academic manner, taking on the character of one who had not only never seen, but, what's more, never wanted to see an urban centre any larger than the little town of the *Sunshine Sketches*. That Mrs. Leacock, accustomed to the refinements of a city, entered into the spirit of the place furnished further proof of her readiness to defer to a husband whose real happiness lay in the rural life.

More often than not the summer cottage housed guests from near and far, with Prof. René du Roure possibly the most regular and decidedly the most welcome. But Leacock's own routine never varied. The practice of retiring early, with an equally early rising, was jealously maintained in the interests of a regular writing schedule. After 10 P.M. it became Mrs. Leacock's job to entertain the visitors. In the morning Leacock would work away from 5 until 10 and then would spend the rest of the day outdoors, fishing or gardening.

The man who had written to his mother a dozen years earlier that the sad world could pass him by, that he wanted to retire at fifty-five and settle for a rustic existence was in part at least realizing his wish. He managed to spend on the average four and a half months anually near Orillia, on his modest "farm" which gave him the utmost pleasure—a strange reversal of the detestation he constantly expressed (right up to the end) of his childhood farm existence.

Opinions vary on his competence as an agriculturist. Undoubtedly a paddling of ducks regarded him as a gentleman farmer. Leacock had taken pity on his ducks, so far removed were they from the water's edge. It occurred to him they deserved more considerate treatment and a solution materialized quickly. He dug a shallow ditch from the duck enclosure down to the lake. Gratefully the ducks obliged by using the miniature waterway. On Lake Couchiching they swam with gay abandon—swam clear out of sight, never to return. Leacock was surprised and hurt.

For his own benefit and for the comfort of friends, it was a house rule of the summer residence that there should be a decent supply of alcoholic beverages at all times. Prohibition occasionally militated against this regulation, though never for very long. The professor had persuaded himself—and others, for that matter—that this particular law of the land (or, to be exact, of the provinces) was a stupid and harmful piece of legislation and an invasion of an individual's private rights. Moreover, it was an impractical law since it could not easily be enforced. As had been demonstrated in the United States, it would breed crime. And, apart from the personal inconvenience, the hypocrisy of the thing irritated him. There still were ways of getting a drink:

> It is only necessary to go to a drugstore and lean up against the counter and make a gurgling sigh like apoplexy. One often sees these apoplexy cases lined up four deep.

In his "Letters to the New Rulers of the World" he included, expectedly, one epistle to a prohibitionist in his best mocking manner:

> Before I begin this letter let me explain that, of course, I am myself a believer in prohibition. I think that water, especially clear, cold water—I don't care for muddy water—is a beautiful drink. I had a glass of it the other day, and it seemed wonderfully limpid and transparent—almost like gin.

How people had carried on in the old days simply beggared the imagination. He dreaded the very thought of the life he had led:

> I remembered that very often in the middle of the morning we used deliberately to go out from our business and drink a glass of lager beer. Beer, sir, as you yourself are aware, contains neither proteins nor albumen. It has less nitrogen in it than common starch, and is not nearly so rich in effervescent hydrogen as ordinary baking soda: in short, its food value is not to be compared with tan bark or with common mucilage. Nowadays, if I find that I flag at all in the morning work, I take a little nip of baking

soda and a couple of licks of mucilage and in a moment I am willing and anxious to work again.

As for whisky "and the stronger spirits," naturally nothing could be said in their favor. He had, therefore, only one suggestion to place before the cock-a-hoop prohibitionists: "The sale of whisky should be rigidly restricted to those who need it at the time when they need it, and in the quantity they happen to need." He did not suppose for a minute that the Supreme Court of the United States would have any difficulty in interpreting such wording.

Whenever Leacock went to the U.S.A., the first thing he packed was a large flask. He never was without it on his various speaking engagements below the border. In the winter of 1920 that is where he was—at Wesleyan University, Middletown, Connecticut. This particular visit was going to mean more to him than his otherwise routine speechmaking chores. He found out that Middletown was situated near Hartford, with its Mark Twain house on Farmington Avenue. He would contrive to get there somehow. But his host, Dean Frank W. Nicolson, had anticipated Leacock. Nicolson, a Canadian and a well-known after-dinner speaker himself, arranged to drive him to Hartford. There Leacock was shown over the home in which *Huckleberry Finn* and other Twain masterpieces had been written.

At about the same time, in another part of the United States, a twelve-year-old boy had been asked by his family what he wanted for Christmas. Young Colin G. Jameson lived on his father's ranch at Wolf, Wyoming. A keen reader and a lad who believed in aiming high, he told his parents that he would like a complete set of Stephen Leacock's books, though he held out little hope of ever realizing his wish.

Jameson, Senior, conveyed the request to the humorist's publishers in New York. They, in turn, communicated with Leacock, who proceeded to have the books shipped to Wyoming. With them went a sheet of Leacock signatures so that the boy could cut them out and paste one in each book.

In a covering letter to the family, Leacock wrote:

Your son's taste should be encouraged by both myself and my publisher. Consequently I am directing the latter to send him anything I may write in future.

Forty-nine years later Colin G. Jameson remembers that the professor stuck to his promise but that the publisher did not:

> Later I received a copy of *The Unsolved Riddle of Social Justice* (which I have never read). But the thought of that autographed set of wonderful nonsense still makes me mentally "ride off in all directions" (although not at this ranch, of course).

This sort of thoughtfulness, which took many forms, endeared Leacock to friends, students and associates. Young men graduating from his department were helped to get jobs. Leacock often paid the cost of publishing his students' papers or theses. He kept the Political Economy Club going by underwriting all its expenses, including that of the annual photograph.

As though he hadn't enough on his plate, Leacock accepted another appointment—that of lecturer in the social science department, which had recently been created. At the same time he added still another academic undertaking. In cahoots with René du Roure the professor inaugurated a course, in French, dealing with the history of the government of France, with French social development and so on. This academic load was intensified when the university made him a member of the Faculty of Graduate Studies and Research.

There were those in and out of McGill (including Mrs. Leacock) who wondered if the whole Leacock performance—administrator, lecturer, public speaker, writer, man about town, father confessor—might not eventually prove deleterious both to the quality of his work and to his health.

The words of critic Henry Seidel Canby describing writer Christopher Morley could just as accurately have been applied to Leacock:

> A rusher in and out, bubbling with ideas like a soda fountain, a wit, a wagster, an Elizabethan philosopher, with one of the few minds I know perpetually enjoying its own versatility.

Even the humorist's loyal and admiring English publisher, John Lane, considered the moment appropriate to administer a salutary warning. From New York he wrote:

> Your recent books have not been so well received in England, as your four or five earlier ones, either by the critics or the public.

Lane went on to imply that perhaps his author had been biting off more than he could chew, adding "and there's a very general feeling, even in Canada, that you are now writing snippets for high prices."

If Leacock replied to this paternal stricture or took cognizance of it at all, no record of his reaction remains today. It is said, however, that when a few years later Leacock's mother warned him that he was writing too much and too fast he left the house in a rage.

Now instead of reducing his activities, he extended them. A fresh endeavour began quite innocently at a small dinner party Leacock arranged at the University Club. His guests were the ubiquitous B. K. Sandwell, John Murray Gibbon, head of public relations for the Canadian Pacific Railway, and Professor Pelham Edgar, educator, author and fellow teacher with Leacock at Upper Canada College.

Inevitably the conversation revolved about the Canadian Copyright Act, which had just undergone several vital amendments in the House of Commons.

The real cause for alarm among this quartet—all writers—was the provision that deprived an author or his voluntary licensee of the sole right to reproduce a work of art, and contravened the principles of the Revised Berne Convention. A book publishers' lobby had been at work. Neither Leacock nor his fellow authors liked the situation. With the aid of postprandial libations a decision to protest against the offending clause was reached. It was agreed that an expertly organized and publicized dinner, to be attended by as many Canadian writers as possible, ought to gain support for the campaign.

At the gathering itself some months afterwards, such was the unanimity of feeling that the moving spirits behind the widely reported affair found themselves with a brand-new, properly constituted organization on their hands. Born that night, it bore the name The Canadian Authors' Association. A committee of this association went to work on copyright matters and two years later an amendment to the offending clause in the 1921 act was passed to the satisfaction of all authors.

Somehow Leacock made time in his crowded schedule to attend four convocations at which he became the recipient of honorary degrees—an LL.D. from Queen's, a Ph.D. from the University of Toronto, a Litt.D. from Dartmouth and another from Brown.

Sir Arthur Currie warmly congratulated the humorist on his return from the Brown convocation. But Leacock was bent on business at the time. He wished to report the case of a student's indiscipline and sought the principal's permission to deal with it in his capacity as head of a department.

Currie had a soldier's impatience with a lack of order. In a typical fit of righteous indignation the former general roared: "The damned young scoundrel. I'll deal with him myself." And with that he began to issue instructions by telephone. Just as he was informing Leacock what course he proposed to take, in walked one of Currie's army officers, whom he had not seen since France. With what Leacock described as "that wonderful recognition and affection Sir Arthur kept for his officers," the principal rose to meet the man.

"Come right out to lunch with me. My morning's all over—but wait a few minutes in the outer office, I've got to deal with a damned young scoundrel they're sending over to me."

The officer grinned. "I'm the damned young scoundrel. They sent me over."

With that embarrassing incident laughed off, Leacock still had some business to transact with the vice-chancellor. He set the stage by apologetically recalling that hardly had he joined the staff seventeen years earlier than he had asked for and received a special leave of absence in order to deliver a series of lectures on imperial defence in Ottawa. He then told Sir Arthur that a mere three years after that event, he again had been granted a leave of absence of several months duration when he embarked on a globe-girdling lecture tour for the Cecil Rhodes Trust.

"Well," interjected Currie before his professor could proceed further, "where do you wish to go now and for how long?"

The rhythm of his painstakingly prepared approach had been broken by the military man's plain speaking, and Leacock hesitated for a moment. Finally he blurted out that an opportunity had arisen for him to make a series of speeches in the United Kingdom. The professor put before the principal correspondence with a firm of agents and promoters in London. The space of time involved would be about three months.

"When?"

"In the late fall."

It was now the spring of 1921. Sir Arthur promised a reply before the summer vacation set in. By that time the board of governors had acceded to Currie's plea on behalf of his professor and friend.

X

Banishing Gloom

With his wife and young son, Stephen Leacock took first-class passage (all expenses having been underwritten) from New York in mid-September 1921. Either the voyage proceeded without incident of any kind, or else he could not be bothered recording anything about it. As he put it, "During the last fifty years so many travellers have made the voyage across the Atlantic that it is now impossible to obtain any impressions from the ocean of the slightest commercial value." He went on, however: "One of the steerage passengers, we were told, was actually washed overboard: I think it was over board that he was washed, but it may have been on board ship itself."

The arrival at Liverpool provided an opportunity to indulge in faintly invidious comparisons of the respective ways of British and American customs officials, with the latter coming off second best. Leacock dilated on the behavior at ports of entry of English as opposed to U.S. bureaucrats.

> Without wishing in any way to disturb international relations, one cannot help noting the rough and inquisitorial methods of the English Customs men as compared with the gentle and affectionate ways of the American officials at New York.

Sarcasm rather than satire, the reversed element of truth in this observation (as it applied at the time) underlined the fact that Leacock, like Mark Twain, was a not-so-innocent abroad. In similar vein he dealt with the immigration inspector at Liverpool who ostensibly did not appear to care if Leacock might be a Trotskyite or guilty of moral turpitude:

> I was determined to rouse him from his lethargy. "Let me tell you," I said, "that I am an anarchistic polygamist, that I am opposed to all forms of government, that I object to any kind of revealed religion, that I regard the State and property and marriage as the mere tyranny of the bourgeoisie, and that I want to see class hatred carried to the point where it forces everyone into brotherly love. Now, do I get in?"
>
> The official looked puzzled for a minute. "You are not Irish, are you, sir?" he said.
>
> "No."
>
> "Then I think you can come in all right," he answered.

When he "came in," the Canadian received a public welcome for which he had been quite unprepared. His publisher and his lecture bureau had seen to that. Fleet Street had been alerted and it considered the visitor to be of sufficient importance to warrant special interviews. Flattering editorials greeted him. One national newspaper described Leacock as the enemy of misery, a condition not unfamiliar to the great portion of the British populace at that stage of postwar readjustment.

Earlier the stage had been set by a special welcome in *Punch*. Charles L. Graves, a member of the magazine's staff and cousin of the poet Robert Graves, composed some engaging verses under the heading "To Stephen Leacock":

> The life that is flagrantly double,
>   Conflicting in conduct and aim,
> Is seldom tainted by trouble
>   And commonly closes in shame;
> But no such anxieties pester
>   Your dual existence, which links
> The functions of don and of jester—
>   High thought and high jinks.
>
> Your earliest venture perhaps is
>   Unique in the rapture intense
> Displayed in these riotous Lapses
>   From all that could savour of sense,

Recalling the "goaks" and the gladness
  Of one whom we elders adored—
The methodical midsummer madness
  Of Artemus Ward.

With you, O enchanting Canadian,
  We laughed till you gave us a stitch
In our sides at the wondrous Arcadian
  Exploits of the indolent rich;
We loved your satirical sniping,
  And followed, far over "the pond",
The Lure of your whimsical piping,
  Behind the Beyond.

In place of the squalor that stretches
  Unchanged o'er the realist's page,
The Sunshine that glows in your Sketches
  Is potent our griefs to assuage;
And when, on your mettlesome charger,
  Full tilt against reason you go,
Your Lunacy's finer and larger
  Than any I know.

The faults of ephemeral fiction,
  Exotic, erotic and smart,
The vice of delirious diction,
  The latest excesses of Art—
You flay in felicitous fashion,
  With dexterous choice of your tools,
A scourge for unsavory passion,
  A hammer for fools.

And yet, though so freakish and dashing,
  You are not the slave of your fun,
For there's nobody better at lashing,
  The crimes and the cant of the Hun;
Anyhow, I'd be proud as a peacock
  To have it inscribed on my tomb:
He followed the footsteps of Leacock
  In banishing gloom.

[© – *Punch*. Reprinted by permission.]

Graves had taken in the full range, to date, of what *The Spectator* termed "Leacock's whole budget of absurdities." That the *Punch* gesture bespoke the feelings of the reading public in the United

Kingdom became obvious by the list of bookings for Leacock's lectures. In the course of the succeeding eleven weeks his commitments embraced fifty-two addresses throughout England and Scotland, from Brighton in the South to Aberdeen in the North.

Nor was it a matter of a single stock talk. His hosts were given a choice of four subjects—"Frenzied Fiction," "Literature at its Lightest," "Laughing with Leacock" (readings from his own works) and "The Drama as I See It." The latter attracted attention in the press for its sweep of theatrical history and its understanding of contemporary trends on the stage, both British and American. Once more there was evidence here of the author's love of drama, both as a playgoer and a potential playwright. Of his general platform technique *The Spectator* noted: "His jokes are often produced by the magnifying-glass method, which is the same as the method of exaggeration, which, again, is the same as the reductio ad absurdum."

For special occasions—several universities were included in the itinerary—Leacock had ready the draft of a speech entitled "The Economic Man." In one instance, at least, he started on this theme, but soon drifted away from it. A student then working towards his Ph.D. describes the scene at Glasgow University in November 1921:

> He addressed the students in the Men's Union. He got a packed audience and, almost uniquely, a number of professors attended. His subject was announced as "The Economic Man," but he made no reference to him at all, keeping everyone convulsed with his witticisms. In reply to the vote of thanks, he said: "I think you have here in Glasgow the finest university in the world, bar none.' Then, supposedly *sotto voce*: "I said the same thing at Edinburgh yesterday and I'll be saying the same thing at Durham tomorrow."

One of his London appearances coincided with the founding of the Canada Club, an institution which has since continued to hold annual functions at which distinguished men and women speak. In the course of his remarks at this inaugural dinner, Leacock departed from his text to comment on British complaints about the high rate of their personal income tax. He told his audience that the English were far better off than Canadians. The latter's income tax scale may not be so high, he said, but the sales tax and other hidden imposts resulted in a greater financial strain upon the individual than was the case in the United Kingdom.

Following press reports of the speech, letters to the editor poured into newspaper offices. Leacock was taken to task for meddling in Britain's domestic fiscal affairs.

While this storm in a teacup was raging in Fleet Street, Leacock took part in an informal get-together at the London School of Economics. At the end of the evening a group of six undergraduates came forward to thank Leacock for breaking into his heavy schedule in order to talk to them. Inevitably, the controversy in the newspapers was raised. The professor leaped at an opportunity to have some fun. Addressing the six students Leacock in all seriousness put forward a suggestion:

> Wouldn't you boys like to see your names in the papers? Quite legitimately, I mean. If, for instance, you agree with what I said at the Canada Club, why not—each one of you—write a letter to the editor—either *The Morning Post* or *The Daily Telegraph*—and state your considered opinion. From the trend of the letters which have appeared so far, I need some support.

Unhesitatingly the students followed the Leacock proposal and, in due course, their letters appeared in the editorial columns. When next the professor came to London he made a point of looking up the students to thank them and ended up by taking them all to dinner at the Savoy Grill.

One of those nineteen-year-olds—Frank Cyril James—almost twenty years later to the day would become principal and vice-chancellor of McGill University.

As the royal progress went from strength to strength, the humorist began to discover that he did not know the citizenry of his native land (nor they, him) as well as he supposed would be the case. Exposure to a wide variety of audiences in a compressed period of time caused him to formulate a national stereotype of men who chair meetings. He tried to laugh them off, yet some of them really riled him. Example: an evening at a philosophical meeting in the Midlands—

> The chairman rises. He doesn't call for silence. It is there, thick. "We have with us tonight," he says, "a man who is well-known to the Philosophical Society (*here he looks at his card*), Mr. Stephen Leacock." (*complete silence*) "He is professor of political economy at—" Here he turns to me and says, "Which college did you say?" I answer quite audibly in

the silence, "At McGill." "He is at McGill," says the chairman (*more silence*). "I don't suppose, however, ladies and gentlemen, that he's come here to talk about political economy." This is meant as a jest, but the audience takes it as a threat. "However, ladies and gentlemen, you haven't come here to listen to me." (*this evokes applause, the first of the evening*), "so, without more ado (*the man always has the impression that there's been a lot of "ado," but I never see any of it*), I'll now introduce Mr. Leacock." (*complete silence*).

Then there was the case of the clerical chairman in a small centre in the south of England. According to Leacock the local vicar's introduction went as follows:

"Not so long ago, ladies and gentlemen, we used to send out to Canada various classes of our community to help build up that country. We sent out our laborers, we sent out our scholars and professors. Indeed, we even sent out our criminals. And now (*with a wave of his hand towards me*), they are coming back."

Daringly risking censure from south of the border, Leacock held up Scottish audiences as the best of the lot. They possessed "the best taste and the best ability to recognize what is really good." In a word, they were rapturous over Leacock. He went further. He cited reasons. The Scots were truly educated people in the sense "of having acquired an interest in books and a respect for learning." The English were all right for that matter, though their primary purpose in attending lectures took the form of seeking solid information. By contrast, American audiences were principally interested in *seeing* the speaker, rather than listening to him.

Prior to his meeting in Aberdeen, the professor had been entertained by a stuffy local celebrity, who wanted the Canadian all to himself. Over dinner the host mentioned that he had just heard a very funny new story which his guest might wish to add to his repertoire.

A woman in a Scottish village had died and the funeral proceedings were under way. The coffin was borne to the small cemetery where one of the pallbearers stumbled on a jutting rock. The coffin fell to the ground, broke open and the corpse came alive. But she did not last long and the solemn ceremony took place one more. The coffin was carried along the same path. When the pallbearers reached the jutting rock which had caused consternation before, the twice-bereaved husband warned, "Now, steady, boys!"

Leacock laughed heartily. He asked permission to inject it into his discussion of "Frenzied Fiction" that evening. At an appropriate moment in the lecture, he told the story. There was a pall of silence in the hall. Only the humorist and his host in the audience laughed. Aghast at the reaction, Leacock was knocked off his stride and barely recovered for the balance of his address. He made a point to find out at the conclusion of the program what had happened. The chairman quickly explained. It wasn't a new joke. It had gone the rounds in Aberdeen for weeks and here was a famous jester relating it as though it were his new creation.

What Leacock said to his dinner host, if he spoke to him at all afterwards, may also be imagined. But the yarn was brought back to Montreal and served its once humiliated narrator well on many a private occasion.

Assured at the outset that wherever he went he would face sellout crowds, Leacock the businessman seldom overlooked any possibility for self-promotion. He kept peppering his publishers with reminders of where and when his next lecture would be given, and agitating for proper window displays of his books in the towns where he was billed to speak. He wrote, for instance, to the manager of a large bookshop in Birmingham, urging him to close his premises early and release his workers for the purpose of attending the meeting. Thus, he argued, the bookstore's staff would find themselves in a more advantageous position to push his wares.

Whenever it could be fitted into the busy round, hospitality from fellow members of the craft was extended to Leacock in abundance. Writers of the standing of Hugh Walpole, H. G. Wells, Arnold Bennett and John Galsworthy made a point of contacting the visitor. That shy, curious Scotsman of letters, Sir James Barrie condescended to see Leacock, who thought the circumstances surrounding the audience a bit odd. The popular actor Cyril Maude had made the arrangements and accompanied the Canadian to Barrie's residence in Westminster. On arrival they were ushered into a darkened sitting room, where the playwright received them reclining on a settee. A desultory conversation ensued until the name of O. Henry cropped up, whereupon Barrie came to life and Leacock was in his element. Barrie recalled a report in *The Times* on Leacock's arrival in London to the effect that the humorist had stated that his admiration for the work of O. Henry was "on this side idolatory." Much as he himself liked O. Henry, Barrie thought this a bit much. To which Leacock replied: "I don't care. I stand by every word I've written of that magician." The brief session came to an end amicably and to Leacock it meant a great deal.

It remained for the head men of *Punch* to be constantly attentive to the humorist. Sir Owen Seaman, the magazine's editor, had presided over Leacock's initial London meeting. E. V. Lucas, a wit of the first magnitude, readily took a liking to the professor. Among other things they held in common was a love of Scotch. Lucas offered to drive Leacock down to Hampshire so that he could, for the first time in forty-six years, revisit his birthplace and other childhood scenes. Had it not been for the convivial companionship ("I have drunk whisky with you in a car for 80 miles," Leacock wrote Lucas later), the professor, on reflection, thought the whole idea a mistake. As already noted, the reminder of the humble nature of his early years proved to be repugnant to Leacock. Like others before and after him, he considered, "It is better not to go back to the place you came from. Leave your memory as it is. No reality will ever equal it."

The inadvisability of having his family accompany him on the hectic trek across the British Isles was understood before they undertook the journey. Mrs. Leacock and Stephen Jr. stayed put for the most part in the South, looking up and staying with friends, and seeing the sights. However, all three went to Oxford together and lived at The Mitre, regaled by university officials and townsfolk.

Having addressed the Oxford Union—by his own reckoning, one of Leacock's most satisfying engagements—he was invited to breakfast next morning in one of the undergraduate rooms at New College. Here some former McGill students entertained him, and here he laid the foundation for one of his most often quoted essays, "Oxford As I See It." This would form a part of his next book, *My Discovery of England*, then in its formative stage.

Leacock had, of course, visited Oxford before and in any case was thoroughly familiar with its history. The breakfast discussion, however, afforded him a student's-eye view of the traditions and regulations of the famous seat of learning. The enthusiasm of his young hosts for everything about the ancient surroundings set the tone of the piece he was planning to write.

His views on higher education were already well known. He had often fulminated against the examinations system in America. He had foreseen and condemned what was even then taking place in the New World—mass production of degree holders. Woman's place in this scheme of things he had settled to his own satisfaction.

He was soon to say, and to repeat many times in print and on the platform:

> If I were founding a university—and I say it with all the seriousness of which I am capable—I would found first a smoking room; then when I had a little more money in hand I would found a dormitory; then, after that, or more probably with it, a decent reading room and a library. After that, if I still had money over I couldn't use, I would hire a professor and get some textbooks.

In the learning process, environment counted more than anything else with Leacock. Without this "the passive recipient of lectures" could only be a note-taking machine.

At the breakfast session he had been impressed by the students' praise of the institution of the tutor.

"We go over to his room," they told Leacock, "and he just lights a pipe and talks to us. We sit around with him and he simply smokes and goes over our exercises with us."

From this and other evidence Leacock concluded "that what an Oxford tutor does is to get a little group of students together and smoke at them. Men who have been systematically smoked at for four years turn into ripe scholars. If anybody doubts this, let him to go to Oxford and he can see the thing actually in operation. A well-smoked man speaks and writes English with a grace that can be acquired in no other way."

The professor on the other side of the Atlantic was, by comparison, a woeful creature. Anticipating by forty years the complaints of the activist students of the sixties, Leacock went on:

> The American professor has no time to be interested in a clever student. He has time to be interested in his "deportment," his letter-writing, his executive work, and his organizing ability and his hope of promotion to a soap factory. But with that his mind is exhausted. The student of genius merely means to him a student who gives no trouble, who passes all his "tests," and is present at all his "recitations." Such a student also, if he can be trained to be a hustler and an advertiser, will undoubtedly "make good." But beyond that the professor does not think of him. The ever-

lasting principle of equality has inserted itself in a place where it has no right to be, and where inequality is the breath of life.

Was this the Victorian dreaming of days beyond recall; or did he really believe that the march of what he called the mechanical side of education could even then be reversed? There was no doubt in the minds of the young men and women who sat under him in the twenties that their mentor had convinced himself that it was not too late. With the handwriting already on the academic wall, he strove to develop the attitude of the tutor if not the actual conditions. He succeeded in imparting an air of intimacy in his classes despite the fact that the surroundings resembled impersonal schoolrooms.

Nor did he stop at this. Using undergraduate publications as sounding boards, Leacock pressed for such amenities as dormitories at McGill and any other university which might listen to him. Dormitories would ensure what the student needed most—continued and intimate contact with his fellows:

> Students must live together and eat together, talk and smoke together. Experience shows that that is how their minds really go. And they must live together in a rational and comfortable way. . . . If a student is to get from his college what it ought to give him, a college dormitory, with the life in common that it brings, is his absolute right. A university that fails to give it to him is cheating him.

Towards the end of Leacock's life, in the latter thirties, McGill did finally get a dormitory, though it accommodated less than two hundred students. In the postwar years two more men's residences were built, with a total capacity of some five hundred and fifty boarders. Had Leacock's advice been taken there would have been a dozen such buildings.

The Oxford experience was clearly the highlight of his tour, especially the opportunities it brought him to come face-to-face with students. Unlike Mark Twain, he was not offered an honorary degree. In his heart of hearts he had hoped that this might happen, crowning a tour which would shine in his memory. From every other point of view it had been a success, with financial results which brought his 1921 total earnings to twenty thousand dollars. Much as he loved money, however, the three months in the United Kingdom had, more importantly, bolstered his spirit and reinforced his self-confidence.

The Leacocks traipsed over to Paris for a few days before finally embarking at Le Havre for home in mid-January 1922. The ten days at sea were not wasted. The literary explorer was now ready to record *My Discovery of England.*

XI 🎋

Literary Lucre

Within two months of his return to Montreal from his British triumph, Stephen Leacock finished the manuscript of *My Discovery of England*. By early March it was in the hands of his publishers, whose letter of acknowledgement may well have cooled the professor's ardor. A Dodd, Mead editor wrote: "I must confess to a feeling of disappointment that it is not actually fiction, but, at any rate, it is most amusing. . . . You may be sure we shall do all we can to make it a success here."

The author had not done all he could to make it a success. Leacock's compulsion to be in print as soon as possible after an idea had come to him began to govern again. There had been good time to ponder the composition of "Oxford as I See It"; the balance of *My Discovery of England* had not enjoyed equal premeditation. Yet it contained some of his most thoughtful work.

Leacock was cheered by a letter from President A. Lawrence Lowell of Harvard, who told him: "I enjoyed your remarks about Oxford in your *My Discovery of England*. We are trying here the plan of a general examination, and tutors who 'smoke at their pupils,' and I really think it is working well."

However, the professor was short-tempered with critics who considered that the book was a pale imitation of Mark Twain's

Innocents Abroad. He had been irked by similar remarks which had been made about the chapters on Paris in *Behind the Beyond* six years earlier. By his own admission Leacock was not above borrowing once in a while from other authors, dead or alive. It is one of the tricks of the trade. But his reply to university colleagues who twitted him was to the effect that neither Mark Twain nor anyone else held a monopoly on themes, at some of which Leacock was ready to admit he was better.

The point to be borne in mind, of course, is that *My Discovery of England* was conceived and written as a book, with a homogeneous field of enquiry. Such an extensive, unified structure was far from being Leacock's strong point. In essence, he was an essayist, practised in the art of light, terse comment. The demands of a long narrative were beyond him. He knew it and acknowledged it.

Superficialities (e.g., the chapter on the British and American press—long since inapplicable, anyway) and the sapient passages concerning Oxford apart, the book included some of the parodist's most effective shafts, notably those which he directed at English politics, at the rubberneck tourist in London, and at the already cited unsatisfactory chairmen of public meetings. But he was too intent on the alluring American market; the U.S.-oriented references often tended to blunt the humorist's barbs.

With prohibition once again annoying him at home, Leacock harked back to the Scottish portion of his tour. Because he loved the people and their principal product, Leacock expanded delightedly on what he considered to be the Scotsman's pragmatic and sensible outlook:

> . . . there is no fear that prohibition will be adopted there: and this for the simple reason that the Scotch do not drink. . . . Because they manufacture the best whisky in the world, the Scotch, in popular fancy, are often thought to be addicted to the drinking of it. This is purely a delusion. During the whole of two or three pleasant weeks spent lecturing in Scotland, I never on any occasion saw whisky made use of *as a beverage.* I have seen people take it, of course, as a medicine, or as a precaution, or as a wise offset against a rather treacherous climate; but as a beverage, never.

In his own England, seat of government and heart of Empire, political morality raised a kind of ironic cheer from Leacock. The main differences between the systems of the New World and the

Old Country seemed to be that "our politicians will do anything for money and the English politicians won't; they just take the money and won't do a thing for it."

As for the Mother of Parliaments, its leisurely charm, breadth of interests, tolerance and patience, all impressed the visitor. The debates, for example:

> . . . When the English introduce a really large question as the basis for their politics, they like to select one that is insoluble. This guarantees that it will last. Take, for instance, the rights of the Crown as against the people. That lasted for one hundred years—all the seventeenth century. In Oklahoma or in Alberta they would have called a convention on the question, settled it in two weeks and spoiled it for further use. In the same way the Protestant Reformation was used for a hundred years and the Reform Bill for a generation.

During the closing weeks of Leacock's travels in the United Kingdom, the Canadian political pot had come to the boil. In December 1921, Arthur Meighen went out as Prime Minister and an untried figure, William Lyon Mackenzie King, came in. King had recently been elected to head the previously split Liberal party. While members from the province of Quebec held half of the government's seats in the House of Commons, a newly organized group calling themselves the Progressives won a sizable representation, so that King's position could only be said to be weak.

As a political scientist, Leacock kept his eye on the new party, which had drawn its strength from Ontario and the West. Earlier he had sensed the restiveness in the western part of the country and predicted in college circles that if a reform movement were to show its head, it would begin west of the Great Lakes. The conservative Conservative professor could not help but be suspicious about what shape any proposed reforms might take.

He had his reservations, too, about the new government. Questioned in the classroom at this time, Leacock ventured to think that Mackenzie King and the Liberals were up to no good so far as the professor's beloved imperial ties were concerned. He used to say that he could not dislike a man because he was a Liberal. That would be too much trouble; there were too many of them. Conscious of the fact that World War I had loosened rather than tightened Empire bonds, especially in Canada's case, he felt that if a break were to come, Mackenzie King would be the one to engineer it.

A younger departmental colleague described Leacock's stand succinctly: "He, before Winston Churchill, saved the British Empire every Monday, Wednesday and Friday, at 3 o'clock in room 20."

While Leacock as a lecturer now took on an even more assured air, he remained the orthodox economist, with only a superficial knowledge of neoclassical economics. He did manage to find time to become familiar with Alfred Marshall's *Principles of Economics* and the latter's Cambridge school of economic theories. If he were loath to admit that he might be a wee bit behind the times, one of his associate professors was not at all backward about asserting it.

Drs. Leacock and Hemmeon shared a course on banking, the former taking the first term, the latter concluding the course. It may have happened more than once, but certainly there was one occasion when Hemmeon, opening the second half of the course, and clipping his words through thin lips, said: "First of all, gentlemen, you will forget everything Dr. Leacock told you in the earlier part of this course."

Technically, Hemmeon may have been right. The more advanced arguments about, say, the quantity theory of money may possibly have eluded Leacock. Yet the man's great humanist qualities suffused the classroom. His lecture notes may have been dusty in more ways than one, but the expansive mind surveying the contemporary scene soared. His historical sense did the rest. His whole approach was historical—richly so.

At one point Leacock announced to his students that he would give a series of six lectures on the problems affecting the deepening of the St. Lawrence waterway. After the fourth lecture, an enquirer asked a member of the class, "How far have you got in deepening the St. Lawrence?" The student replied: "The first white man arrived yesterday."

The enquirer referred to above had his own following at McGill, including Professor Leacock. The Arts building, naturally, had a janitor, and the janitor had a peculiarly apt name—William Gentleman. Leacock's liking for him, plus the affection of generations of undergraduates for him proved the measure of this man. An athlete in the days of his youth, an old soldier, Bill Gentleman dispensed counsel, when sought, as a veritable father confessor. Unquestioningly, the professoriate heeded Bill's advice on matters ranging from the preservation of the premises to the welfare of its occupants.

Once when the humorist hailed the janitor with "Good morning, Gentleman," everyone within earshot replied, "Good morning, sir." Ever after, the professor changed the daily greeting to "Good morning, Mister Gentleman."

My Discovery of England had pleasantly surprised the publisher, though the author took its success for granted. By 1923 the book had gone into three printings in the United States, two in Canada, three in England, and a contract had been signed for its translation into Japanese.

While he was writing it he had been in correspondence with his agent on another idea: "If the *Saturday Evening Post* wants a series of burlesque plays (not in dramatic form but on the model of *Behind the Beyond*) I'll do them as soon as I'm clear of *My Discovery of England*."

Nothing came of this so far as the magazine was concerned. Nevertheless, Leacock wrote the burlesques and a syndicate had some success with them. Automatically they went into book form. In April 1923, *Over the Footlights* flooded the bookstores and caught on, its comic pseudo-playlet-style farces and paradoxes supported by some pieces in the essay form.

Ridiculous and helter-skelter as his modest ventures into the theatrical medium were, he returned periodically to that medium. His love for any brand of stage make-believe knew no bounds. If there happened to be a road show in town, he and a party of friends were in attendance; if not, vaudeville would do. The students' revue productions were a source of delight. Strains of Thespis were in his blood.

What he did with his extensive knowledge of the theatre was, of course, quite another thing. *Over the Footlights* swept the drama of the day into swirling gales of guffaws for those susceptible to free-swinging parody.

Cast Up by the Sea (which was eventually to be professionally dramatized) in five very short acts ripped into the kind of melodrama beloved of the actor-manager's school. The preserve of the movie "western" was invaded in *Dead Man's Gold*, but with not too much success. Leacock's liking for revue sketches found him in technically good form with *The Raft,* in which desperate survivors talked desperately. Greek tragedy, Ibsen, Russian drama were also all fair game.

The Soul Call, for all its nonsense, really represented another crusade. The prevalence of cheap sex in literature, on or off the stage, brought out Leacock's old-fashioned views on the subject. What he called a "Piffle Play" (the sub-title ran "in which a man and a woman, both trying to find themselves, find one another") took dead aim at the class of drama which

> . . . always deals in one way or another with the Problem of Marriage. Let it be noted that marriage, which used to be a sacrament, became presently a contract, and is now a problem. In art and literature it used to constitute a happy ending. Now it is just the bad beginning.

That the would-be playwright was seriously contemplating an excursion into the commercial theatre could be assumed from a warning to his publishers. Once more he stipulated keeping the dramatic rights, airily adding that "there are various other things which can be turned into acting with the stroke of a pen."

If the role of a novelist failed to interest him—as we have seen, we have his own word that he thought himself incapable of filling such a role—he came very close to an association with the stage. Indeed he once mentioned to a friend that if P. G. Wodehouse could do the libretto and lyrics of a musical comedy, he (Leacock) couldn't see why he shouldn't follow suit.

Was there not a "P.G." or Noel Coward touch in this bit of doggerel about the founding of "The Straits Settlements":

> Tell me now, will you please relate
> Why do they call these Settlements straight?
> Does it mean to say
> That the gay
> Malay
> Is too moral to quarrel in any way?
> Does he never fight
> On a Saturday night,
> When he's drunk in his junk
> And his heart is light?
> Have they got no music, no whiskey, no ladies?
> Well, it may be straight, but its gloomy as Hades.

Almost as an afterthought, Leacock tucked into the back of
Over the Footlights a threnodic study of "The Faded Actor." It
had appeared the year before in a Toronto magazine edited by a
friend of his. "A brief discourse on the art and the true artistic
temperament," the essay sang of the sadness of the mummer who
might have been. Here was the artist supreme,

> ... pure of the taint that is smeared across the arts by the money rewards
> of a commercial age. He lived too soon to hear of the millions a year
> that crown success and kill out genius; that substitute publicity for fame;
> that tempt a man to do the work that pays and neglects the promptings of
> his soul.

It is not stretching a point to conclude that here was not so much
the faded actor as a self-portrait of the reflective jester.

In the summer of 1923 the rural tranquility of Orillia was disturbed by the excitement caused by the visit of a special lacrosse
team. It comprised undergraduates of Oxford and Cambridge—
Englishmen, Canadians, Americans, Australians, South Africans,
New Zealanders—who had embarked on a tour of North America.
Among the Canadian players were a future chancellor of the university of British Columbia, Sherwood Lett, and a young man destined to become a Nobel prize-winner and Prime Minister of Canada,
Lester B. Pearson.

It is not clear how such an aggregation came to be booked for a
game in this particular part of Ontario. But it was important
enough to attract the then Prime Minister, W. L. Mackenzie King,
who threw out the first ball. Another notable witness of the contest,
of course, was Stephen Leacock. It was insufficient, however, for
him to remain a mere onlooker. Ahead of time he had cooked up
a plan which took the form of a ceremonial ball on his Old Brewery
Bay estate the evening of the game. The party so impressed the
athletic scholars that they invited themselves back a day or so later
for tea. They got tea. Leacock said he had a sore toe, and drank
whisky.

Throughout that summer he fussed over another book, as though
My Discovery of England and *Over the Footlights* were not suffi-
cient for one year. The new one did not require very much work.
He had persuaded his publishers—against their will, one guesses—

that a collection of some of his earlier odds and ends would go down well with his addicted audience. He called the result *College Days,* a volume which the most dedicated Leacockian could not with any honesty regard as anything but a mistake.

In the preface Leacock wrote that *College Days* was being presented "without apology," that it included pieces which he had written gratis for the University of Toronto's *Varsity,* McGill's *Outlook,* Harvard's *Advocate,* Princeton's *Tiger* and other "idealistic" journals.

A good deal of his amateurish and topical verse crept into these pages, one of the more agreeable of which was called "Idleness":

> Let me lie among the daisies, with my stomach to the sky,
> Making poses in the roses, in the middle of July,
> Let me nestle in the nettles, let me there absorb the dew
> On a pair of flannel breeches with the stitches worked in blue.

Another, a fifteen-stanza effort, "The Dean's Dinner" had caused a ruction on the campus fourteen years before. Leacock read it at a function given by the beloved Dean Moyse to the professors of the Faculty of Arts and Sciences. It named names and there were a few references that could not be construed as altogether kindly. To make matters worse, and unaccountably, Leacock calmly took the manuscript down to *The Herald,* which published the poem.

It took some time for the tumult to die.

A short essay in *College Days* reverted to his own teaching days. While there was breath in him no opportunity was lost to bewail that period in his career. In "Memories and Miseries as a Schoolmaster" he raked over the boredom and drudgery which he claimed to have suffered, consoling himself that he had tried never to be harsh or brutal to the schoolboys.

Perhaps he hadn't been. However, he could hardly be described as the soul of diplomacy with their parents. While in London he told the editor of *The Times* how he had dealt with one parent:

> Fathers and mothers—you know how tiresome they can make themselves by interfering with the schoolmaster.
>
> I remember a man who used to check his son's lessons. Once, opening the boy's exercise book, I came on a note, "How is it, after being with you three months, Robert knows no Latin?"
>
> Under this note I wrote another: "Probably his ignorance is hereditary."

College Days did contain one pensive little essay, "The Oldest Living Graduate" (it had first appeared in *Old McGill*, 1922, and has since been employed frequently and usefully in the cause of fund raising by a number of universities).

Now that his third book within seven months was failing to create literary history the professor proceeded to do what he had intended to do at the time of his son's birth—make a will. (A member of Leacock's law firm remembers how, in later years, the professor made a fetish out of adding or subtracting codicils. His legal advisers always knew what to expect when the humorist turned up in their offices.) He had evaded a second duty, too. He had a book to read, had had it for a number of weeks. It was about himself, but not by himself. It came from the pen of Peter McArthur, the mentor and friend who had published Leacock's earliest writings. It was called *Stephen Leacock.*

But this duty could wait one more week. He had a date, or hoped he would have, with some theatrical people—vaudevillians then playing a week's stand at Loew's Theatre. Headlining the bill were Jack Norworth and Nora Bayes. Leacock had never met them, but he knew all about them. In private life they were Mr. and Mrs. Latter; Nora was a musical comedy star of considerable magnitude, Jack a composer and actor. The Ziegfeld Follies and several Broadway revues had featured Miss Bayes. The pair collaborated on the popular song "Shine on Harvest Moon," and Norworth wrote the lyrics for "Take Me Out to the Ball Game."

Leacock, who had "caught" one of the earlier performances of the engagement, sent his card backstage hoping that Norworth would call him at the club. Norworth ignored this and two subsequent messages. As this diamond in the rough told a close friend later, "Hell, what did I have in common with a dignified, 'gates-ajar' collar professor of McGill University?"

Finally, a note arrived at the dressing room. It was couched in the terms of an imperial summons: "Professor Leacock will meet Mr. Jack Norworth at the University Club at twelve noon tomorrow."

This was Norworth's version of what followed:

This University club was the sorta place God would have a hard time gettin' in. But I wanted to find out what the old geezer had in mind. So

I went. The attendant at the desk told me the professor was waiting for me in the reading room, which I found—part of the tomb where there was a window or two—and there was the professor, loose collar, tie any old how, and all. He was a figure to appal a monarch, let alone a vaudeville bum like me.

Leacock greeted me with befitting dignity. I was pretty nervous and all I could think of was: "How are you, professor? How do you feel?"

The professor said, loud and clear: "I feel like s--t!"

Well, anyway, after that shock wore off a little, I stuck out my hand, with my chewin' tobacco in it. "How about a chaw?" I asked.

He said: "I'd love it!"

So we sat there chewin' and cussin' and talkin' about vaude and actors and musicals and what it was like to write songs—and havin' a perfectly dandy time!

Norworth returned to Loew's understandably flummoxed by his host. Why had Leacock wanted to arrange this meeting? Apparently not to see the pretty Nora, the more famous of the two, who hadn't been asked. Leacock showed a detailed knowledge of Norworth and Bayes being headliners and songwriters, that much was obvious. Maybe he just enjoyed a good tobacco-chewing companion, Norworth mused. The experience completely stumped him, but he never forgot it.

The plain truth was that, as has already been noted, the professor courted the stage and anybody on it. He never lost his boyish enthusiasm for it and for everything about it. And, much as he was inclined to taunt the medium, the same applied to the world of motion pictures.

Leacock had learned that the recently wed Mary Pickford and Douglas Fairbanks would be in Montreal in the course of a continent-wide tour designed to display the ideal marriage, Hollywood style. Quietly he extended an invitation to the stars to a private dinner at his home. But when a prominent film-struck businessman learned of the coup his crony was pulling off, he pleaded with Leacock for the privilege of meeting "America's Sweetheart" and her equally famous husband. Leacock warned his friend that the affair was to be a small and private one but that he could drop in briefly for a cocktail at 7 P.M. When Leacock, who had gone to the station to meet them, and the celebrated cinema couple arrived at the Cote des Neiges residence they were confronted on the steps with the recumbent figure of the tycoon, a bouquet of roses lying in disarray on his chest. The scent of the flowers fought a losing battle with the aroma of whisky.

The conversation over dinner may only be surmised. Not long after, however, Leacock revealed to his intimates that it had been suggested he ought to try his hand at a scenario, which the Pickford-Fairbanks team would be pleased to consider. Leacock said he would keep this in mind.

When they had departed, the humorist at last got down to reading McArthur's book, *Stephen Leacock*, which had been brought out as a volume in the Makers of Canadian Literature series.

These two men had, up to a point, trod a common trail. Both were raised on Ontario farms. Both gained teaching certificates at the Strathroy Collegiate Institute (McArthur obtaining his three years earlier). Both attended the University of Toronto (McArthur only for a year). They shared the gift of humor and the wish to write. And both wrote snippets for the same magazines—*Judge*, *Life*, etc.

But, by the time Leacock was eyeing a professorial career, McArthur had become editor-in-chief of *Truth* in New York, a forerunner in style and flavor of today's *New Yorker*. Thanks to McArthur, there appeared in the pages of this periodical several of the sketches that were, in *Literary Lapses*, to make of Leacock an international figure.

Because he knew his man intimately, McArthur got closer to the bone than any of the academic commentators have managed to do in their solely subjective judgments. He saw in the satire, for instance, how Leacock could be "sometimes aroused to indignant scorn," plying a "satiric lash that is none the less lacerating because it is light." McArthur thought that his friend lacked the cold ferocity of the master satirist; instead, "he rages at the impossibility of getting things right, then finds refuge in his marvellous gift of laughter. If he cannot help us, he can make us laugh and forget." Recognizing the overwhelming autobiographical nature of Leacock's work, McArthur made a most important point: "Possibly he finds forgetfulness himself in his outbursts of fun-making." This would hold true long after McArthur died in 1924.

The professor let everyone know that he liked *Stephen Leacock*. For the most part he had reasonable cause to react in this way. Yet the sensitive nature can hardly have overlooked McArthur's disparagement of his tendency to listen unreservedly to the "siren call of the publisher" and, more especially, to this:

> His great danger is that he may be misled by an insistent and profitable demand into the modern evil of speculation—an evil with which he has dealt in his literary essays—and will give too free a rein to his genius for fun.

Whatever the points he saw or missed in the McArthur assessment, however much John Lane's wrist-slapping may or may not have meant, despite the cautions of his New York publisher, Leacock uncloaked in a letter to his American agent the chief end in his personal catechism: "I admit I am very commercial and like money."

It follows that he liked the year 1923, in which his income of forty thousand dollars—derived from his latest books, recent reprints, royalties from early works, syndication, and from speechmaking—nearly trebled that of the Prime Minister of Canada.

XII

Tragedy

Considering the dollar's purchasing power in the middle 1920s, a forty-thousand-dollar income placed Stephen Leacock squarely in the ranks of the affluent. Being one of their class could he now, as he had consistently done, chide the rich? He would, for he considered that he had none of their bad habits. He had certainly striven to reach his present position, from which he could enjoy the comforts of life; but he could not be listed among the recklessly extravagant.

At the age of fifty-four it could be said that Leacock's position satisfied the conditions of the recipe for artistic creation which had been enunciated by Matthew Arnold:

> The three things that improve genius: proper exertion, frequent exertion and successful exertion. . . . The three things that support genius: prosperity, social acquaintance and applause.

"Proper exertion" might have been the only thing in some doubt. His "very commercial" inclination took command and remained in command throughout the 1924–25 span; so much so that he tended to overlook certain matters closer to home.

To be sure, he could not be indifferent to the disappointing progress of his son's health. The boy was not growing as fast as he should have been for his age. Nor could he be less than worried over his wife's flagging energy and general dispiritedness. An apparently minor accident on the golf course the previous summer, when Mrs. Leacock was struck on the breast by a hard tee shot, appeared to have no connection with her subsequent depression and loss of weight.

In his extramural work, Leacock refused to be discouraged when submissions to magazines were turned down. A commissioned contribution to *College Comics* resulted in a rejection slip. As a matter of course, he got paid for it; paid twice, actually, due to a bookkeeping error. He coolly accepted both cheques without demur!

For an American syndicate Leacock had been doing a "How I . . ." series of articles—How I Do This, That, etc. (Robert Benchley blithely poached the same idea later on). His readiness to stretch out his material for the sake of another dollar was in evidence again in a note to his agent: "If you think we can get away with one or two more, I'll see what I can do about it." But no more were wanted.

Remembering the Pickford-Fairbanks suggestion about film scripts, he set the wheels in motion regarding the possible sale of his books to the movies. He instituted negotiations with the Famous Players-Lasky Corporation. These overtures met with little interest in Hollywood.

Undismayed, Leacock addressed the business of getting out his annual collection. *The Garden of Folly* unhappily proved to be a prophetic title. It was one of his few books to suffer the ignominy of one edition only. Its preface contained some observations which the author himself might usefully have taken to heart.

In discussing his particular literary specialty, Leacock stated:

> Humor cannot exist alongside of eager ambition, brisk success and absorption in the game of life. Humor comes but to those who are down and out, or who may have at least discovered their limitations and their failures.

It was in the same preface, also, that an oft-quoted statement made its appearance:

> I have always found that the only kind of a statement worth making is an overstatement. A half truth, like half a brick, is always more forcible as an argument than a whole one. It carries further.

As professor and humorist alike, Leacock excelled at throwing half-bricks.

Aside from one or two of the "Letters to the New Rulers of the World," which were included in these pages, *The Garden of Folly* could offer only one funny piece truly representative of Leacock at his best. This dealt with the "prevailing degeneracy" of the smooth-shaven face, and he gave it a pseudo-historical treatment:

> The growth of the clean-shaven habit in this epoch is becoming a serious national menace. In twenty years the entire nation will be clean-shaven. The moment is now. It is time for the people to pause and realize what whiskers have meant to human civilization.
>
> We turn to the records of history; Adam—he had a dark brown beard, slightly pointed; Noah—he had a long white beard, that reached his waist. Imagine Noah clean-shaven and with his eyebrows darkened with black dye, and with little beady eyes looking down under a straw hat! You can't? Of course not. And yet that man saved our whole human race.

In fact, shaving appeared to present Leacock with insoluble problems; every morning his face bore a new crop of nicks and sticking plasters. Presumably he would have wallowed in the 1970s, with their proliferation of hirsute appendages.

Despite all his domestic cares and university responsibilities, Leacock undertook two extensive lecture tours in the United States, besides making one fully reported speech at home. In this address to the Export Club of Montreal, Leacock coupled an account of the uncertain political and economic situation in Canada with a repetition of his old cry for firmer Empire ties and for more British immigrants. He concluded with the dogmatic statement that "the silliest thing this country could do would be to cut itself loose from the help and co-operation of the British people." He suspected what was in the mind of Mackenzie King, who was even then scheming for independent nationhood, despite his shaky parliamentary position. Nor was this address a dying gasp for Leacock. He was to return again and again to his imperialist stand, which is what Leslie Frost meant when he described Leacock as having been "out of tune with reality."

The professor's latest foray below the border concentrated on the "Valley colleges"—in the Connecticut River Valley, which included quite a constellation of star institutions of learning. On this round he took as his theme "Heroines of Literature," a subject obviously designed chiefly for female consumption.

Mrs. Robert V. Boname, of Rye, New York, then an undergraduate at Smith College in Northampton, was among those present when Leacock arrived in the John M. Greene Hall, its 2,000-seat capacity filled to overflowing:

> I can't remember if he limited his heroines to American literature, but the passage that has stuck in my mind was his reference to the heroine of the romantic Old West whose chivalrous rescuer encloses her decorously in his tent, and then goes out and sleeps on the cactus.

Yet the warmth of the reception (plus the fee) from the hordes of women, young and old, would do nothing to reduce his reservations concerning their sex.

Following a decent spell at his college desk, off he went again, this time to the American South, armed with texts he had used during his English trip. To these he had added some new talks about Charles Dickens, Mark Twain and O. Henry. The term "text," however, is hardly accurate. His themes and main arguments were merely sketched out, partly in shorthand, on pieces of hotel notepaper, backs of old envelopes and postcards, and sheets torn from exercise books.

In Virginia, just before an engagement at the University of Richmond, Leacock revealed for the first time a quirk which in future would become a fixation regarding the press, and which will be examined at length in due course. On this occasion a young reporter, John Archer Carter, had been despatched by the editor of the Richmond *News-Leader* to the hotel where the visitor was staying. The assignment called for a substantial interview with the Canadian.

This is what happened, in Carter's words:

> When I rapped on the door of his suite, the door swung open and there stood a big man, with a large, longish face and a mass of greying hair parted on the side, and he did not look like any humorist I had even seen. Political scientist, economist, mortician or chief mourner, maybe, but not a humorist, surely. He was all solemnity when he thrust into my unready hands five sheets of Hotel Jefferson stationery, each sheet cluttered with ascending lines of virtually indecipherable writing.
>
> "How do you do," Dr. Leacock said from a sad mouth. "That's the

interview with me. I've already written it. Wrote it while waiting for you. Saves us time and bother. Both of us. You'll wish to read it? Oh, naturally! Come in, come in!"

Dutifully, the youthful reporter sat down and laboriously went through the scrawl before him:

Professor Stephen Leacock, of Montreal, head of the Department of Economics at McGill University, who is lecturing this week at the University of Richmond, had a brief chat this morning with a representative of this journal.

Dr. Leacock spoke in his characteristically humorous vein of his increasing difficulty in being interviewed by the press.

"I have grown to have so many friends," he said, "in so many places and of such different ways of thinking that I can't say anything at all without losing some of them. For example, I hold very strong views on the Volstead Act, but I daren't say what they are. I'd like to tell you how beautifully the Quebec system of government control works, but I mustn't. I have strong views on Evolution and Fundamentalism. In fact I truly believe that all adherents of one side are soft in the head, but I won't say which. I either think that Mussolini is the hope of the world or the death knell of democracy. People who fly across the Atlantic are either damn fools or heroes. In fact, all my opinions are too violent for friendly intercourse.

"But I am here on a mission which fortunately is not controversial at all. I am giving three lectures out at the university on the relation of the great humorists of the world to social progress. The lectures are to deal with Charles Dickens and Mark Twain, and O. Henry, with a hint here and there on the side that I am doing a little good myself. That's why I don't want to give an interview. Good-bye."

It was not good-bye for Carter. He had the tenacity of a good newspaperman. After buttering up the professor on his journalistic prowess, Carter wore him down until he was asked to stay. They talked like a couple of old buddies. Towards the end of the chat Carter explained that, in order to get off the hook with his editor, he would have to write something himself and could he use one or two of the stories Leacock had just spun? The humorist cheerfully agreed.

One of these yarns disclosed what some of Leacock's academic analysts have chosen to refer to ominously as the "dark" side of the man.

Carter reported the conversation:

"You know, because I was something of an authority on O. Henry, I was delegated you might say, to seek out any of his unpublished material that might be lying around after his death in 1910. So I advertised widely. There would be ample payment for any O. Henry material worthy of publication. After that, the deluge. And it struck my office exclusively. People from all over the land mailed me what they declared to be O. Henry stories. Within a few weeks manuscripts were cluttering up my desk, and they lay in piles all over my office. Very terrific stuff, believe me. I was disgusted to observe how many . . . " He paused, seeking a word.

"Phonies? Creeps? Fakes?" I suggested.

"Phonies," he said, "is the word. How many there were in the country. First disgust, then nausea, then anger. Madness, you might say. So one morning I pushed all the manuscripts off the desk and then picked up one. chosen at random. It was atrocious! And some lady had mailed it to me. I shouldn't have written to her as I did, when returning the manuscript. What I said was on the macabre side, and not in the best of taste. I was sorry afterward . . . but I was very angry.

"I wrote something like this:

" 'Thank you, madam, for sending me this story by the late O. Henry, which I am returning because it doesn't quite fill our needs. However, it is amazing and astounding and miraculous, and the reason for that is that obviously the story was written by O. Henry after his brain had been removed.'

"No, I shouldn't have written that, but I was angry."

The swing around the southern states had put another feather in the, by now, much-decorated Leacock cap. But it had also proved to be tiring. Added to this, on his return to Montreal he came face-to-face with the fact that Mrs. Leacock was not so well as she had been before he left on his speechmaking rounds. The two decided that a medical checkup should be arranged, but that it could wait until she had spent the summer at Old Brewery Bay, where rest and fresh air might effect an improvement. Meanwhile, Leacock began to entertain doubts about the competence of the pediatrician advising on the condition of Stephen, Jr. The father proposed to seek further counsel from friends on the staff of the Faculty of Medicine.

In the spring of 1925, as an alumnus of the University of Chicago he rallied to a call from that institution, which was conducting a campaign for funds totalling seventeen and a half million dollars. Leacock wrote to his old friend there, Dean Gordon J. Laing:

I have just learned that the University of Chicago is asking for seventeen and a half millions. I regret that I had not known of this sooner, but I hasten at once to enclose my cheque for seventeen and a half millions with my best wishes for the continued success of my Alma Mater.

In entering this subscription on your list I would like to ask you not to mention my name but just mark it as from "A Friend."

The only stipulation or caution I would like to make in regard to this donation is in reference to the cashing of the cheque. It ought to be cashed very carefully. The ideal thing would be to cash it during a total eclipse of the sun. But that, I believe, will not take place for 218 years. There is, however, a total eclipse of the moon next month and it might be possible to get away with it during that. But failing an eclipse, I would like to say that when I was a student at Chicago they used to cash my cheques at a little delicatessen store on Cottage Grove Avenue, and I am sure if this cheque were taken there they would cash it without hesitation.

After being cashed, this cheque should be laid in a warm place, not exposed to the damp, and covered up at night.

I have not yet learned just for what purpose this seventeen and a half million is required. Of course it will not go far. I have heard it said that it is to be used to buy a complete outfit for the basketball team and pay their return fares on the Illinois Central to Terre Haute. Others say that it is for plumbing.

But I should like it to be distinctly understood that in giving this money I leave the use of it entirely free. I know by experience how easily an up-to-date University can get away with seventeen and a half millions. If the President tells me a year hence that he dropped it on the street or lost it in a game of mah jongg I shall know that it has merely gone the way of many other millions and has been absorbed without a trace—*spurlos versenkt*—in the great cause of education.

*   *   *

I had only just written the above when I became aware that I have been laboring under a misunderstanding. On looking again at the Campaign Extra and the other documents before me I see that it is seventeen and a half million dollars that is wanted. I am so sorry. I had to get mixed up. I was thinking of marks. When I wrote my cheque I had German marks in my mind and hence my misunderstanding. As to seventeen and a half million dollars, I am sorry to say it is out of the question. I haven't got it. There is no use disguising the fact and I may as well say it straight out. I have not got seventeen and a half million dollars. Since I left the University of Chicago I have not got along very well, and if I were called upon tomorrow to raise seventeen and a half million dollars I couldn't do it without borrowing it from one of the other professors at McGill University, or asking the bursar to advance it to me against my next five hundred years' salary.

Under the circumstances all I can do is to ask you to keep my cheque. You cannot cash it except at an enormous discount or by sending it over to Checko-Slovakia. But it may at least stand as a token and symbol of gratitude to my Alma Mater as the evidence of an affection which neither time nor distance can diminish.

That cheque is nowhere to be found today.

During the vacation months of 1925 the nation buzzed with political activity, in which Leacock refused to participate but which never failed to fix his attention. Prime Minister Mackenzie King had been running the country with the uneasy backing of the Progressives, whose free trade ideas found no sympathy in Leacock. The government's popularity, if that term could be used at all, suffered further when a high federal sales tax was imposed.

Rumors of a general election solidified into a decision by Mackenzie King to go to the polls in October. Much to Tory Leacock's delight, the Conservatives doubled the number of seats they held in the previous parliament. They fell short of winning a majority, however. King continued in power, with the ever more grudging support of a couple of dozen Progressives.

Talk at the time that both major parties had been angling for Leacock's active support and possible candidature appeared to be just that—talk. Leacock had quite enough to do for the present. Yet he was never too busy to lend a hand in undergraduate affairs.

For the annual classbook of 1925 Stephen Leacock answered the call of the young editor-in-chief, T. F. M. Newton, for a contribution with an article which urged a project that was to have far-reaching results. He pleaded for a real literary journal at Mc-Gill—something over and above *The McGill Daily*, which "needed nothing but the news, murders and rum-running to put it in line with the metropolitan press." Given a cause, the professor's vigor knew no limits. In the columns of the student newspaper he continued his campaign: "It is plain to me that in this matter of a college journal we either lead the world or else we come at the tail of the procession. I think I know which we are doing."

Because of this kind of prestigious drumbeating, some of the editors of *The Daily* were moved to resign and, joined by other students who shared their feelings, set about finding funds for the creation of the kind of literary magazine Leacock had been espousing. The initial issue of *The Fortnightly Review* made its appearance in November with a lead article by the humorist on the nature of a college. With his manuscript he had enclosed "a more substantial testimony of one Canadian dollar" to boost the cause.

Beset by financial problems, the bold venture lasted less than two years. Its importance, however, lay in the fact that it served as an outlet for the creative energies of a whole clutch of future poets and writers of considerable magnitude. Led by A. J. M. Smith in the early stages, this gallery included poets Frank R. Scott and A. M. Klein, and Leon Edel, who would become the world authority on Henry James. That these young men who eventually were to prove a new force in Canadian literature found a place to try their wings at this time owed much to the stimulation of Stephen Leacock.

Even as he wrote and spoke with great persistence on such an apparently minor matter, an air of profound despondency pervaded Leacock's household. Trix had finally paid a visit to her doctor, who, in agreement with a visiting overseas specialist, diagnosed cancer of the breast. The thoughts of husband and wife inevitably went back to the golf course accident which had happened months earlier.

Desperately the professor sought advice and assistance from the abundance of medical knowledge in the university. An operation was performed; but it only confirmed first opinions that the disease had reached an advanced stage. Nothing, counselled the experts, could be done.

Leacock refused to accept the awful finality of this advice. He remembered the visiting specialist Dr. Blair Bell, of Liverpool, England. Leacock knew somebody in Liverpool, a Dr. J. George Adami, who had been professor of pathology at McGill up until 1919, when he was appointed vice-chancellor of Liverpool University.

Despite being gently warned that any further efforts must be fruitless, Leacock cabled Adami. Yes, cabled back Adami, Bell enjoyed a high reputation, had in fact evolved a lead treatment for cancer which had had some clinical success. Adami heartily supported Bell's experiments.

"Tell Bell, then," Leacock replied, "that I shall bring my wife over. We shall sail immediately."

Adami had already been told by Bell of the hopelessness of Mrs. Leacock's case.

Leacock then approached another friend, Sir Edward W. Beatty, president of the Canadian Pacific Railway, and also chancellor of

McGill, who acted with typical directness. In a CP ship scheduled to sail within two days, a miniature hospital was set up and staffed by two nurses. The tragic little group—Dr. and Mrs. Leacock, young Stephen and Mrs. R. B. Hamilton, Trix's mother—set sail on what the humorist could not believe would be a futile journey.

Dr. Adami's widow, now Mrs. Marie Monsarrat, of Bath, Somerset, remembers with clarity the arrival and the subsequent sad events:

> Blair Bell had made all the necessary preparations for receiving Mrs. Leacock in his nursing home. But on her arrival he realized that he could do no more at this point other than to alleviate her condition, which deteriorated rapidly. She died on Dec. 14th in her forty-sixth year. . . . She was a beautiful woman, and devoted to her husband and her little son, and Dr. Leacock was equally devoted to her. . . . When all was over, my own father (in Holy Orders, Church of England) took the funeral service at St. Luke's Church, after which the body was taken down to the ship. We saw them all away.

A vast outpouring of sympathy for the distraught humorist came in the wake of the news. Messages of condolence flowed into McGill by the hundreds and were duly relayed to Liverpool. The cable from Sir Arthur Currie read: "Courage, Stephen, we are all with you."

On the day following her husband's fifty-sixth birthday, Mrs. Leacock was buried in St. James Cemetery, Toronto. The original intention was that this would be a temporary resting place. Throughout the following years Leacock kept saying that his wife's body should be moved to the Leacock family plot at the church of St. George's at Sibbald's Point, not far from Old Brewery Bay. But no action was ever taken.

The twenty-five-year marriage had been marked by a deep mutual admiration and understanding. With Trix's stage background and Leacock's passion for things theatrical, the world of the actor represented a very real common bond. Her chief interests had centred upon music, golf, tennis, and some women's groups, activities essential since she had a husband who was largely immured in his literary pursuits, away on speaking tours, or absorbed in university affairs. She knew when to remain in the background, calm and rather serious, when to come to the study in Montreal to laugh at the latest funny pieces read aloud, when and how to be the good hostess. It was rumored that she often seemed overawed by the distinguished figures with whom her husband mingled. But her great virtue rested in a self-taught accommodation to a difficult and demanding disposition. By the laws of the Victorian lares and penates, Trix had her pedestal, but a man's always stood several inches higher.

In every instance where relatives and friends have been asked to epitomize Leacock's attitude towards his wife, the one word which invariably crops up is "adored."

In this connection there comes to mind a wistful passage in his posthumously published *Last Leaves*:

> The real adoring husband overtalks his wife, over-dominates her, pays with unexpected presents for easy forgiveness of his ill temper, and never knows that he adored her till it is too late, for she cannot hear it.

XIII

"Smiling at Grief"

Leacock's sorrow remained a private thing. He did not withhold himself from the daily round, as many another in his place might have excusably done. At the beginning of the 1926 term the public figure was as visible as ever. When classes began, he began, as though all that had happened had been forgotten. It hadn't, of course. As an intimate of the family has said, "When Trix died, a bit of Stephen died, too." Professor René du Roure rose to the occasion. Constantly at Leacock's side in the off hours, the Gallic sprite saw to it that the riotous billiards games at the club were renewed.

The pain of the preceding months aroused in the professor a determination to make a personal contribution to the fight against cancer. He started by donating one thousand dollars to the Medical Faculty toward initiating at McGill the new Liverpool lead treatment. Various drives for cancer research funds found in him a ready supporter. For the next ten years he hardly ever overlooked an opportunity to speak on the subject. Once, at a luncheon of the New York Cancer Committee, he attacked cancer quacks and seriously recommended the death penalty for any practitioner proved to be such. When the King George V Jubilee Cancer Fund made its appeal on a world-wide scale, he gave money and talks on the fund's behalf.

Closer to home Leacock devoted his wholehearted attention to his son's physical problems. After consultation with the dean and other friends in the Faculty of Medicine, Leacock dispensed with the services of the doctor in attendance on Stephen, Jr. In his place came the brilliant thirty-six-year-old specialist Dr. Alton Goldbloom, who later related the experience in his forthright autobiography, *Small Patients.* "So began a friendship with Stephen Leacock which lasted until his death. I was fortunately successful in the treatment of his child."

It was a protracted treatment, and Goldbloom's patience must have been strained to the limit when the boy's father occasionally looked for advice elsewhere. While the family were in Liverpool, Leacock had visited a noted pediatrician in that city. He also went to New York to consult "the leading exponent of endocrinology in Gotham." In this instance, however, he did approach Goldbloom, who in turn checked the Manhattan doctor's credentials with a specialist at Cornell University. Of the New York physician, Dr. O. Schloss of Cornell wrote: "I don't believe he ever does his patients any harm."

A constant stream of correspondence flowed between Goldbloom and the humorist. One note from Leacock poignantly ran: "I think he's growing. But I hate to measure him." Later—very much later —the professor jubilantly recorded: "You will be very pleased to learn that Stevie at last shows a definite and apparently rapid growth." A family acquaintance believes that for years the parent harbored a deep feeling of personal guilt about the son's condition.

Of his long pleasant association with Leacock, Alton Goldbloom remembered the "sheer brilliance intermingled with naïvete and medical credulity," though he paid tribute to Leacock's "insight with regard to pediatrics that I would gladly have wished on the antagonists and scoffers in the Faculty of Medicine." And the doctor recalled, too, this little incident:

> One morning when I called, a very old lady was with him: it was his mother. He introduced me in a typical Leacock way. He put his arm around me and led me to the old lady. "Mother," he said, "here's the most fortunate doctor in the world—his patients live."

The "very old lady" had then reached the age of eighty-one. Some years previously she had undergone surgery for a cancerous growth and had regained her full health, although she walked only with the aid of canes. She now lived in a comfortable little home at Sutton, near Orillia, which had been purchased by her children. It was named Bury Lodge after her old childhood home in England, and was full of the Imperial mementoes which must have had such an effect on the young Leacock—objects from India, Africa and other far-flung countries, acquired in them by far-flung relatives; while in every nook and cranny were piles of old numbers of *Punch* and *The Illustrated London News*. The Empire was still very much a reality at Bury Lodge and at the lake-side cottage four miles away which Mrs. Leacock rented in the summer for the benefit of her grandchildren.

After Trix's death a readjustment of Leacock's domestic organization had to be faced. The secretarial duties of Grace Reynolds, who joined him in 1924, were extended to embrace part of the management of the establishment. She undertook the oddly assorted assignments with a cheerfulness badly needed at this time. A governess was also added to the ménage for the purpose of looking after the boy's educational requirements.

Meanwhile Leacock's literary conscience plagued him. In 1925 he had failed to publish a book. He moved to rectify this omission by gathering together his magazine writings of that period. They were brought out under the title of *Winnowed Wisdom*.

If anybody had been inclined to think that the steam might have gone out of "Leaky Steamcock," they were due for a surprise. The pieces had all been written before the onset of Trix's tragic illness. They displayed the humorist's favorite hyperbolic form on a wide variety of topics. At one extreme he dealt pointedly with "How We Kept Mother's Birthday," an admonishing lecture on the thoughtlessness of males towards the distaff side of a household. The book also contained a burlesque, "The Laundry Problem." Here Leacock went to work with rolled-up sleeves on the people to whom the family wash is entrusted:

I have never witnessed at first hand the process of a modern incorporated laundry company using up-to-date machinery. But I can easily construct in my imagination a vision of what is done when a package of washing is received. The shirts are first sorted out and taken to an expert who rapidly sprinkles them with sulphuric acid. They then go to the coloring room where they are dipped in a solution of yellow stain. From this they pass to the machine-gun room where holes are shot in them and from there by an automatic carrier to the hydraulic tearing room where the sleeves are torn off. After that they are squeezed absolutely flat under enormous pressure which puts them into such a shape that the buttons can all be ripped up at a single scrape by an expert button-ripper.

The collective sense of humor of laundry managements probably had worn thin ages before this Leacock onslaught took place. However, while other irate customers could be mollified or recompensed fairly easily, Leacock's pitiless attack could not be ignored. Laundries, large and small, proclaimed their innocence loudly, chiefly in letters to the humorist. One establishment went so far as to threaten obliquely that court action might even be considered. Leacock dealt with them all by return mail and nothing worse happened. But he did tell one McGill group that the article had the effect of improving the handling of his own personal linen. The class naturally didn't believe him. His students could see no difference.

It is worth noting, however, that this was the only recorded instance of any kind of protest, organized or otherwise, against Leacock's irreverent treatment of institutions or individuals.

Also in *Winnowed Wisdom* the author included his "outlines" of Shakespeare, Evolution, and Recent Advances in Science, which had already served him well in speeches and in periodicals. He summarized the Darwinian theory and reviewed the accomplishments of Madame Curie on radium, Einstein on relativity, and his old colleague now Lord Rutherford on his great pioneer work at McGill on the atom.

Leacock dedicated the book to the Average Man, "a poor shrimp" if ever there were. If he intended to be amusing, he succeeded only in being abusive so far as Mr. Average was concerned. This Average Man, he found, was weak on religion, but strong on morals, having spent only one week of his life in the penitentiary. "Taking an average of theft and dividing it by the population, it appears he has stolen only two dollars and a quarter. And he never tells a lie except where there is some definite material advantage."

Unflinchingly he went on to size up the Average Woman. Predictably, he discovered even less admirable statistics. In point of intellect she "cannot reason and cannot think. But she can argue." Having regard for the fact that the Average Woman "cannot read, except love stories," he could see no purpose in dedicating the book to her.

It was in this preface that he stated a fundamental tenet of his philosophy. He would, he said, "like ever so much to start a movement of getting above the average."

Just as *Winnowed Wisdom* arrived in the bookshops in 1926 so did another, this one about Leacock and entitled *Oh, Mr. Leacock!* From the pen of an English scrivener, Charles K. Allen, the book purported to take Leacock's frivolities seriously and then to take him to task for his attitudes. Parodying a parodist is always likely to produce boredom. Allen's effort did not escape such a fate. But Leacock's New York publishers wanted to know what their prize Canadian thought about *Oh, Mr. Leacock!* The professor replied: "A fad of mine. I never take any clippings or as far as I can never read anything about myself." Quite untrue! Hadn't he absorbed every word that Peter McArthur wrote about him a mere three years before?

Still wearing the mask with its "perpetual half-smile," to quote Dr. Goldbloom, Leacock realized the best antidote for his recent sorrows was to keep himself busy. He set about composing several serious articles, the most important of which reiterated his views on "The Work of the University." Uncompromisingly he stood for selectivity in admitting students, for keeping enrolment within manageable limits, for eschewing courses which ought to be confined to specialized schools, and, above all, for education which went beyond routine teaching. He warned once more against expansion and "a wilderness of functions" in the modern university.

In his own college work he did not lack topical material with which to stimulate the increasing number of young minds in his charge. The country's political instability was all grist to a lecturer who liked to roam far and wide in his enquiries, and to the devil with strict curriculum. It was just this sweep of his humanist touch which excited the curiosity of his listeners. The warmth of his personality, the full, deep voice with a hint of laughter in it, the accent reflecting his English origins, the easy-going delivery, the method of relating present events to a larger historical context—these were the characteristics which helped set him apart from his fellows.

Leacock made the most of the matters of the moment. In June

1926, a Customs scandal broke upon the nation. Corruption had been unearthed in this government department, and it involved the French Canadian Minister of Customs and Excise. Events moved swiftly. Mackenzie King met defeat in the House of Commons and immediately sought the dissolution of parliament. The Governor-General, Lord Byng, a British World War I hero, refused to act on the Prime Minister's advice; instead, he asked the leader of the opposition to form a government.

An unholy howl went up from the Liberal ranks led by King, whose resignation Byng had demanded. Had not the representative of the Crown misread his viceregal authority? Yes, asserted King. No, retorted Meighen, the Conservative leader, with equal tenacity. But Meighen's brief regime collapsed under the pressure of this constitutional wrangle, and a general election ensued. Mackenzie King again occupied the seat of the mighty, this time with a comfortable working majority. Since the Progressives had been virtually put to rout, Canada now returned to a two-party system.

Once more Leacock held aloof from the hurly-burly of the political arena. Yet, the better to watch the action, he broke a long-standing rule and remained in the city that summer. This also gave him the opportunity to accede to an oft-expressed request from René du Roure. The diminutive Parisian aristocrat had been conducting a French summer school at McGill for several years. Its mounting reputation drew people from all walks of life and from distant parts of Canada and the United States. He knew his economist friend would be impressed once he saw it in operation. Leacock, whose fluent French required neither summer nor winter schooling, showed a great deal of interest in du Roure's accomplishment. Dr. Alan Leslie, of Los Angeles, looks back to those days, describing how the humorist dropped in for informal chats and "occasional post-prandial libations" in the office of the school's director, or chatted with out-of-town students in an informal, friendly, witty way. "It was plain to all," writes Leslie, "that Leacock's friendship with du Roure was a substantial one."

Those of us who were members of Leacock's classes at this time hold memories of the way in which national issues enlivened the political science discussions when the fall session opened. Leacock may have been shaky on economics, but he could match the best when considering the science of government. ("Had he concentrated on political science," a former associate, Dr. Eugene Forsey, has said, "he could have produced a work of lasting value.") He was particularly eloquent defending the action of Lord Byng. British and Tory to the core, he had no choice.

There was less to celebrate, he felt, in the events which were taking place over in London. There Mackenzie King attended an imperial conference at which a formula for a new United Kingdom —Dominions relationship was hammered out, with significant contributions from the Canadian Prime Minister. For the time being the Empire stood intact. But the fact that some of its individual members were now well on their way to autonomy convinced Leacock that he was probably fighting a losing battle. The Empire did seem to be breaking up. He would not give up easily in his fight to preserve its unity.

Early in the new year Leacock surveyed with pardonable pride two accomplishments outside the run of his regular work. The dramatized version of *Behind the Beyond*, referred to in an earlier chapter, had come to the end of its run in London. The modest proceeds—$305 was Leacock's share of the royalties—failed to dismay him; on the contrary, the *succès d'estime* bolstered his morale.

In addition, the professor's name now figured in the list of contributors to the Encyclopaedia Britannica. In his preface to *Sunshine Sketches*, Leacock had expressed his preference for creative writing, topping it off with the remark: "Personally I would sooner have written *Alice in Wonderland* than the whole *Encyclopaedia Britannica*." A quarter of a century later the publishers of that storehouse of knowledge approached him to prepare some articles for the thirteenth edition. These took the form of short accounts of five of Canada's provinces. He went on writing for subsequent editions—at two cents a word. ("That is what," he expostulated to a colleague, "is paid for *truth*. Fiction of course comes higher, and humor is more expensive still.")

On March 8, 1927, Stephen Leacock was surprised to receive a letter from Horatio Bottomley. A promoter-cum-publisher, Bottomley had founded a successful periodical, *John Bull*, in England. He had also become involved in a gigantic financial swindle, for which he was sent to prison. In his letter Bottomley told Leacock that while he was serving his jail term in Maidstone Prison some six years earlier he had read some of Leacock's work. Now Bottomley proposed to restart *John Bull* and hoped that Leacock would contribute "a regular light piece."

The Bottomley letter ended:

> Do not think too badly of me for having been sent to prison. . . . After all, O. Henry (of whom you are a born successor) was there, too, wasn't he?

Leacock must have answered Bottomley, but no copy of his reply was kept. In any case he had other things on his mind. Dr. Goldbloom recommended a change of scene and climate for Leacock's son, now nearing thirteen and now referred to by everybody as Stevie (his students always called Dr. Leacock Stevie, but never to his face). The pediatrician suggested the sunshine of Florida or thereabouts. The boy's parent, ever conscious of prohibition in the United States, thought the addition of sea air might help. Forthwith he announced that he would take the youngster to the south of France.

That some close friends of the professor were also planning to visit Europe more than likely had something to do with this decision. They were Mr. and Mrs. H. T. Shaw, he a successful Montreal businessman, she—nicknamed "Fitz"—a former intimate of Mrs. Leacock. Fitz was to play an increasingly important part in the professor's life.

Early in May the party set sail from Montreal for Liverpool— Leacock, father and son; Grace Reynolds, secretary; the Shaws with their young daughter, Peggy; and the Shaws' governess, whose job was to look after the children.

En route to France, the humorist really intended to discover England, in the approved tourist fashion this time. He arrived in the land of his birth as a doting father, with nothing on his mind except relaxation and enjoyment. There were no press conferences with snooping Fleet Street reporters. No announcements of his presence were made, nor did he want any. Other than meeting his publisher, dining with one or two old acquaintances and writing a column-length article "On Literature" at the request of the editor of *The Times*, the stay was strictly for pleasure. While Mr. Shaw treated Miss Reynolds to dinners and dancing, Stephen Leacock and Fitz made the rounds of the West End theatres.

After a few days in Paris, the group reached Biarritz, where, with a short incursion into northern Spain, they soaked up the Mediterranean sun for several weeks. Leacock had never permitted himself so much time off from his literary labors. He even allowed himself to forget about his early rising habit. It goes without saying that 1927 ran its course unmarked by a Leacock publication.

That he took the needed rest was just as well; the plans for 1928 called for the construction of a new house at Old Brewery Bay. And on his return to Canada in the autumn he systematically began to pour out enough magazine pieces to warrant another volume. When the latter, *Short Circuits*, appeared a few months later, it became only too apparent that this, his largest collection to date, would undoubtedly have benefitted from severe pruning. His publishers didn't think so; on the contrary, while the book was in preparation, borrowing a phrase from their star author, they pleaded with Leacock to "squeeze it out" to 50,000 words. He obliged, with several thousand words over that figure.

"Too much, too hurriedly" summed up the views of the critics. Even such an incurable Leacock devotee as S. Morgan-Powell, of *The Montreal Star*, reluctantly agreed.

Yet the fact that he had gone out into the marketplace with hastily prepared wares had some virtue: some of the contents of *Short Circuits* were useful in that they told a lot about the author. For all his attempted adaptation to the screaming twenties, Leacock revealed himself as what would now be described as "a square."

In the epilogue he stated: "If this book has in it any general theme, it is the contrast between yesterday and today, between today and tomorrow; the contrast between the life of the past and that of the future." Actually, it concentrated more on the past and the present, and the present contained many features which he disliked.

The movies and radio, both of which showed every sign of becoming an integral part of man's existence, annoyed Leacock, who treated them as passing fads. He made jokes about each medium in public and was to continue to take pot shots at each in print. Their mechanical character worried him. Though he owned an automobile in the country, he cheerfully kept it until it was old and decrepit, and could never bring himself to drive it. To him this kind of conveyance only added to the deplorable speed of living and could not begin to provide the joys of the old horse and buggy. The usual dollop of extreme exaggeration did not conceal the deep-seated nostalgia for other days and other ways.

In a hotchpotch of parodies he called "Short Circuits in Current Literature," Leacock let go at the literary trends of the decade, or, that is, at what he thought were the main trends. Unlike *Nonsense Novels*, in which he disclosed a deadly familiarity with the types of books he sought to assail, the commentaries in *Short Circuits* showed a lamentable ignorance of contemporary writing. At this point one is driven to the conclusion that, as in his reading in economics, Leacock had left his general reading well behind him. What an opportunity he had to have fun with the likes of the "lost generation" of the jazz age, with Dreiser, Fitzgerald, Hemingway, Mencken, Ezra Pound, Somerset Maugham, James Branch Cabell, James Joyce and Gertrude Stein, especially the last! Yet he avoided parodying them. The explanation can only be that his knowledge of them and their works was so superficial as to make it risky to toy with them at all.

Yet here Leacock advanced an argument about books for juveniles which seems to be lost on those in the 1970s who bewail the influence of violence-filled books for children. The humorist thought it wrong to "soften" stories for youngsters, because "they prefer them rough." The grownup might be vulnerable, but not the child. In the matter of terror and violence the children "look clean over it, or past it, or under it." And he concluded:

> The moral of all of which is, don't worry about the apparent terror and bloodshed in the children's books, the real children's books. It only represents the way in which little children, from generation to generation, learn in ways as painless as can be followed, the stern environment of life and death.

One of the saving graces in this 1928 bill of fare was his application of mathematics to the game of golf, which pinpointed the foibles of humans who indulge in this sport. Leacock tried but could not make a go of the pastime. In his youth he had played cricket at U.C.C. and for Sutton and Orillia; later he enjoyed a game of croquet on the lawn at Old Brewery Bay. Golf he never mastered. But he knew enough about the rules of the game and those who broke the rules to feel safe in enunciating some human equations. The diversity of reasons which could be cooked up by a player for not being at the top of his form fascinated Leacock— "the barking of a dog always puts him off his game; so do children; or adults, or women. Bad news disturbs his game; so does good; so also does the absence of news." He was certain all this could be expressed mathematically through the theory of permutations and combinations:

> Let us say that there are altogether fifty forms of disturbance any one of which puts Jones off his game. Each one of these disturbances happens, say, once in ten days. What chance is there that a day will come when *not a single one of them occurs*? The form is a little complicated but mathematicians will recognize the answer at once as $x/1 + x^2/1 \ldots$ $xn/1$. In fact, that is exactly how often Jones plays at his best; $x/1 + x^2/1$ $\ldots xn/1$ worked out in time and reckoning four games to the week and allowing for leap years and solar eclipses, it comes to about once in 2,930,000 years.

When, in 1969, the Canadian Government issued a commemorative postage stamp marking the centennial of Leacock's birth, philatelists the world over were reminded of a forgotten amusing little essay in *Short Circuits*. The McGill Graduates' Society widely circulated a brochure of Leacock quotations, which contained this extract from his "Stamp Album World":

> Whenever a part of the earth contains a sufficient number of people to need stamps, the people all get together and join in forming a government the purpose of which is to issue stamps. If the stamps are to have a man's head as a design, the country is placed under a king, the person selected for the king having the kind of features needed for a stamp. The British Royal family makes such excellent stamps that it is thought that they will be kept at the head of Great Britain for a long time to come. On the other hand, the Emperor of Brazil had to be deposed in 1889, his whiskers being too large to go through the Post.

Unfortunately the foregoing bright, specialized jocundities were sparsely sprinkled throughout the sixty-four subjects of *Short Circuits*, which deserved the poor reception it experienced. No wonder the flood of the writer's royalties had ebbed from a peak of forty thousand dollars in 1923 to half that amount in 1928.

It has been seen what a factor money played in governing Leacock's life. He was more than ever concerned about it now that the house-building scheme at Old Brewery Bay had already got under way. There had been difficulty in financing the cottage he had erected in 1919, to the point that the place fell far short of his desires. One day, he then promised himself, a new and larger structure would rise on the property. In 1922 he had even drawn up detailed plans for it.

The old frame house, too close to the lake anyway, was knocked down. The site of the new structure stood back from the shoreline a hundred yards or more on a rise of ground affording a much better view of Lake Couchiching. He had provided for nineteen rooms in all, with his own bedroom and study occupying a secluded wing. He insisted on oak panelling for all the walls, and a fireplace in the living room, the dining room, the study and all the bedrooms. At the back of the new house, overlooking a small lawn and garden, a glassed-in gallery served as a spacious sunroom, while at the front a wide verandah ran nearly the full length of the building, with an open balcony above it. The supreme touch was to be found in the basement—an ample, fully-equipped billiard room ("I've played billiards all my life," he once said, "and I play now every bit as well as when I began.")

The house was, of course, less than perfect, even though Leacock seemed to be blind to its faults. The bedrooms may have had fireplaces but they didn't have running water. On the other hand a leak in the roof provided some unwelcome running water.

The surrounding grounds included a tennis court and a sundial on which the proprietor had engraved Browning's lines from *Rabbi Ben Ezra*: "Grow old along with me! The best is yet to be" and, on the base, "Brevas Horas—Longos Annos."

A trout stream not far away had been leased. Money meant nothing where fishing was involved. Leacock stocked the brook with fifteen thousand dollars worth of speckled trout. To the end of his life he remained addicted to fishing. When Karsh the photographer visited Old Brewery Bay to photograph Leacock he spent days on the lake with him before he was able to complete his mission and return to his studio.

Old Brewery Bay now stood ready for all comers. And they came in their dozens, old friends and new, for the summer, for Christmas and for the Easter holidays. All were invariably greeted with the hospitable question: "Will you have a drink?" Each guest

Stephen B. Leacock, Litt. D.; Lindley M. Garrison, LL. D.; Herbert C. Hoover, LL. D.
THREE RECIPIENTS OF HONORARY DEGREES

(30) Leacock was among a distinguished trio when he received an honorary degree from Brown University, Providence, Rhode Island, in June 1917. The formal occasion apparently did not over-awe him. *(Courtesy of the Brown University Archives)*

(31) In 1919 the boathouse at Old Brewery Bay was built according to Leacock's specifications. The upper story was his private preserve, where he did much of his writing. *(Courtesy of the Public Archives of Canada)*

(32) The main drive on the lower campus of McGill University in 1919, with the Arts building in the centre. *(Courtesy of the McCord Museum of McGill University)*

(33) The scene of Leacock's lectures, the Arts building, has remained unchanged down the decades although the interior was made over in the latter 1920s. Photo taken in 1922. *(Courtesy of the McCord Museum of McGill University)*

LECTURES BY

STEPHEN LEACOCK

The Master Humorist.

SUBJECTS:
"FRENZIED FICTION"
"LITERATURE AT ITS LIGHTEST"
"LAUGHING WITH LEACOCK" (Original Readings)
"THE DRAMA AS I SEE IT."

Literally speaking Stephen Leacock has made nations laugh. He talks in a most fascinating manner. If there is any truth in the theory that a laugh is healthy, and that nations must smile to survive, then Stephen Leacock is an international asset. He makes people laugh—and they laugh at the right things. The world gains in cheerfulness through the efforts of such men. He is a real humorist, and his wholesome fun is irresistible.

STEPHEN LEACOCK WILL BE AVAILABLE FOR LECTURES IN GREAT BRITAIN FROM OCTOBER 4th TO DECEMBER 31st, 1921.

For further particulars, Terms, etc., apply to Stephen Leacock's Sole Agents:

THE LECTURE AGENCY, Ltd. (GERALD CHRISTY)

The Outer Temple, Strand, London, W.C. 2.

Telegrams: "Lecturing, London."   Telephone: Gerrard 2899.

(34) This British lecture agency's fly sheet was circulated in 1921 prior to Leacock's lecture tour of the United Kingdom. The photograph dates from 1914. *(Courtesy of The McGill Daily News)*

VEHICLE FOR LITERARY EXPRESSION IS NEEDED AT McGILL --- LEACOCK

The need for some kind of a journal which will afford to the students of McGill a proper vehicle of literary expression was stressed yesterday by Dr. Stephen Leacock, head of the Department of Economics and Political Science.

Dr. Leacock, pointing to the numerous literary publications in various colleges throughout the United States, maintained that they turn out a class of journal which McGill has not aspired to for nearly 25 years.

"I understand that the question of having a Literary Supplement connected with the McGill Daily has become a subject of very keen controversy among the students," he declared. "I think it would be improper for me to interfer in any way in such a controversy and I prefer not to do so.

"But I would like to draw attention to what I think the urgent need at McGill for some kind of journal which will afford to the students a proper vehicle of literary expressions and a proper training ground for learning to write.

"The Daily is excellent for disseminating news. But I fear that a journal of that kind is of very little use in training students how to write in a literary way and in helping students to be interested in culture and literature in the general sense.

"A Daily publication has the faults that go with its very existence. It is bound to be to some extent flamboyant exaggerated, and noisy. It is bound to see the little routine of our daily college life under a huge magnifying glass. It can take no interest in people who are as dead as Homer and Shakespeare, and it will take an exaggerated interest in little transitory things such as student elections. In point of literary style it teaches the wrong things. It inculcates false notions of the things called 'pep' and 'punch,' and the passion for immediate effect.

"Let me repeat that I am not saying a word against the Daily but merely trying to show the conditions under which it labors and how nearly useless it is as a vehicle of culture.

"I do not know whether our students are aware of how completely isolated we are in this matter. Every college in the United States of first or second or even tenth rank has a literary journal. There are dignified and deserving journals of a literary and deserving character flourishing at Kalamazoo College, Muskingum College, at Denison, and at Allegheny College in Meadville, Pennsylvania. I mention these because I happen to have seen them within the last year or so. These are little colleges with nothing much to recommend them beyond poverty, and hopefullness, and a few sound traditions. But they turn out a class of journal which we have not even aspired to in McGill for nearly 25 years.

"In England and Scotland literary journals at every great school and at every great college without exception are regarded as an essential factor in college life.

It is quite plain to me that in this matter of a college journal we either lead the world or else come at the tail end of the procession. I think I know which we are doing."

GOOD TOE DANCER

"She is a good toe-dancer."

"You're right, but she never uses her own toes."

Not to withdraw after making an error is itself a new error.

—Confucius.

(35, 36) Leacock frequently appeared in the *McGill Daily News* either as a newsworthy character or as a contributor. The article above dates from the edition of March 4th, 1925; that below is from October 28th, 1925. (*Courtesy of The McGill Daily News*)

(37) Beatrix Leacock at Old Brewery Bay.
(*Courtesy of the Public Archives of Canada*)

(38) Leacock as the McGill campus knew him about 1925. The bulky clothes, the loosened tie and the prominent watch-chain were all trademarks. *(Courtesy of the Public Archives of Canada)*

(39) Leacock's friend, General Sir Arthur Currie, principal and vice-chancellor, McGill University, 1919-33. *(Photo by Arnott Rogers Batten, Ltd., courtesy of the McGill University Archives)*

(40) Immaculate in spats, René du Roure (centre) is surrounded by staff members of his French summer school, about 1922. *(Photograph courtesy of Mrs. Clifford Powell)*

(41) Leacock in winter attire about 1928.
(Courtesy of the Public Archives of Canada)

could do as he wished during his stay so long as he understood that the host could creep away from any festivity early in order to preserve the lifetime habit of early rising. Guests were under compulsion in only one respect. The large living room had been equipped, with great premeditation, to accommodate a rudimentary stage curtain. Plays were presented in that room, plays which the host wrote, and for which the casts were drawn from any company at hand. Dinner, too, was usually quite an event; even ordinary family dinners were often marked by amusing place cards composed by the host, who would dominate the proceedings with great good humor.

Into this inviting country home and the residence in Montreal there entered a refreshing influence in the person of one of Leacock's nieces, Barbara Ulrichsen. On his return from Europe the professor had written to his sister Carrie, who lived in the United States. He thought that it might be mutually helpful if her daughter would come to McGill and serve as his secretary, the post earlier filled by Grace Reynolds, who had left to take up a library course. He would guarantee Barbara's tuition fees and provide her with an allowance into the bargain. Typically, the academic uncle asked for her high-school record to be forwarded. On that he acted promptly with the co-operation of Dr. Ira McKay, the dean of the faculty.

For a decade, until she became Mrs. Donald Nimmo in 1937, Barbara Ulrichsen far exceeded the "make-herself-generally-useful" stipulation of her uncle. Sensitive at all times to the busy professor's literary activities and to his barometric moods, she became amanuensis, chatelaine and constant companion at a very important stage in the humorist's career. At the same time she distinguished herself scholastically, going on after graduation to her master's degree.

"Ba," as Leacock affectionately dubbed her, was to prove a godsend.

XIV

Depression

With his two houses in order, himself fit and fifty-nine, Stephen Leacock distributed all over North America "a memorandum for the use of lecture committees." The fruits of the lecture circuits in the United States promised to be as high as one thousand dollars per appearance, plus expenses, depending on the status of the speaker. Leacock often rated five hundred dollars. Much as he bemoaned this sort of work, the attractiveness of the fees offset any dislike he may genuinely have felt for it.

The circular drew the attention of the agencies and organizations to the two kinds of public lectures available from the humorist. Referring to himself in the fly sheet as "Mr." Leacock, the professor announced his preparedness to take on education and democracy, the outlook for literature in the present century, the evolution of modern democracy, or the social teaching of the great humorists. These were topics "in which anything humorous in the treatment is merely incidental."

The second group of themes, he announced, "are intended to be of a purely humorous and amusing character as their main feature, but to contain also a substratum of philosophy and common sense." These were the old standbys of frenzied fiction, literature at its lightest and latest, literature and progress, and "What I Don't

Know About the Drama," all of which had stood the test of time.

During the winter of 1929 Leacock gave over most of his weekends and statutory holidays to fulfilling engagements both in Canada and the U.S., bolstering his revenue accordingly. This was just as well, since revenue from his books was sinking every year.

One booking in Boston had to be cancelled, however. Saddled with a special duty by Sir Arthur Currie, the professor decided to make the most of what in most other hands would have been a routine task. It had to do with a courtesy visit to McGill by the first Japanese ambassador to Canada.

As an outcome of the 1926 Imperial Conference, the Canadian Government appointed a minister to Washington the following year, to France in 1928, and now to Japan. The Japanese reciprocated by sending Iyemasa Torkugwa to Ottawa.

When Leacock received his brief to extend McGill's welcome to Torkugwa, he suddenly thought of a student in one of his classes—a Japanese prince of the blood royal. On the strength of an insouciant personality, this T. R. Makiyama enjoyed a considerable popularity with his classmates, some of whom retain memories of his extra-special racoon coat and his spotless grey fedora worn at a jaunty angle.

The Leacock scheme called for addressing the Japanese envoy in his native tongue. The professor had mastered several languages, but this would be a definite challenge. So he dragooned Makiyama into doing a coaching job. Leacock wrote the introductory remarks, pressed the youthful prince of Nippon to translate, then together they went over it, word by word, until Leacock managed the correct intonation.

Torkugwa's visit went off with flying colors, highlighted by the humorist's dexterous performance in Japanese, which he handled—according to the ambassador—with charming fluency.

(A footnote to this episode brings us to that fateful day, December 7, 1941, and the Japanese attack on Pearl Harbor. In Washington on that weekend the official delegation from Tokyo which had been negotiating with the Americans included a Japanese prince. His name was T. R. Makiyama!)

A less exacting and highly nostalgic undertaking confronted Leacock with the acceptance of an invitation to chair a dinner in Toronto. The occasion at the Royal York Hotel on September 14,

1929, marked the centenary of his old school, Upper Canada College.

The record of the dinner leaves the reader in no doubt that a good time was had by all. Leacock was in absolutely top form. All his introductions were regularly punctuated by laughter, including the moment when he began to address the chair and then remembered with apparent confusion that he *was* the chairman.

The humorist seems to have had the audience eating out of his hand. Indeed, one of the speakers actually began his speech with a mock apology for having been responsible for selecting the chairman—a sure sign that the chairman was a very successful choice.

Introducing the Canadian Minister of Trade and Commerce, Stephen Leacock remarked:

> I am going to call upon the Honorable James Malcolm, towards whom I feel a bond of sympathy that is very difficult to express in words. He came to U.C.C. in 1898 and in 1899 he was the only one among some three hundred boys who had the manliness to say, "Stephen Leacock is going, and I am going to leave with him."

Occupied as he had been with his university work and his outside lecture commitments, the humorist had not neglected his obligations to various magazines and newspapers. And out of these contributions came another volume, *The Iron Man and the Tin Woman, and Other Futurities*. And while the economic bubble had yet to burst on Wall Street—only a few weeks later, as a matter of fact—Leacock's New York publishers were obviously already worried. They argued that their author's 20 per cent terms were too high for the trivia he had included in *The Iron Man*. But the professor was a formidable bargainer. A compromise went in his favor.

Looked at as a whole, and compared to some of his earlier productions, this book must have been a disappointment to many ardent followers. *Short Circuits* had offered only a few genuinely funny pieces. *The Iron Man* had even fewer. Leacock was straining, had been noticeably straining for some time. Six years previously Peter McArthur had pointed the finger at the humorist's weakness for grinding out material without regard to quality. The professor had paid no heed, sticking to his habit of squeezing the lemon dry. Now the lemon seemed to be dry.

A sense of the ridiculous is as nothing without a sure hand, and in this volume Leacock's hand missed all along the way, or nearly all the way. In "Jazzed Journalism" he had a good idea to start with. What would happen in a newspaper when various editors and specialized columnists were switched to one another's jobs? But the amusing possibilities ended in mere silliness. "In the Golf Stream" found him playing with one of his least favorite games again, reviewing the season at the golf club:

> Where do we stand in our gain or loss of human affection? How are we on brotherly love? I fear that it is only too evident that with each season we lose a little more. In my own case several valued friendships have come to an end over various little points of the game. They say that Scotland is mostly a lonely country of empty spaces and the people keep to themselves to an amazing degree, trusting no one and never speaking. I think I understand it. They began golf there 400 years ago.

This is not taking something out of context. It is the principal muddled point of the piece.

(Today, in McGill's McLennan Library, one of several copies of *The Iron Man* bears a sticker reading "from the estate of Harry Barker." It is inscribed "To Harry with kindest regards." Harry was one of several mop-pushing assistants to Bill Gentleman in the Arts building. He fancied himself a poet, and thought nothing of stopping staff and students to recite his latest composition. Shakespeare was on tap if you cared to wait, which Leacock often did.)

It is impossible to know if the professor realized that his little essays and stories had been losing their sharpness. It's a safe guess that he did not. He appeared to be satisfied, and the nineteen thousand dollars he would earn from his literary efforts in 1929 pointed to the probability that a lot of his customers were still satisfied, too. But the line on his personal financial chart pointed downwards.

The line on virtually everybody's chart dipped into a seemingly never-ending dive in October with the crash of the New York stock market. Although the effect was not immediate, the resulting chaos in the United States inescapably would be felt in Canada. Shares nosedived on the Montreal and Toronto exchanges. But Leacock was enough of an economist to have chosen his investments with care and on good advice. When the deluge came, his own portfolio was small but sound. He had not, as the rumor ran, "lost his shirt" in the crash.

The great economic depression left Leacock's usual optimistic beliefs in a state of disrepair. He was deeply distressed "about the failure of society, and economists in particular," to account for and deal with the sudden turn of events and the aftermath. But if all his firmly embedded orthodox concepts had been shaken to the roots, he was held steady by the support of the staff with which he had surrounded himself in the department. These were clear-thinking men with an objectivity their chief lacked. They included Drs. J. C. Hemmeon and J. P. Day, assisted by such up-and-coming scholars as Eugene Forsey, John Culliton and H. Carl Goldenberg.

Goldenberg, who was to rise to national prominence as a pre-eminent labor-management negotiator, witnessed many gleeful incidents in these rough times. One of them involved the then president of the Royal Bank of Canada, Sir Herbert Holt.

Leacock and his youthful assistant were strolling along Sherbrooke Street on a sunny afternoon. They were passing the front entrance of the exclusive Mount Royal Club (Leacock's Mausoleum Club) when a limousine drove up and disgorged the multimillion-aire figure of Holt.

Sir Herbert nodded to the professor, burbled a perfunctory "Good day," and proceeded up the steps.

"Good day," Leacock replied cheerfully. "And how are things, Sir Herbert?"

"Bad, very bad," muttered the banking potentate, and with that he entered the club.

Turning to Goldenberg, Leacock shook his head with mock seriousness and said: "I really feel sorry for Holt. I wish I could do something to help him."

But, as everyone who suffered through that stark period knows, chuckles were pretty much at a premium. Even Leacock wore a grave expression. While trying to sort out what was going on around him, he had brought to completion a hefty book on a pet topic—imperial co-operation. Published in the spring of 1930, when millions on the American continent were beginning to feel the pinch, it was called *Economic Prosperity in the British Empire*.

Written in a strain of the highest optimism, it put forward proposals for the consolidation of imperial credit, advocated an integrated and reciprocal tariff system in order to capture world markets, and proposed "the establishment of a system of mutual co-operation for a development in common of the vast potential wealth of the Empire." It also argued for "the expansion of its present limited population."

Leacock belabored that last point. An empire of some 450 million surely required no expansion. However, this total embraced millions of Asiatics and Africans, whom the professor more or less dismissed. His interest lay in the 66,500,000 white population. "None of the Dominions want to link up their economic life with the good will or bad will, the aspirations, the hatreds and the convulsions of the welter of peoples who live in British India and the Indian states. . . . What is wanted is a conference between nation and nation, between white men and white men." This stoutly stubborn Anglo-Saxon even managed to refer to New Zealand's Maoris as "savages."

The then pro-Empire *Montreal Star* editorially praised the principles laid down in the book. *The Times* of London presented a more detached analysis:

> It bristles with questionable epigrams, skates lightly over practical issues and waves aside both economic theory and statistical method. Few economists will be impressed with the shortcuts the author takes "through the jungle of statistics," or with his pieces of "financial magic" in which something is made out of nothing.

Other serious journals of opinion also took the professor to task for talking in airy generalizations, from the heart rather than from the head, betimes salting important problems with irrelevant humor. But Leacock was cheered by backing from an unexpected source. The Orillia Board of Trade rose up, bought a thousand copies, and mailed them to every British M.P. and to numerous newspaper editors in the United Kingdom.

The "shortcuts" which *The Times* mentioned marked much of Leacock's economic writing. Figures and details had never been the professor's long suit. He was content with broad theories, and others were left to deal with statistics. But, as Dr. Hemmeon would say, economists deal in facts.

Nor were the fictional exercises entirely free of this fault. He tended to brush off, or at least contend lightly with research and verification. He liked to say, with a gurgle, that the best way to write about Eskimos and the Far North was to sit by one's roaring fire

at home, with a glass of whisky at hand. Thus positioned and pro-
visioned, one's imagination could the better conjure up the desired
atmosphere.

It could be taken for granted that at least one prominent person
had little time to pursue the Leacock call for imperial preference.
Prime Minister Mackenzie King had other worries. He was very
slow to move to un-pick the tangled skein of the Depression; if
rising unemployment and the diverse demands of the provinces
alarmed him, he betrayed no sign of it. Quite the contrary: un-
guardedly, he made the stupid remark that he would never give "a
five-cent piece" to any province governed by a Conservative administration. That statement would cost him a few million five-cent
pieces in political power.

Cannily—as he thought—King called a general election for mid-
July. Political wiseacres were willing to wager that Wily Willie's
strategy was to hand over the Depression, lock, stock and barrel,
to the Tories and let them sink beneath its burden in the economic
slough of despond. Ultimately, his diary entries were to reveal that
this was not the case: King felt confident he would win. He didn't.

Stephen Leacock now had a friend at court in the person of the
pompous, autocratic, wealthy Richard B. Bennett, who not only
took over the reins as Prime Minister, but into the bargain appointed himself president of the Privy Council, Minister of Finance
and Secretary of State for External Affairs. He kept such a close
eye on his other ministers that once, when Bennett was observed
walking alone on an Ottawa street oblivious to all and sundry, a
local wag opined that he was holding a cabinet meeting.

The unlikelihood of Bennett offering Leacock a portfolio in his
government has already been stressed by the Hon. Leslie Frost.
That the pair would have made strange political bedfellows is obvious. Certainly they shared everything that was Tory, up to and
including a sentimental attachment to the Crown as an institution
and to British royalty as a family group. Yet, for a lasting friendship, a personality transformation in one or the other would have
been imperative. Either Bennett would have had to develop a sense
of humor, which he completely lacked, or Leacock would have had
to give up being funny, and drinking alcohol as well. The odds were
about twenty million to one against in each case.

It seemed to be sufficient for Leacock that someone who thought along the same lines now headed the government of the country. Half-hearted approaches were made to the professor to try for a seat in the July campaign, but he wasn't having anything of it. Undoubtedly he was content to console a McGill colleague. Dr. Cyrus Macmillan, head of the English department, who had been King's Minister of Fisheries, had been beaten in the election.

With politics out of the way for the moment and his sixtieth birthday approaching, the humorist was able to add to the overflowing, ceiling-high bookshelves in his Cote des Neiges study a couple of anthologies of his work. Both his English and American publishers marked the occasion of his birthday with collections of what they deemed to be his best pieces published between 1910 and 1929. *The Leacock Book* appeared in Britain, *Laugh with Leacock* in the United States and Canada. Each paid tribute to the man in his twentieth year as an author.

In the preface to *Laugh with Leacock*, the editor concluded with this note to the author:

> A moment ago I confessed that before making this selection we dropped a hint to some of your friends that this was a jovial occasion in which they might perhaps wish to join. All of what they said in reply may not best be printed for the public eye, as perhaps now and then too intimate and laudatory for anything but a sincere and secret blush; yet never were truer words said than the graceful compliments that they have paid you, which we are appending in the order they happened to reach us.

There followed brief tributes from fifteen American writers, among them:

George Ade—Stephen Leacock has achieved the distinction of being a happy combination of the drawing-room Englishman and the liberated and unconventional American.

Irvin S. Cobb—I can't pick out my favorite Leacock story, because all Leacock stories are favorites of mine. How are you going to choose one pearl from a string of perfect pearls?

Donald Ogden Stewart—I owe Stephen Leacock a great deal—so does every contemporary American humorist—but I would prefer not to know the exact extent of my debt. Ignorance is golden.

Nunnally Johnson—Writers of humor I have found to be a most poisonous crew, none of them seeming to have anything but loathing and contempt for the stuff of any other. I can think of but two names that are exempt from this harpooning, and Mr. Leacock's is one.

Gelett Burgess—Though I say it as shouldn't, it takes a fine scientific mind to write good nonsense, and Stephen Leacock has placed himself in the class of Edward Lear, Dodgson, Barrie, Oliver Herford and the author of Felix the Cat.

In his contribution to the birthday round-up, Chic Sale (pen name of Charles Partlow) pointed out that Leacock had been one of his closest friends, which was quite true. A vaudevillian, Sale won acclaim as an impersonator of rural types on the variety stage, in Broadway revues and eventually in Hollywood. Leacock had met him as an actor before Sale published, in 1929, that extraordinary disquisition on outdoor toilets, *The Specialist,* which sold a million copies in a very short time. Sale had been Leacock's guest at the University Club and on one occasion visited Old Brewery Bay. *The Specialist* clearly appealed to the bumpkin in the professor. But, according to Mrs. H. M. Little, a constant member of the Leacock circle, when the humorist and Sale got together, neither one cracked a smile. They were both dead serious about their common pursuit of the comic muse.

Solemnity, as a matter of fact, happened to be a product in too ready supply as the Hungry Thirties began to gather momentum. The catastrophic effects of the Depression found economists, academic and otherwise, floundering in their efforts, at first to explain the global breakdown of the system, and then to concoct remedies for it.

Bennett already had summoned parliament in emergency session shortly after his assumption of office. Relief work in all forms and in all parts of the nation assumed some of the hysteria which seemed to have the whole continent in its thrall. The initial tariff and monetary policies which the Prime Minister initiated were along the lines that Leacock had been advocating for years.

Although his own financial position was relatively secure, Leacock rushed into print, ill-advisedly, an assortment of new and old sketches on the subject of prohibition, which still obtained in the U.S.A. and in parts of Canada. His *Sunshine Sketches* town had elected to string along with the "drys," much to the annoyance of its most famous citizen. This, as much as anything else, served to convince him that further shafts of wrath directed at restrictive liquor laws would be justified and welcomed. The book attracted only a limited audience.

Wet Wit and Dry Humor could hardly have been more aptly named. In large part it was rubbishy; and most of the book's merits were to be found in the older pieces in which he had given vent to his hostility towards busybodies who dared to dictate what people ought to drink, and when and where.

While some of this was probably acceptable to readers living under the then prevailing conditions, the writer went to extremes in his account of "A Butler of the Old School." Here he created vintage brands of water which had their origin in such rich sources as French taps, the Johnstown flood, ditches, canals in the Netherlands, ancient parish pumps and so forth. To thirsty folk unable to procure their favorite brew (and these weren't many, such was human ingenuity) this kind of spun-out jest may possibly have appeared funny.

Whether or not this sketch emerged from an actual incident that Carl Goldenberg carries in his memory is neither here nor there. But it will serve to illustrate how Leacock regularly tried out his jokes "on the dog" before submitting them to his publisher.

It was the professor's pleasant conceit to usher in each college year with a dinner party at his home. The members of his departmental staff were his guests. In making preparations for this particular function one year, the realization struck the widower that all his associates and assistant professors were unmarried. He didn't want a stag affair. The resourceful Barbara Ulrichsen was pressed into service to select some appropriate co-eds, whose attendance would ensure a mixed party.

At the well-stocked bar which dominated the large dining room one of the more demure young ladies gave her order—a glass of water. At the sound of the word the host spun around with a look of incredulity.

"Water? Water?" Leacock uttered. "Ah, yes, I remember water about forty years ago. Barbara, get out that very good water we've been saving for forty years."

For the greater portion of *Wet Wit and Dry Humor* spontaneous parody eluded the author. "Confessions of a Soda Fiend" furnished a prime example of how hard up Leacock had been for fresh fun.

The condemned sodaolic began the sad story of his dissolute life:

> I was born of a family in comfortable, if not affluent circumstances, of parents of sincere, if not profound convictions, in a home that was educated if not cultivated, in a house that was rough cast if not brick, with plumbing that was effective, if not open.
>
> I often sat at my book till long after nine at night, even till nine-thirty, or nine thirty-five. . . .
>
> To my mind a good woman is one of the greatest things on earth, second only perhaps to a good child or a good man.
>
> I had soon abandoned all attempts at serious study; spent my whole evenings hanging round Sunday School and choir practice.

Humorist and critic Will Cuppy stated in his corner of the preface of *Laugh With Leacock* that the Canadian "is the real grand-daddy of the best ones of the day."

As Leacock entered the sixth decade of a febrile life, the question stood: Was "grand-daddy" wearing out, his vitality deserting him, the well running dry?

One could believe anything about Stephen Leacock at this stage —except that anyone could possibly apply to him the word DRY!

XV

Sunshine and Sadness

*The physiology of wrinkles can
be very telling and accurate.*
Leo Tolstoy

In 1932 the furrows of the humorist's brow and the creases at the
mouth corners ran deeper. These had the effect of underlining the
strong character of Leacock's leathery face. The clear grey-blue
eyes, and the cleft chin jutting out above a neck which sank into
hunched shoulders implied more resolution than ever before. His
initial shock at the economic catastrophe appeared to have subsided. Once again he dug himself out of a melancholic mood.

Politically, things were going well for Leacock. Though most of
his beloved Empire had become the Commonwealth by virtue of
the Statute of Westminster in the previous year, the professor's
economic ideas were shared by Prime Minister Bennett. The Imperial Economic Conference of 1932 produced a number of agree-
ments and bilateral trade pacts which found favor with the McGill
theorist, who had got in a word ahead of the gathering with *Back
to Prosperity: The Great Opportunity of the Empire Conference*.
This little book of just over a hundred pages won considerable
attention in Canada, the United Kingdom and South Africa. A

Canadian Liberal organ commented: "He is in deadly earnest, as only a humorist can be with supreme common sense when he wants to be, about the empire's thinkers and doers doing more than those of any other nation to solve the world's common problems." Whether or not Bennett gave ear to Leacock's pointed piece of advice is debatable; the Prime Minister seldom listened to anyone except himself.

One person to whose opinions Leacock paid increasing attention was Mrs. H. T. Shaw. Between the two of them there developed a growing attachment. She and her husband, it will be remembered, accompanied the humorist and his son on a European jaunt in 1927. Yet, prior to that, May, or Fitz Shaw had been an intimate of Mrs. Leacock. The Shaws were not only neighbors in Montreal but also at Old Brewery Bay, where Fitz maintained a country house a mere hop, skip and jump from the Leacock home.

Little, if anything, has been written about the relationship between Stephen Leacock and May Shaw following the death of Trix. There have been, however, plenty of rumors, notably one which was gleefully bandied about in Orillia. There the tale-bearers whispered that the author of *Sunshine Sketches* "was keeping a woman," that she lived near him, and that a path between the two residences had become well trodden.

Hearsay gained some support from an incident which involved the ubiquitous Professor René du Roure, who frequently came to Old Brewery Bay as a welcome guest, indeed almost as a member of the family circle. On one of these trips du Roure, delayed on business in Toronto, thoughtfully wired his colleague:

I will be with you tonight. [signed] Rene.

When the message arrived at the Orillia telegraph office, the acute accent on the final vowel of du Roure's Christian name naturally did not appear on the ticker. Without that accent, René became a feminine name and proof positive to the girl operator that the rumor of a "kept woman" had a basis in fact. Soon the town of Orillia rang with the name of "the woman." When the story reached the collective ear of Leacock, Fitz and du Roure, their voices rang with laughter.

Twelve years Leacock's junior, an attractive, artistic, lively blonde, forthright in her views and behaviour, Fitz had proved a good foil for the more restrained Trix. When the 1930s arrived, the Stephen-Fitz companionship had developed into deep mutual affection; nor could it be said that any attempt was ever made to disguise the fact. In the city they regularly dined at the club, often in the company of a friend, Mrs. H. M. Little, widow of a noted gynaecologist. Mrs. Little recalls the spirit of gaiety which Fitz contributed to Leacock's life, plus an outspokenness which delighted the professor. In his last will and testament, he was to leave May Shaw five hundred books from his library—the titles to be of her own choosing. The copyright of his unfinished autobiography also stood in her name.

In 1932 with renewed energy Leacock applied himself to three more books before the year's end—two collections of humor and a "biography" of his lord and master, Mark Twain. In the same period he edited, with an introduction, the journal of Louis Armand de Lom d'Arce, Baron de Lahontan, seventeenth-century French soldier-memoirist who travelled among Canada's Indian tribes. Unfortunately, the Canadian publishing house which commissioned *Lahontan's Voyages* went bankrupt when the pressrun had hardly begun. Leacock received not a cent of compensation. Only a few copies survived the debacle.

Of the two light works, in charity a veil should be drawn over the first, *Afternoons in Utopia*, in which the author gathered together some stray magazine confections dealing chiefly with some pet hates—socialism and Communism. The blunted wit of these pieces demonstrated how little, as Carl Goldenberg has pointed out, Leacock understood Leftist philosophies. Here the professor's prejudices so got in the way that his otherwise sharp sense of the ridiculous lost its cutting edge.

The "squeeze" strategy again came into play with *The Dry Pickwick*. The obsession with prohibition led him to turn out this compilation almost on the heels of *Wet Wit and Dry Humor*. Yet *The Dry Pickwick*, although it had precious little to do with Dickens' character, had its merits. Leacock's effervescence could not be bottled up permanently. In these pages a diverting excursion called "The Flying Carpet" found the writer turning a trite idea into an amusing story. The airborne rug took tourists on trips to the Arctic, Tibet and Africa where the respective denizens were occupied with such Western problems as the gold standard and golf. It transpired that, despite the disparate climes, regional differences were barely discernible. But in "Come and See Our Town" the humorist displayed a brash indifference to repetition of theme and treatment. The same notion had already been stretched to the limit in *My Discovery of England*, and it would be used again. Recurrence of everything from plots to phrases dotted the corpus of his work, either by accident or deliberately, in all likelihood the latter. Perhaps he relied on his readers' short memories.

How and why at this time he tackled a study, however brief, of Mark Twain can be explained only by a palpable determination to build up his bank account, which had been radically affected by the Depression; more important still, he was determined to ensure security for his sixteen-year-old son, who was now away at school and doing brilliantly.

Though Leacock referred to his *Mark Twain* as a biography, this was a misnomer. In the main a succession of endearing generalities, the slim volume undoubtedly aimed at an appreciation of the genius whom Leacock venerated and to whom his indebtedness may be traced in many ways. Whatever the motive, Leacock did not mean to waste much time on research. But in any case, he disdained minutiae, alike as an economist and as a writer of fiction. In *Mark Twain* he either skated breezily over or omitted entirely whole areas of the Samuel Clemens story.

"It would be tedious as it would be purposeless," he wrote with apologetic abandon, "to follow all the comings and goings of Mark Twain and his family in the years that followed their return from Europe." Frequently he resorted to Paine's life of Twain and other sources in an offhand referential manner as though to say, "If you really want detail, go elsewhere." Time, to Leacock, was of the essence. Yet this *Mark Twain* has a place in the immense bibliography of the American's life and works. The modest Leacock tribute added its own special brand of fluffy informality.

The two men afford interesting similarities and contrasts. Clemens died in 1910, the year that *Literary Lapses* catapulted Leacock into the limelight. It seemed as though a tradition was simply going to be continued. Theirs were common gifts for broad burlesque, grotesque exaggeration, juxtaposition of irrelevant ideas, and casual shifting from one comic pose to another. A love of personal anecdote and a general lack of reverence were also shared.

Tolstoy's physiology of wrinkles could be applied to both, and a psychology of dress equally so. Twain, painstakingly groomed, with his spotless white suits; Leacock, unconcerned, yet with a suggestion of studied casualness in his expensive yet rumpled tweeds. Each protested loudly against the tiresomeness of lecturing in public; each continued to indulge in it with apparent relish. Their platform styles differed radically. Twain's deadpan seriousness often reached the point of wrathfulness. As though to prove he was not following in the steps of the American, Leacock developed, and used superbly, the trick of laughing at his own jokes well before the punch line.

The pair deplored class distinction, particularly hereditary aristocracy. The Canadian refused to include the British royal family in his condemnation of inherited titles. Twain confessed that, "like all other human beings," he himself had reverence for rank, no matter how much he might scoff at it in print. Leacock concurred in Twain's observation that "it does rather look as if in a republic, where all are free and equal, prosperity and position constitute *rank*." While they twitted *rank*, each had attained *rank* and revelled in the concomitant amenities. Both were quick to anger. Twain made more money. Leacock was more careful with his.

Although the professor was much better off financially than most of his station in 1932, he made some curious decisions. On May 29 the Canadian Press carried an item from Ottawa stating that Leacock "had been placed upon the retired list of Fellows of the Royal Society of Canada. He tendered his resignation a few days ago as 'a matter of personal economy'." In the following weeks, on the same pretext, he terminated his membership in other organizations, notably The Canadian Authors' Association. In neither of these cases could the prevailing fee have been deemed a hardship. For undisclosed reasons Leacock began to cut costs, even as his production increased at a considerably accelerated rate.

As a public figure and a slightly eccentric academic, yarns about him always abounded. There were always people who could be counted upon to believe the worst about him. In the late spring of 1932 an overwhelmingly obscure young female evangelist came to Montreal to stage a kind of revivalist meeting in a small downtown hall. At the conclusion of her spiel about sin, and before she embarked on a question-and-answer confessional period, the lady announced to the crowded auditorium her pleasure in having in her audience such a distinguished man as Dr. Stephen Leacock. Pointing at a middle-aged, grey-haired man in the front row, she asked if he would begin the exchange of views by stating his personal worries, be they business, women or wine.

She could not be accused of mischief-making, since the man she addressed did bear some resemblance to the McGill figure. But the gentleman, embarrassed for being singled out at all, mumblingly explained he was not Leacock. While he did not identify himself, he happened to be a member of a prominent Montreal family. In those circles which thrive on twisting facts for the thrill of it, the story got about and was mangled in the process, to fade only after it had discommoded the professor to a considerable degree.

Such annoyances failed to depress a spirit bent upon rescuing mankind from the woes of the day. Through the winter of 1932–33 he had worked on *Stephen Leacock's Plan*, a pamphlet of eighteen pages designed "to relieve the depression in six days, to remove it in six months, to eradicate it in six years." His attack, and the cures, were not as frivolous as the subtitle sounded. Leacock plumped for immediate action to get the economic machinery of the Western world into gear again. Solutions for the permanent welfare of society could await healthier times.

Like his economics lectures, *Stephen Leacock's Plan* consisted of an elementary approach, enlivened by ear-tingling metaphors. The complexities of the Depression were swept aside. Holes had to be plugged quickly, work for the workless to be found in short order to revive desperate minds. The rebuilding of slums on a massive scale was essential anyway and would serve two obvious purposes —stimulate employment and production. Ever present was a Leacock fear that a solution would be found in the creation of socialist states rising from the ashes of capitalist economies. Predictably, he rushed to the side of individual enterprise and the profits system, which "is as old as Adam and Eve and as respectable as either of them." Central to his scheme for recovery was a proposal to reduce the gold value of the dollar from twenty-three grains to seventeen grains, permitting issuance of more money against existing reserves without spawning more inflation.

Leacock pushed his plan to the top. He sent a copy of the pamphlet to President Roosevelt, another to Prime Minister Bennett. He spoke before an audience of business and professional men at the

University of Cincinnati. When the FDR Brains Trust initiated a far-reaching economic program, Leacock contentedly remarked that his ideas were now being adopted. Like his own plan, this statement was simply an oversimplification of the facts.

When, however, facts were flouted, Leacock made a point of setting the record straight—sometimes dramatically. Graham F. Towers, a former student and friend of the professor and the first governor of the Bank of Canada, recalls an incident which took place in 1932.

The world-wide collapse of gold standards after 1930 supported the position of those opposed to their continual use. Great Britain had gone off the gold standard in 1931. But for some mysterious reason the government of Canada persisted in its contention that Canada was still on the gold standard. This, says Mr. Towers, just was not so, "as anyone with a smattering of economics knew." It got under Leacock's skin and he proposed to do something to disprove the government's stand.

The professor went to his bank and drew out ten thousand dollars in legal tender. "That," explains Mr. Towers, "at the time meant one or two-dollar bills which were then the only legal tender, apart from the large denomination bills used by the banks for clearing purposes."

Leacock then proceeded to the office of the Assistant Receiver General in Montreal, put the considerable package of bills on the desk, and demanded gold in return. Somehow the government officials had got wind of his impending visit and paid him as inconveniently as possible in the smallest coins.

After a while Leacock decided to ship his gold to the United States. Strangely, however, neither the express companies nor any other shipper would undertake to do so. The months went by, Leacock still saddled with the coins. Then the government wrote to him to call in the gold.

Leacock had accepted the gold coins at face value, but Graham Towers reports that when the professor returned them "he had to suffer a deduction for loss of weight through wear and abrasion, so he didn't get back what he had put in. However, if Leacock lost the battle, he won the war. He had proved that Canada was not on the gold standard."

But at least one muddle involving Leacock was straightened out amid the confusion of the early thirties. The industrial and business magnates who comprised McGill University's board of governors discovered a strange oversight in their past operations. A quarter of a century earlier, in 1908, the board had instructed Principal Peterson to ask "Dr. Leacock to take charge of the work of the Department of Political Economy, until the board is ready to proceed to the appointment of a professor."

As has been seen, in 1908 Leacock "took charge" in no uncertain manner. Thereafter it had been assumed by all concerned that, functioning as department chairman, Leacock *was* chairman. Not so, however, since the governors down the years seemed never to have remembered to be "ready to proceed to the appointment of a professor." At last in 1933 they realized the oversight and Leacock's formal appointment was quietly entered in the minutes. This did not involve an increase of his college stipend; he'd been receiving the salary of a departmental chairman throughout the twenty-five years.

Forgetfulness in the tradition of academic absent-mindedness could not be charged against Leacock. If unimportant routine matters sometimes confused him, lack of consideration for other human beings could not be numbered among his shortcomings.

A colleague had brought to his attention a second-hand bookstore where exquisite bookbindings could be obtained at bargain prices. Always on the lookout for good values, Leacock paid a visit to the store, a tiny, dusty establishment tucked away in a downtown area around the corner from several derelict pawnshops.

He found a boy of sixteen or so behind the counter, made his purchases, got into conversation with the youthful bookseller, and learned his name—Louis Melzack.

Why, Leacock wanted to know, was the lad not at school? The explanation revealed that Louis had abandoned his educational plans in order to help his father run the business. The professor probed further. Was Louis utilizing his opportunity to read books to further his learning? Yes, but the reading took haphazard form. Leacock casually named some books he thought the boy ought to tackle; and said that if there were no objections, he might from time to time drop in to check on the results.

Being in an out-of-the-way location, the Melzack store required some effort to reach it. The humorist, however, proved as good as his word. As much to act as a kind of unpaid tutor as to browse, Leacock appeared often and young Melzack, thus encouraged, benefitted accordingly. Thirty-five years later Louis Melzack would become the most aggressive and best-informed bookseller in the country, the proprietor of more than twenty shops across Canada.

The tight daily schedule, which began before dawn as it had done since the childhood farm days, became extraordinarily flexible when it was a matter of helping others, especially former students. One of these, S. R. Norris Hodgins, of Ottawa, Ontario, recounts an incident which occurred about this time.

Leacock had shown more than passing interest in Hodgins since he, after graduation, had written a humorous guidebook entitled *So This Is Quebec.* Not long after the publication of this effort, Hodgins, then a professor at Macdonald College, Ste. Anne de Bellevue, undertook to edit an anthology to be called *Some Canadian Essays.* Without Leacock, of course, this would not have been an anthology. Hodgins therefore telephoned for an appointment. When, eventually, he entered Leacock's Arts building office, there were two other visitors. But they could wait, said the professor.

Hodgins takes up the story:

"Which of my gems do you think of including in your anthology?"

The piece I had selected was an article entitled *The Decline of the Drama,* which had been one of a syndicated series he had later expanded into one of his annual volumes. When I told him of my choice, he asked if I had a copy of it with me as he couldn't recollect how the thing went.

I gave him the copy I'd made, and he began reading it to himself. That he enjoyed what he was reading was evident from the grin that spread over his face. But it was too good to enjoy *solus.* He began reading it aloud to the three of us present; then, rising and taking an oratorical stance, he finished by declaiming it in ringing tones.

"My God," he exclaimed, "that's good stuff, isn't it?"

Well, of course, it *was*; so he had no argument from us.

"And about permission . . ." I began.

"Certainly you can put it in your book," he said heartily. "It's a textbook, isn't it?"

"Yes—one of Nelson's *Teaching of English* series."

"Why, you're doing me a favor. Just imagine: Little Mary comes home from school and says to Mother, 'Ma, who is this Stephen Leacock who wrote such a funny piece in our schoolbook?' Her mother says, 'Mary, a big girl like you doesn't know who Stephen Leacock is! You ought to be ashamed of yourself. I'll get you a whole set of his books for Christmas.' "

Leacock explained to Hodgins that the syndicate would have to be consulted about permission to publish and that he would write them immediately. In fact, he scribbled a note then and there, pointing out, "otherwise I sometimes forget."

A fortnight passed without any word. Hodgins wrote to the professor to enquire about the delay. Back came the Hodgins letter with Leacock's reply scrawled in the margin: "And a good reason, too! I've just found my letter in my coat pocket. However, this time I *have* mailed it."

For years Leacock had been putting off what he knew would be a labor of love—writing a book about Dickens. As long ago as 1928 he had told some of his students, off the record, that he proposed to work on a serious account of the novelist's impact on America. More pressing matters intervened, until in 1933 he set to work with determination; in an amazingly short space of time *Charles Dickens, His Life and Work* came to the market. Though his admiration for the Victorian writer fell only a little short of idolatry, Leacock's ingrained moral sense shone through the mists of adoration, so that he could view with cool objectivity the man himself, the while lavishing often indiscriminate praise on the artist. As in *Mark Twain*, the professor's appraisal of his subject dealt largely in broad conclusions and surface judgments.

The power and influence of Dickens' writing had never ceased to fascinate Leacock. Ever since the short study in the 1916, *Essays and Literary Studies*, the Canadian, who never managed completely to overcome his own Victorian roots, had discussed, lectured on or written about various aspects of Dickens' character and work. Now he had a good deal to say about his hero's shabby conduct in the domestic sphere, though the views expressed shot off at curious tangents. He could not condone Dickens' behavior towards his wife, but he paid no attention whatever to the writer's mistress. Instead, Leacock gave himself over to such blind statements as "In him was nothing of the philanderer, the Lothario, the Don Juan," and "In all the records of his comings and goings there are no surreptitious pages." This was nonsense, and Leacock must have known it to be so.

But his *Charles Dickens*, after all, bore the stamp of a personal document rather than that of a detached biography. Leacock made no bones about his bias. However ill researched, the book contained some shrewd observations, even though the author placed too much emphasis on the part that humor played in Dickens' novels. His praise for *A Christmas Carol* was of course entirely expected, since he himself had made the theme his own in a half-dozen or so little essays. In concert with many other critics, Leacock found *Hard Times* hard to take, generally dismissing it as a waste of time. He may or may not have heard of a colleague's assessment of *Hard Times*, that this novel was "the best of Dickens since it is the shortest."

Today one does not go to Leacock for a profound understanding of Charles Dickens' private life or public performance. His *Charles Dickens*, however, like his Twain treatment, has the virtues of a sympathetic and informed mind.

Having concluded a highly active twelve months, Leacock was suddenly confronted with a totally saddening event. As 1933 drew to its close so, too, did the remarkable life of Sir Arthur Currie, affectionately referred to by many an undergraduate as "old guts and gaiters." At fifty-eight he wasn't old, although he had aged markedly throughout the previous four years. The cause lay not in himself so much as with a man previously unknown to him. The latter had in the late twenties published an allegation that Sir Arthur, as commander of the Canadian Corps, had malevolently sent troops to their death in France, well aware that the World War I armistice would be concluded within a matter of hours.

The charge, as unsubstantiated as it was cruelly promulgated, understandably cut deep into Currie's big and generous heart. Whatever qualities he may have lacked, integrity was not one of them.

To clear his name, Sir Arthur considered recourse to the courts. Close friends, Leacock among them, advised the beloved McGill principal to avoid such a course, to let the hue and cry die a natural death. On several occasions during their almost weekly informal chats, Sir Arthur and his professorial companion reviewed the choices of action. Finally, the portly ex-general made the decision to sue.

The case, heard in a small courtroom in the town of Port Credit, Ontario, became a cause célèbre in 1928—long-drawn-out and venomous at times. Judgment was found in favor of Sir Arthur, who won nominal damages. To deny that this was a Pyrrhic victory was to have no notion of the killing personal experience of the already heartbroken plaintiff.

With a stern sense of duty, Currie carried on, the impassive outward appearance a very inaccurate reflection of his inner feelings. He even found occasion to visit the Far East on official business. Following his return to McGill, Leacock jokingly asked him if, while in Honolulu, Sir Arthur had happened to witness the hula-hula girls in action. Indeed, the principal had seen them. With ponderous seriousness he launched into a stout defence of the beauty and grace of an art then generally regarded in the West as sexy stuff. This contribution to terpsichorean knowledge from a university vice-chancellor made headlines throughout the continent.

The tribulations of 1928, on which were superimposed the gathering administrative worries of the Depression, had steadily taken their toll. On November 30, 1933, Sir Arthur Currie died.

On the day of the state military funeral, there appeared in the columns of the Montreal *Herald* some of the most evocative passages ever to come from Stephen Leacock's pen:

It is as a great soldier that the world at large mourns General Currie today. It is right that it should be so. His great achievement was in arms. Those who know tell us that he was one of the great generals of the war; and that if the war had continued, his record, scarcely more than begun, would have placed him among the great captains of the ages.

But there are those of us who were not privileged to know him in this wider horizon. Our memory of him is that of his thirteen years as our principal at McGill. There he sat in his college office room, ready and accessible to all of us. Beside him was his pipe with plenty of strong tobacco and plenty of strong language to keep it burning.

There was a man! I have known many college principals and presidents, —a poor lot most of them, with a few brave exceptions here and there. But there was never one to match up to General Currie. College presidents, as a lot, must bow to the rich and fawn for benefactions. Not so General Currie. He thought no more of a plutocrat than of a ninepin. College presidents must be careful what they say and how they say it. Not so General Currie. He said what he thought and he said it in his own way —which was a forceful one. He knew some of the strongest words in the language. Nor was there ever such honesty as his.

For General Currie owed no responsibility to any man. For that he looked elsewhere. Never was there a man so deeply religious in the real meaning of the word. He lived, in peace as in war, with the consciousness of the imminence of death. For him life was but a pathway to something else, and he walked the path with a sense of its meaning and its end that never left him for a day. Beside him as he walked was the shadowed curtain of the infinite.

General Currie knew nothing of scholarship in the narrower sense of the term. His dusty, shabby professors were always a sort of mystery to him. He never could quite understand whether they were researching or loafing. When he first came to us, he imagined that the professors were always buried in the library, each lecture planned and prepared like Vimy Ridge.

Later on he was a little disillusioned. "Some of these gentlemen," he said, only that was not the name he used for them; he had a simpler one, "don't research at all." They were like hens who wouldn't lay. But disillusioned or not he was unfailing in the devotion of his leadership.

We never had the place in his heart that he kept for his generals. Nor had we the right to it. His generals were always there in his mind, all nicknamed and labelled, as General Currie loved to name people. Indeed as time went on, we too dropped into our nicknames and labels. No one but General Currie would think of a professor of seventy as "Bill." But he had to have it so. He could not bear a world of idle dignity and pretences.

There were those of us who served under him at McGill to whom there came during his principalship those dark hours that at some time must shadow every human life. And there General Currie was beyond words, —a tenderness of sympathy, an affection for those in distress that no language can present and that no gratitude can repay.

Now it is over. We have laid him to rest. Yet we who served with him at McGill can only hope that somewhere in the sound of the martial music and the measured step of his soldiers, his soul might hear the shuffling feet of his dusty professors, out of step and out of breath, but following him,—as they had been wont to these thirteen years,—as best they could.

The day after the burial of Sir Arthur, Stephen Leacock wrote to his mother:

I send you by this mail *The Herald* with pictures of General Currie's funeral . . . On the Saturday before he was taken ill (which happened on Sunday) I had him to lunch with me at the University Club with 4 others, all his old friends. . . . It was the last thing he went to: after the lunch we drove up with his wife and son in his car to the football game, and that was the last I saw of him. . . . He was fine and happy that day because I had invited old friends of his. . . .

In the memorial service, I mean the funeral service, the Bishop read prayers, which I enclose. . . . I don't think that they are in the rubric, are they? I think that Bishop Farthing made them up. . . .

I hope to be up for some time at Xmas . . . and Stevie and I will drive

over to Sutton on Xmas morning and see you but not to stay to dinner. . . .
but as I go to Orillia on the 21st., if the roads are good we will drive over
& see you before Xmas, as I have a turkey to bring. . . .

Yr. affec. son,
Stephen Leacock.

It was Agnes Leacock's last Christmas. She died on January 19,
1934. She had entered her ninetieth year a fortnight before her
death.

XVI

Distress Signals

Agnes Leacock must have been a singular person. She had borne herself and her eleven children through testing times, uncomplaining, undemanding. Loyal to a fault so far as her spineless husband was concerned, almost alone she brought up the large family, with wise and loving care. Her piety stood her in good stead.

Stephen Leacock held her dear, fully aware from his youngest days of the burdens imposed upon her and of her adaptability to changing circumstances. Like most of his brothers and sisters, to the end he had shown a sympathetic attentiveness. An omnivorous and critical reader, she never wanted for good books, which Stephen selected and supplied. Not long before her death he had presented her with a life of Cardinal Newman.

Though he was seldom a churchgoer and never openly subscribed to creeds or dogmas, Leacock's childhood grounding in ethical matters, administered by his mother, left its mark. Up to a point Leacock, in his rough way, may be said to have been a religious man in the sense that

> . . . a religious man means a man who lives in the daily consciousness of the transience of life and the imminence of death. Such a feeling carries with it a supreme sense of duty, and a sense of tolerance towards all men. It leaves no time for anger and for hatred. Time is too short.

191

He had said as much of Sir Arthur Currie. But this quotation came from *Lincoln Frees the Slaves*, a book which appeared shortly after his mother's death. Leacock had long been fascinated by the career of the great emancipator, "round whose name had gathered one of the great myths of history." Hero-worshipper that he was, the author nevertheless addressed himself to the business of setting the record straight, as he saw it. Lincoln, he wrote, "is credited with capacities which he never had and with a foresight which he never showed . . . nearly everything about his career is seen in a false light and glorified beyond recognition."

It was not his intention to swell the already overmanned ranks of the debunkers of his day. Leacock simply sought to make the point that, while the great man's political powers had been vastly overrated, he was one of the elect of mankind. To a certain extent Leacock came down on the side of the South; otherwise the respective causes received a fair hearing. There were, as there had to be in Leacock's method of working, the usual number of sweeping generalizations, without any shading or supporting evidence.

For example:

> The red man would not work; he would rather die. The acceptance of death and the scornful tolerance of pain were among the redeeming features of a race whose fiendish cruelty for cruelty's sake forfeited their right to live.
>
> Those who know properly the history of such a tribe as the Senecas—cruel, filthy and cannibal—will harbor no illusions about the "noble red man." But work the red man would not. The black will work when he has to, but not otherwise. The white man cannot stop working.

Fitz Shaw received one of the earliest copies. She apparently had expressed her own views of Lincoln and the slavery question. Leacock inscribed the end papers of her copy thus:

> With sincere apologies to *Mr. Punch* for recalling the form of his match-less poem of 1865, *You! lay a wreath on murdered Lincoln's bier*, etc. . . . .
> > You! undertake to read a Lincoln biography,
> > Without even a working notion of American geography,
> > Who could not possibly define
> > Mason and Dixon's line,
> > For whom a Lincoln is a touring car
> > And Henry Clay the name of a cigar
> > Or Gettysburg a fatal day for France
> > And Robert Lee a Carolina dance!

Yes, even you! But let me first I pray
From certain misconceptions clear the way.
Lincoln was not the same as Washington,
No, he was not the man called Uncle Tom,
Oh, no, his soldiers never called him Stonewall,
The novel is quite wrong you got that from.
Your grandmamma remembers when they hanged him?
I think she's got him mixed with poor John Brown.

What's that you say? It's all come back at once?
How silly to have spoken like a dunce.
Lincoln! Of course, how could one ever pause,
Lincoln! the Hero of the Southern Cause!
Now that you're qualified please take a look
And find your views supported in this book.

Fitz did not hesitate, as Trix would have done, to argue on any subject with the humorist. Such a formidable adversary held no fears for this chirpy good companion. Her sprightliness enlivened many a discussion in the Old Brewery Bay house which her husband had purchased for her use. According to a mutual friend, "Mr. Shaw never liked the house and my information is that he really never stayed there. He preferred a more lively summer holiday and he would go to Bigwinn Inn well north of Orillia that was then owned by his brother, where there were bright lights and entertainment."

Shortly after the Lincoln appreciation, Leacock turned his hand to an anthology, *The Greatest Pages of Dickens.* In between the well-chosen passages from Dickens' work, the professor sandwiched extracts from his biography of his literary hero. This was another manifestation of the "squeeze" policy. Almost simultaneously another Leacock anthology was published. Called simply *Stephen Leacock,* the selections were made by E. V. Knox of *Punch* for inclusion in an English library of humor, and re-entitled *The Perfect Salesman* in the American edition.

At about the same time as these books began to replenish the Leacock treasury in a modest way, another close friend died suddenly in his mid-fifties. Dr. H. M. Little, one of the country's most respected gynaecologists, left a widow and a young family. It was typical of Leacock to take a personal interest at once and to lend a methodical and practical hand.

With the reliable help of René du Roure, Leacock conceived the idea of setting up a French luncheon club, to which all and sundry would be invited and at which only French would be spoken. Mrs. Little, who would supervise the activities, could use her own substantial residence for the purpose. As an added incentive, long-range plans called for a series of special speakers.

Professionally organized and publicized, this little institution carried on without interruption during the winter season for four days each week up until the beginning of World War II. Attendance, including people from the French-speaking population, ranged up to eighty-five guests. Visiting VIPs from overseas were usually roped in to give talks. This was the first organized effort in the Canadian metropolis to spread the word of the French language amongst adult English citizens. Looking back, Mrs. Little's only regret continues to be that the charge for admission and bounteous repast never exceeded one dollar.

Emboldened by this successful departure from his normal routine, against his better judgment Leacock accepted an assignment of a very different order. He signed a contract to do a series of talks on that new-fangled medium which he had so often joshed in print and in fact really hated—radio. Joseph E. McDougall, a bright young advertising agency executive, had talked the professor into it. McDougall had known the humorist before, when, as editor of a Toronto comic magazine, he had printed some of the professor's articles. Now his theory was that Leacock's deep, well-modulated voice, which so entranced his listeners from speaking platforms, made him a "natural" for radio.

The terms of the agreement were, to say the least, a little out of the ordinary. Leacock would read bits and pieces from his books on a weekly variety show (thirteen weeks, provisionally) for two hundred dollars per broadcast. But there was a provision that on the evening of the show Leacock would give a dinner party at his home and then invite all his guests to the studio to sit with him around the microphone as a very special claque.

As Lovat Dickson has written of H. G. Wells, Leacock "had the clever man's need of an audience"; but Leacock needed a large and variegated audience, not just a small group of well-wined and dined admirers. Everything about the drab surroundings defeated the performer, especially "that box on a stick," as he defined the microphone. The formerly unfailing trick of chuckling prior to and during the development of a joke came through the home loud-speakers with disastrous effect. Radio audiences, to whom Leacock had been a stranger in person, quickly concluded that they were listening to a man very pleased with himself without justifying it. They deserted him in waves. Leacock himself very soon realized his unfitness for this sort of thing and asked to be released from his contract after only five shows.

The distressing experience did not affect the Leacock-McDougall relationship, which blossomed into genuine friendship. The younger man often solicited and received good advice from the professor. Joe McDougall cites a sample:

> I once asked Stephen how much I should charge for an article that I had written and with which he was familiar. "Joe," he said, "I have only one rule in these things. When my agent tells me that I am invited to speak before the such-and-such society and asks me what my charge will be, I say to him, 'Harry, find out how much money they have (pause) and don't charge a cent more.' "

The damaging failure as a radio personality—Leacock had sensed a new and abundant source of revenue—was offset in January 1935 by the award of the Mark Twain Medal of the International Mark Twain Society. When Samuel Clemens' centenary celebrations took place at the University of Missouri, Leacock gave the principal speech; the presentation dinner followed at St. Louis.

On his return to Montreal another anniversary awaited him—the first quarter-century of the University Club. He had been not only one of the founding members, but also one of the most consistent contributors to its bar profits. In recognition of both these facts, not to mention his status on the world's stage, Leacock led the list of speakers. The history of this fraternal organization, as he recalled it (standing on a beer keg in the middle of the reading room), revolved entirely about the bar. Speaking extempore he reminded his fellows how well the receipts had been going when World War I broke out and disrupted everything. Many of the two-fisted drinking members disloyally went off to war, leaving him and a few other cronies to support the establishment. The 1914–18 years had been thin ones for the club's ledgers. Then the cessation of hostilities brought victory for the club, too. Most of the guzzlers had come back and resumed their rightful roles as the most important segment of the membership.

Leacock's speechmaking itinerary did not divert his attention from university affairs and from concern over its financial problems. In January he printed privately, marking it "confidential and not for circulation," a four-page pamphlet in which he made known what measures of economy he deemed essential to the continuing fiscal health of McGill. He would, first of all, cut out all subsidies to college athletics. Then he went on:

> Statistics will show that $5,000 worth of us dies each year; with luck, more. . . . Where the senior professor is not far off pension anyway, give him one and compensate the juniors.

These words would come back to haunt him in the near future.

Meanwhile events on the national political scene took a somewhat startling turn when the Conservative Prime Minister, in an era of panacea proliferation, produced a plan for vigorous state action along the lines of Roosevelt's New Deal. Wages, working hours, unemployment insurance, farm credit and marketing were among measures he got through parliament. On the grounds that a Tory could do no wrong, Leacock backed Bennett, stating, "I know where he can get one vote anyway."

Recognizing that a new age required a new view and, to some extent, a regulated society, Leacock had watched the policies being hatched in Washington. In *The McGill News* in 1935 he issued his own warning to any politician within earshot:

> Very naturally the over-obvious solution of socialism—with everybody in the employ of everybody else—is widely advocated. But socialism would merely mean a shift from the frying pan to the fire. Among ideal people it would be ideal. Among real people, it would place us all under the tyranny of a pack of elected bosses—like a city council done large—place us all within the plunder of the crooked, within the laziness of the bums, within the deceit of the interested politician.

By the same token, he conceded that to carry on under the system that suited the industrial world of a hundred years ago would mean in the new world "a forward rush to an inevitable collapse." But any revision of the system must be allowed to go only so far.

"This socialism, this communism, would work only in Heaven where they don't need it, or in Hell where they already have it."

The Prime Minister, with an eye on every possibility in this election year, made a dead set for the professor's active co-operation. However lightly, Bennett consulted Leacock on the drafting of a fresh monetary policy. (In July the Bank of Canada Act was passed, providing for the establishment of a central bank. When Leacock was asked what he thought about it, he quipped: "It will make the rich richer, and give the deserving poor what they deserve.") The humorist received an invitation to contribute a preface to the published radio addresses of the Prime Minister, and he gladly complied.

When the time arrived for the nomination of candidates, Bennett wrote a personal and confidential letter:

> Dear Stephen Leacock:
> A number of our friends are extremely anxious that you should permit your name to be placed before the Conservative convention in the constituency in which you make your summer home. I need hardly say that I am thoroughly convinced that you could render very conspicuous service to Canada in the next Parliament. Your wide knowledge, your great reputation, and your disinterested approach to problems affecting the welfare of the country could not but be of the utmost value. Won't you favorably consider this matter, and thereby give great satisfaction not only to those who know you in the community in which you live, but to the thousands who have read your books with pleasure, as well as to one who subscribes himself, with high esteem and regard,
> R. B. Bennett.

Stephen Leacock, doubtless flattered, did not take the hook. He was in his sixty-fourth year and disinclined to branch into an unrewarding field, with its guaranteed distraction from a full writing and teaching schedule. How he declined is not known. There is no record of his reply. What little consolation was to be salvaged from the Bennett government's whopping defeat at the polls the next October lay in the thought that the professor might well have gone down with his friend. It must also have occurred to him that to have performed in the bear pit of practical politics would have been intolerable to one who repeatedly deplored the "great dearth of honesty among public men."

Not that Leacock was always honest with himself. A former student, who rose to high prominence in the public service of Canada, remembers a revealing incident which he still refers to as a shocking "let-down."

Sydney D. Pierce, a graduate in law, had found a Depression job on *The Gazette* in Montreal. One day he received a call from Leacock. Would Pierce come to the house to discuss an important matter? Pierce went, to learn that the chair of political science at Dalhousie University, Halifax, Nova Scotia, had become vacant. Leacock wished to recommend Pierce for the position.

Frankly surprised, Pierce wanted to know exactly what was involved.

"Oh, constitutional law, political science and related subjects."

"But I've never taken such courses and wouldn't be fitted for the post. Besides, the opening of term is only two weeks off."

"Oh," Leacock shrugged, "I myself am never more than two weeks ahead of my own students in my preparation. Take these books"—indicating a small pile on the table—"read 'em over and accept the appointment."

Pierce took Leacock's advice. He soon regretted it. He knew he was not adequately fitted for the job and he knew that the students to whom he was lecturing knew it. In a few months he asked the university to relieve him of the appointment.

It was a disillusioning experience for the former student of Leacock and he has regretted the whole episode ever since. Looking back on it, he says sadly: "It reflected little credit on Leacock, or me."

It was the tragedy of Stephen Leacock that he always tried to do too much, too quickly. Something had to suffer in the process. He didn't. His work did. He had walked out on his mother in a rage when she had told him so. Perhaps he had known that she was right.

With the winding up of the 1935 spring term, the university staff learned that the board of governors' hunt for a new principal had concluded. Anyone following in Currie's footsteps was bound to be appraised with a very critical eye by the professoriate and student body.

Dr. Arthur Eustace Morgan, who would take up his duties in the autumn, was an Englishman of the old-school-tie breed. He had been selected, the senior governor triumphantly reported, only "after we had combed the United Kingdom with a finetooth comb." When, later on, Leacock had one or two unpleasant brushes with the gentleman, the humorist remarked audibly: "And you know what you get when you resort to a finetooth comb."

To his dying day Stephen Leacock condemned A. E. Morgan for what happened next. So have thousands of others, in and out of McGill, who listened to the professor or read the gossip columns. However, it is now clear that Morgan was never associated with the decision to retire Leacock at the age of sixty-five. He could not have been. The step was taken at a meeting of the board of governors in June. Morgan did not become principal and vice-chancellor until September of that year. The facts came to light for the first time during some research shortly before this biography went to press.

The finance committee of the governors, it transpires, had been looking into the general university situation for some time. Now they were forced to the conclusion, as indeed Leacock himself had been in January, that many economies must be effected, including retirement of several senior members of the staff. Among these senior members was Stephen Leacock, who, in accordance with the decision reached by the board of governors, would have to retire in May 1936.

When word of this decision reached *The Montreal Star*'s David Macfarlane (McGill was his perennial beat), he went to see the fuming departmental head. He caught up with him in the main hall of the Arts building.

"What have you to say, sir?"

Leacock glared at the reporter, paused, then, whirling about, gruffly ordered: "Follow me."

Head down, the professor bulled his way through the crowd towards the second-floor stairway, looking neither right nor left, and certainly not at Macfarlane.

Grunting up the steps, he began to chuckle quietly to himself. The chuckle increased as he neared the office, which he entered and in which his right-hand man, John Culliton, sat at work.

Leacock broke into a laugh as he reached for a sheet of paper, sat down, scribbled something, and tossed it across to Culliton, who emitted a hearty "Haw, haw."

To the reporter, handing him the paper, Leacock exclaimed "Print *that* in *The Star*."

The statement read:

I have plenty to say about the governors putting me out of the university, but I have all eternity to say it in. I shall shout it *down* to them.

Such a nice euphemistic way of telling bosses to go to hell was bound to win wide newspaper coverage. This did—world-wide.

Leacock did not let it rest at this. The fight continued. He firmly believed, along with everybody else, that the new broom had begun to sweep months before it reached McGill. While the dozen others who faced the same fate remained philosophically humble, Leacock bellowed. The situation when the new principal and the humorist came face-to-face did not improve things. Leacock behaved badly. He spoke (as he had written) a lot of rot about being dismissed because of his "senility." Dr. Morgan explained in a letter that retirement at sixty-five would in future be mandatory, adding undiplomatically, "although it is true that the resolution of the governors reserves the right in very exceptional cases to extend that period."

Thus Leacock was told that he was not "very exceptional," as he indubitably felt himself to be. This simply added more fuel to the flames.

An exchange of letters between the departmental head and Sir Edward Beatty, the chancellor, served only to exacerbate matters. A would-be conciliatory note from the CPR president could have done without this passage: "For yourself, I am afraid I have no sympathy. You have had a full life and achieved fame. Beyond that I do not see what reward any man can obtain."

News agencies kept on carrying stories of the fuss. Leacock saw to that, with his spoken and written references to senility and backstabbing. It was an unbelievable display of childish petulance. He himself in January had raised the possibility of just such a course. In June, when it affected him, he played a loud and discordant tune.

Having fired several broadsides to no avail, Leacock realized that he had to preserve some sort of surface calm to make another year at McGill bearable for all concerned. He cut his cloth accordingly. But it was no use. Morgan—"a cold fish," in the words of the principal's secretary—went on causing friction. "Frenzied friction," the humorist confided to a colleague.

Morgan misread the temper of the graduates' community in the course of a tour of the West, when, curiously, he took credit for having "rid the university of professors who prided themselves on wearing torn gowns"—thereby reinforcing the myth Leacock had created about him.

McGill men and women, present undergraduates and graduates, shared the belief that the humorist's services ought to have been retained on a full-time, if altered, scale, possibly in the role of a public relations figure.

His self-respect badly dented, Leacock's greater worry was loss of income. The board of governors declared a pension based on half the average annual salary earned over the last five years. This amounted to $2,750, an amount which was a mere drop in the bucket of his total annual revenue, even reduced as this had been in recent years to about $14,000.

Principal Morgan's tenure of office lasted less than two years. Incapable of adjusting to North American university methods, nonetheless he enjoyed the confidence of the undergraduates. This understanding of youth proved itself after he returned to England, when he organized and directed the whole physical training program of the Royal Air Force in World War II.

With one more college year ahead of him, Leacock set about making plans for the department he had headed since 1908. His recommendations to Morgan, couched in rather paternal terms, were accepted and implemented.

Fretfully the professor prepared to leave belatedly for Old Brewery Bay and a summer of discontent. Contemplation of an assured future designation as professor emeritus did nothing to salve his hurt ego.

Leacock had once explained the derivation of emeritus—"e" from the Latin meaning "out"; "meritus" from the Latin meaning "He ought to be."

It seemed funny at the time. It was no longer so.

A depressed spirit received a temporary lift at this time, however, when the mail brought a letter from India. The writer signed himself Private P. Fitzharris, 2nd battalion, Argyll and Sutherland Highlanders, Rawalpindi, Punjab. The soldier recounted how he had come upon a copy of Leacock's *Frenzied Fiction*. He found it on the floor of an abandoned hut in a village "some forty miles into Tribal Territory where we were raiding a stronghold of the Mohmands. I never knew you existed. I thought W. W. Jacobs was the only author who could make me laugh. You beat him."

Proof that a spark of fun still lurked in Leacock lay in his statement to a newspaper reporter that he had cabled the commanding officer of the Argyll and Sutherland Highlanders at Rawalpindi as follows:

> Stop raiding the tribe and ask them if they can use a first-class economist, prophesy included.

XVII

Paradise Lost

Brooding midst his hens and other Old Brewery Bay livestock on his impending retirement, Leacock found little to gloat over in his accumulated personal correspondence.

The mail awaiting his attention in the summer of 1935 contained a rejection slip from a U.S. magazine editor, who contended that "the piece, while funny on the surface, would be regarded by readers as unjustifiably guying the hapless state of delinquent boys." *Vogue* turned down a submission because it was "dull" and because it employed "out-of-date slang." For the seventh consecutive month a Montreal orthodontist rendered a bill amounting to several hundred dollars for dental work on Stephen, Jr., with a demand to "please settle this account." An obtuse friend had written from England that an Oxford don had told him, "Leacock is never funnier than when writing seriously about economics." And then there were those exchanges between Leacock and Granny.

Granny was Mrs. R. B. Hamilton, Leacock's mother-in-law and sister of Sir Henry Pellatt. Pellatt once exultantly proclaimed that he had gone through a couple of fortunes. One of them was squandered on the architectural oddity in Toronto which he called Casa Loma, a would-be Italian-style castle, which has been described by Bruce West in *Around Toronto* as "a mixture of 17th century

203

Scotch baronial and 20th Century Fox."

Well-to-do herself, Mrs. Hamilton's will had provided for her daughter, Trix. Stephen, Jr., was now the legatee. What Stephen, Senior, wanted to arrange was that his son could come into his inheritance right away.

"If anything goes wrong with my money, and a lot of it has gone already . . ." he wrote Granny. The father feared that so long as Sir Henry went on spending high, wide and handsome, Mrs. Hamilton's own wealth stood in jeopardy. Every time Granny showed signs of coming to an agreement with her son-in-law, either her lawyer demurred or Pellatt managed to change her mind. Leacock persisted. He offered to look after Mrs. Hamilton for the rest of her life if she would meet his wishes. The protracted and frequently caustic correspondence came to an end with nothing settled, though the quarrels were patched up and Granny often lived at Old Brewery Bay. When she died, there was not much left in the kitty.

A more cheerful communication came from Louis Kon, a well-known Montrealer, Communist party member and loyal Stalinist. Kon conveyed the news that a selection of Leacock's writings, including "My Financial Career," had appeared in the U.S.S.R. satirical magazine, *Krokodil*, published by *Pravda*. Kon enclosed a copy of the issue.

A prefatory comment read:

> In his humor, very often exceedingly fine, there is a great deal of sarcasm and irony regarding his contemporaries. . . . We cannot call Stephen Leacock a left-writer, as he is considered at times by the bourgeois critics of America. . . . nevertheless he protests against the American standard of thoughts, art and literature. That's why we think that it will be useful for a Soviet reader to become acquainted with the stories of Leacock.

The humorist replied to Kon that he was "pleased and flattered," and that "it will give me a chance to learn Russian over again." In a follow-up letter, Leacock expressed the hope that he might be able to get his hands on additional copies of *Krokodil*, for which "I will gladly pay in roubles, or in the bonds of the Old Russian government, of which I still hold 8,000."

But the Kon incident revived his flagging spirits only temporarily. Gloomily Leacock reached a decision which he hastily committed to print. He prepared a form letter which he distributed to his agent and various organizations in Canada and the U.S. In it he announced that "I am giving up lecturing and planning to preserve the silence which is golden." The only exceptions would be those engagements to which he had already committed himself. As an afterthought, he tacked on a sentence to the effect that "I hope never to speak publicly in Montreal again." In his *Mark Twain* he had declared that "no one likes lecturing except those who can't do it." But this was not the reason for his threatened withdrawal from public platforms. He was sulking. He had by no means got rid of his huff over his treatment at the hands of McGill's board of governors. Misguidedly, he continued to believe that they had merely rubber-stamped a malicious scheme thought up by Dr. Morgan.

Clearly Leacock had made up his mind to dislike the new principal. In the fall he returned for his last session as chairman of the department in sullen mood. Even his classes could sense that the professor obviously had a lot on his mind.

Edward F. Sheffield, professor of higher education at the University of Toronto, recalls an experience in this autumn term:

> I dropped into a Leacock class just to see what was going on. I was not registered for the course (European economic history), but I was doing what many students did in those days. On this occasion there could not have been more than twenty students in the class, and Leacock arrived late. When he came into the room, he was wearing his tattered, black-turned-green gown, a portion of which trailed behind him. He reached with his right hand for the trailing piece, threw it over his left shoulder as if donning a toga, and then peered at us over his spectacles.
>
> Without a word he turned to the blackboard and in a large scrawl wrote: "Write all you know about France." Then he shuffled to the door, turned, looked at us once more over his spectacles and said: "If you get anything on this, stick it under my door." At this point he left.

Unlike the indulgent Leacock of old? Of course! He acted as though he had had the stuffing knocked out of him. But he pulled himself together for the balance of the academic year—so far as his students were concerned, at any rate.

Meanwhile, despite his constant travelling and despite everything else that had occurred to sear his soul, Leacock had been steadily at work on a book which he hoped would be received as an informed, even definitive, study of the warp and woof of humor. When this book, *Humor: Its Theory and Technique*, went on sale shortly before Christmas, *The Montreal Star* critic bluntly observed: "The idea of anybody seriously attempting to teach anybody else how to be a humorist is something too decidedly ghastly to contemplate with equanimity." There was something to be said for this point of view. Leacock seemed to be posing as a leading spokesman for this particular craft, when in fact he had hardly produced anything of an outstanding nature for a considerable length of time—*Winnowed Wisdom* in 1926, as a matter of fact. He had said in *Mark Twain* that "the truth is, what Mark Twain wrote after 1900 is chiefly interesting because Mark Twain wrote it." If the date were changed from 1900 to 1926, the same truth could now be applied to Leacock.

Humor: Its Theory and Technique approached its uncrystallized subject with high aplomb. From the primitive to the present, the author ranged over the history of mankind's desire for laughter and the various methods which had been devised to produce it. As the arch absurdist, for the most part he left himself out. The examples and samples cited involved the work of others, principally Twain and Dickens, on whom he was prepared to lavish praise ad nauseam. But, as J. B. Priestley would note in *The Bodley Head Leacock* about Leacock's books on humor, his practice was better than his theory: "his own humor was so much superior to his account of other men's."

The Canadian called this work "a book of discovery," when the word should have been rediscovery. Once more he paraded before his readers his conviction that without a broad and kindly outlook humor is impossible, whereas he himself had given the lie to that. S. J. Perelman, who acknowledges Leacock as one of his early influences, would say in a later generation: "Generally speaking, I don't believe in kindly humor. I don't think it exists."

This voyage of exploration with its sentimental and sometimes perceptive record of joys past, conjured up, with a pre-McLuhanesque feeling of doom, a picture of the man of the future:

> Mostly he gets his news through his earflaps. He doesn't read much, because he can fix in little radio books to his ear-plugs. He can look at books only if they have pictures, queer pictures all distorted out of the actual. But he never reads alone. It frightens him. He has to turn on something to relieve him.

Were this to come true, then what would avail, in Jesse Bier's phrase, "the wholesale theories of practitioners of comic literature?" And Bier goes on in his *The Rise and Fall of American Humor*: "The theories in themselves, from Josh Billings, through Bret Harte, Leacock, Mark Twain to James Thurber, W. C. Fields and E. B. White, are either innocuous or particularist. They may point out, in passing, the 'caustic' quality of our native style, or the interminable leg-pulling that goes on, or the ominous character of our comedy, or the dangerous terror and pain it deals in, or the truth it hotly strives for. But they argue from the experience of special careers, which must be surveyed and judged as part of a larger development."

At least Leacock took this "larger development" in a gargantuan stride. After reviewing the whole sweep of humor, he looked at life in large perspective. "Seen through an indefinite vista," he concluded in *Humor: Its Theory and Technique*, "it ends in a smile," and:

> In this, if what the scientists tell us is true, it only offers a parallel to what must ultimately happen to the physical universe in which it exists. Matter, we are told, is not matter in the real or solid sense. It is only a manifestation of force or energy, seeking to come to rest. An atom is not an atom in the sense of being a particle or thing. It is just an area inside whose vast empty dimensions, unmatched forces, stresses and strains are trying to come together and neutralize one another. When they do this—at some inconceivable distance of time—then the Universe ends, finishes—there is nothing left for it but nothingness. With it goes out in extinction all that was thought of as matter, and with that all the framework of time and space that held it, and the conscious life that matched it. All ends with a cancellation of forces and comes to nothing; and our Universe ends thus with one vast, silent, unappreciated joke.

On top of several newspaper and periodical articles, two more books followed in quick succession in the winter and spring of 1936—*The Greatest Pages of American Humor* and *Hellements of Hickonomics*. Of the former, reviewing it at length in the *New York Times*, Robert Van Gelder wrote:

> There are several kind remarks which might be made about Stephen Leacock's *The Greatest Pages of American Humor*, but most of them would be fundamentally insincere, and even the author would not believe them. For Mr. Leacock must have realized some time ago that in setting out to write this book, he tackled one of the most difficult tasks open to

a writer, that to turn out a really good book on humor, hard work and conscientiousness are not enough. One must be inspired.

Van Gelder didn't think Leacock had been inspired and characterized the work as "an embalmer's job." But the critic rejoiced that the Canadian remained an enthusiastic supporter of the reputation of O. Henry. "In a town," he added, "where Saroyan can become a rage, an O. Henry is badly needed, if only to keep the balance straight."

As for *Hellements of Hickonomics*, the author rated this as the prime favorite of his entire lighter output. Surely there must have been a defensive complex at work here. Today he would have the utmost difficulty in finding support anywhere for such a priority. In the preface he said that the book represented his farewell to economics. Leacock excused the preponderant verse treatment of various economic theories and policies with the argument that experience has taught, "we are moved and stimulated to understanding far more by our imagination than by our intellect: more even than by our self-interest."

While the editor of *Poetry* Magazine solemnly weighed the book and found the paradoxes "brilliant but not luminous," by no definition could the professor be ranked higher than a minor versifier. The material in *Hellements*, both in its conception and execution, could only be classed as doggerel with a message—e.g., the tax-burdened citizen:

> Look at his pitiful Overcoat,
> Pinned and fastened about his Throat,
>   Jimmy has got no shirt.
> They taxed it off him, shred by shred,
> Taxed it down to the latest Thread
>   To the very, very end.
> Each time that Industry needed a Spurt
> They tore off a Section of Jimmy's Shirt
>   For a textile dividend.

Certain bankers and classical economists came in for rough handling, but the little volume amounted pretty much to a campus caper.

Hellements may have been a farewell to economics: a pleasanter leave-taking loomed. A small committee waited upon the professor in his Arts building office to ask him to make no engagement for the evening of May 4, 1936. Some friends would like him to be their dinner guest. Knowing what his memory was like, they urged him to take careful note of the date. This he did, then and there, in his diary, remarking, "I grow more and more forgetful these days."

If a letter on file at the Stephen Leacock Home is any proof, the humorist had not overstated the case. He had written to Dr. Gerhard Lomer, the university librarian, to whom he was always sending missives:

> I wish you would send me a copy of G. Ball's *Mathematical Recreations*(?),—if it is called *Mathematical Recreations*, and if it is G. Ball. If not, please send me the book I am trying to think of.

But Leacock did not forget May 4. Complete in a rumpled boiled shirt, with black tie askew, his iron-grey hair making a rare pretense of having been in contact with a comb, he turned up at the Ritz-Carlton Hotel. In the ballroom he was greeted by a hundred and fifty former students (and the spirits of two hundred others in various parts of the world who had contributed).

Like the Irishman who said he'd keep away from it if he knew the town where he was going to die, Stephen Leacock skipped his last lecture at McGill. Instead he gave it that night to his old students.

Save for a few faint references to the recent retirement hubbub— "the time came when the college said it had heard our lectures so often that it would pay us not to give any more"—Leacock rose to the occasion. Sepulchrally he said he had entitled his talk "Paradise Lost," not Milton's, but his:

> This is my last lecture, gentlemen—for I insist on calling you so. I have kept it purposely for you—for you, my old pupils who have had so many from me in the last thirty-five years that one more cannot hurt you. The harm is already done, and you carry, on all the familiar faces which I see about me, that stamp which is set on all my students—an irremovable look of resigned despair.

He went on to extol the environment of a good university, with "the ideal professor—careless and even comic in his dress, gullible to the edge of imbecility, an easy mark for the idler spirits of the class, but carrying somewhere within him that higher idealism lifted above life, that in the end endears him."

The humorist was presented with two red morocco-bound sets of his own works, comprising forty volumes each, one set for the university library, the other for his son. In accepting the gifts, he said:

> May I say that I appreciate more than I can tell you your gift of a set of my works to the college library and of another set to my son. I am told that you were in some doubt whether to let it be Shakespeare's works, or my own. You have chosen wisely. I have not only written more than Shakespeare, but what I have written is worth more. Shakespeare's books can be had anywhere at fifteen cents each, while mine run from a dollar up.

McGill's chancellor, Sir Edward Beatty, sat next to the guest of honor. Principal Morgan was conspicuous by his absence. Sir Edward (whom Leacock considered to be "the Chief Justice who passed sentence on the Senility Gang") gave his blessing:

> Above all, I prefer to think of Dr. Leacock as a man ,of his kindliness, for his inspiring influences—as a man we love and respect and whom, without exception, we are all sorry to see leave the halls of McGill.

So much for lip-homage.

Three weeks later Leacock stood on the Convocation platform to receive from Sir Edward the honorary degree of Doctor of Laws, the citation for which read in part:

> While his published works in the field of economics have, on his own admission, "produced international complications of considerable gravity," his happy labors in another sphere have resulted in convulsions of a different order and eclipsed the gravity of nations.

An outburst of applause and cheering from an audience of two thousand acclaimed the stooped veteran. There were cries of "Speech, speech!" But Stephen Leacock stood silent and just smiled.

He had a good reason to smile over the thoughtfulness of others not yet prepared to write him off as finished academically. In an editorial the *New York Times* saw benefits for any American university which might employ Leacock "to smoke at its post-graduate students," or create a post of resident wit or satirist.

The University of British Columbia offered a professorial appointment in its department of economics. Leacock wrote that he would very much like to go to Vancouver, but he must bow to the pressures of his literary work; in any case, he could not consider returning to educational activities. Similar reasons were given when he turned down an attractive proposition to tour Australia and New Zealand, which he had last visited a quarter of a century before.

An editor on Fleet Street added his voice to those who felt that Leacock should not be allowed to fade away without some special attention for further service. The English journalist stood ready to back a plan to bring the professor emeritus back to his native land. "He would be welcomed."

To this invitation Leacock replied: "Thank you, Mother England, I don't think I'll 'come home.' I'm 'home' now. Fetch me my carpet slippers from the farm. I'll rock it out to sleep right here."

He knew why he felt this way:

> There's another reason for not wanting to leave Canada for England. I'd hate to be so far away from the United States. You see, with us it's second nature, part of our lives, to be near them. Every Sunday morning we read the New York funny papers, and all week we read about politics in Alabama and Louisiana, and whether they caught the bandits that stole the vault of the National Bank, and—well, you know American news— there's no other like it. And the Americans come-and-go up here, and we go-and-come down there, and they're educated just as we are and know all about kilowatts, but quit Latin at the fourth declension. Our students go and play hockey with their students and our tourists going out meet their tourists coming in. . . . We are "sitting pretty" here in Canada. East and West are two oceans faraway; we are backed up against the ice cap of the Pole; our feet rest on the fender of the American border, warm with a hundred years of friendship. The noise and tumult of Europe we scarcely hear: not for us the angers of the Balkans, the weeping of Vienna and the tumults of Berlin. Our lot lies elsewhere: shovelling up mountains, floating in the sky to look for gold, and finding still the Star of the Empire in the West.

As it transpired, Canada itself—or, more correctly, a few of its proselytizing citizens—found something for Stephen Leacock to do. The man who announced he would never lecture again was talked into doing just that, and on a highly organized basis. Sir Edward Beatty had told him: "I still believe your powerful voice and equally powerful pen should be used to combat the inaccurate and loose-thinking which the more vocal members of your profession are indulging in." To Beatty and his ilk the new Social Credit movement and the Co-operative Commonwealth Federation, though poles apart politically, were "loose-thinkers" and therefore dangerous.

So it happened, though a self-styled "old man," Leacock decided to go West. "If I'm too senile to lecture in the East, I'll go West. There no one ever gets old and the good die young."

The Montreal Star's Lord Atholstan, the publisher who had commissioned *Sunshine Sketches* for his newspaper in 1911, arranged with Leacock to supply twelve articles about his trip .

One purpose of the tour would be to discuss agrarianism and financial policies in western Canada. It was also the professor's hope to try to make a contribution towards harmonizing the East with the West, a Herculean task at this stage. The stricken prairies were crying out for help from a central government which, in the eyes of Westerners, was indifferent to their plight.

Another purpose of the visit concerned McGill graduates. "All across the continent where there are no McGill Societies, I will found them—the same work that St. Paul did in England. And when they are founded, I will not say a word about money, but the idea is they will loosen up at the sight of me." The principal reason for the trip, however, was to get material for another book, if for no other end than to prove that he was not yet decrepit.

With the approval of the McGill authorities, his twenty-one-year-old son would take time out from his lectures to accompany his father. ("Stephen Junior, who had been warned in time, studies English and history but no political economy, and says that he knows nothing of Adam Smith except that he wrote Uncle Tom's Cabin.")

On November 25, 1936, the pair entrained at Montreal for an intensive five-province, six-week-long schedule. Leacock's plan "to preserve the silence which is golden" had been pigeonholed.

XVIII

"Adventure Brave and New"

Stephen Leacock's "state of quasi-semi-retirement," as Sir Edward
Beatty put it, took on the character of a triumphal progress as he
toured western Canada. In retrospect it must be accounted an affair
of genuine importance, to himself and his country.

On the darkening international stage Prime Minister Mackenzie
King, in his perfected role of appeaser, had gone East to plead
before the League of Nations against the use of force as a means of
securing peace. In his own way, King ("Canada's Man of Rubber,"
as a recent biographer called him) had the country's unity in mind.
So had Leacock, now playing the part of interpreter between East
and West in the nation itself. Everywhere he went he indicated the
necessity of the re-union and re-confederation of the country, and
referred to the prevailing attitude of the provinces: Nova Scotia
weeping regretfully into the Bay of Fundy over her irrevocable
union, the French Canadians in Quebec harping for a *petite nation*
of their own, the harassed Middle West making its own paper
money, and British Columbia turning a disdainful back with a
"come hither" look towards the Pacific.

The Social Credit did not worry him particularly, which must
have worried his capitalist friends back in Montreal. Rather,
thought Leacock, what were called the "funny money boys" could

213

not make headway towards catastrophe or social upheaval in the face of deeply rooted British traditions. Throughout the trip he virtually ignored the Co-operative Commonwealth Federation, which was to become a political force, if not numerically, certainly by its influence on the two old parties.

His wit tempered the chauvinism which colored his principal speeches. But humor took command completely in the dozen lectures he reserved for gatherings of McGill graduates. These heard him discuss everything from the history of English literature to "The value of Imbecility in Education." At one point he reported to the graduates' headquarters in Montreal:

> I struck also one or two more doubtful cases of graduation from McGill. The barber who cut my hair called me "Professor." He said, "I'll trim it a little full over the ear, eh, professor?" and I said, "Yes, either that or trim the ear." Then, noticing that he had called me Professor, I said, "Are you from McGill?" He answered, "Yes, sir. I left in 1913, came right here to Regina, got a chair here in six months and have done fine ever since! Two other boys came here on the same train and have chairs down the street!" That looked fine as academic advancement, three appointments to chairs in one and the same town! But afterwards, I didn't feel so sure, my ears were pretty well shrouded with towels. He may have said "Montreal," and not "McGill."

The letters he wrote to Barbara Ulrichsen and to Fitz Shaw were full of enthusiasm for the open-arms reception accorded him.

From Winnipeg: "It's just like a come-to-Jesus parade. I talked at the Fort Garry Hotel and they said a little before the meeting, 'This is the record for seats except for the Queen of Roumania.' "

From further West; "This beats the Queen of Roumania."

Still later: "The Queen is nowhere."

From Victoria, where he wound up the tour: "I had the most marvellous success here with a talk yesterday on 'Economic Separatism in the Empire.' They laughed and cried: never was anything like it, they said."

But the grinding journey, at once an act of vindication and an act of devotion, had tired him. When the excitement died down, he wrote home: "Please God, I won't have to lecture any more. It's too hard."

Too hard? The pace he set himself on returning to Montreal

would have compelled a man half his years to think twice. He dashed off in jig time the twelve articles on his Western experiences for *The Montreal Star*, which gave them a prominent presentation. Expanding on these, he produced *My Discovery of the West*. This book, which won him the Governor-General's literary prize, displayed remarkable prescience. The professor foretold the future course of Social Credit. It would maintain "a tradition of its origin," but its fundamental preachment would become "a sort of sacred ideal which it is supposed to represent, too holy for current use." What he then had to say about constitutional reform would not begin to be tackled in anything more than political platitudes until well into the 1960s. His observations concerning the relationship of Canada and the United States still remain valid.

Yet there were three more books in the works in 1937. Half-heartedly he had assembled *Funny Pieces: A Book of Random Sketches*, as may be gathered from the preface: "This book in all is so peculiar in character, so fragmentary and so discursive, that I should not dare to have put it together if it were not for the past indulgence of my readers." It was asking a lot of his readers, however previously indulgent. In the same preface Leacock spoke proudly of borrowing an idea from his son, "whose work is now appearing in school and college journals."

Funny Pieces revived the controversy over his retirement and that of several other prominent staff members from McGill the previous year. A reviewer in *The Morning Post* of London remarked on this: "Wiser than the governors of that imposing institution, we have no intention of depriving him of his Jestership, believing as we do that humor, like sound wine, improves with age."

Possibly the best demonstration of Leacock's best wit in *Funny Pieces* cropped up in a diverting satire on the diplomatic settlement of international misunderstandings—a dispute between Mr. Hyphen Jones and Mr. Asterisk Brown about the back lane which separated their backyards. Their semi-official communiqués led to grave tension, which was not relieved until an acceptable formula was found. This rings so true that quite likely it had its basis in one of the many little squabbles that the manorial Leacock used to encounter (or cause) amongst the denizens of the Orillia area.

Since the thirties began the humorist had introduced more and more reflections of a serious nature into his annual clowning.

Funny Pieces had its share, including one of the most quoted passages concerning university life. Leacock's ideal professor went like this:

> His class?—you can't keep him out of it. Preparing his lectures?—that's no more work than a lion getting up his appetite. People who do not live in colleges cannot understand the unworldly absorption of the professor's task. Poets talk of the joy of the springtime—of the month of May breaking the hills into green and filling all the air with rapture. The "merry month of May," says the poet. I know a merrier one. Give me the murky month of February, with the snow blowing on the window pane of the classroom, the early darkness falling already and the gaslight bright in the classroom. That and a blackboard, and a theorem, and a professor—the right kind, absorbed, ecstatic and a little silly. Give me that and the month of May may keep its fronds and toadstools as it will.

Other days and other ways, no doubt; but as a once-upon-a-time self-portrait of Stephen Leacock, this would be hard to beat.

Funny Pieces, which also contained a reprint of his tender refusal to return to "Mother England," was followed by a selection of speeches he had delivered on both sides of the ocean. Called *Here Are My Lectures*, and interspersed with trifling anecdotal items, the book testified to the humorist's versatility. But, since these pieces had been written for and were dependent on the author's unique brand of theatrical performance, on the printed page they suffered greatly from the lack of the vital element of spontaneity.

One Canadian critic took a positive stand on *Here Are My Lectures*, however:

> Let Leacock fans know, then, that although his retirement may have somewhat disturbed his spleen, it has not impaired his sense of the ludicrous and unerring aim at the pretentious. His lament is "when people say to me, you'll be able to finish the History of Political Theory, I answer, to hell with it."
> Never mind the political theory, professor.
> Give us some more lectures.

At the behest of a Toronto investment firm, Leacock then turned his attention to an outright promotion job, a consideration of the importance of nickel to Canada in world markets. The monograph forcefully conveyed the nation's pre-eminence as a producer of the metal. (For a quick buck he would do this sort of thing from time to time. A couple of years later, for example, Leacock was commissioned by The Royal Trust Company to produce a pamphlet entitled *Other People's Money*, although this was not published until 1944.)

As he worked unremittingly, others also worked on his behalf. In March President Lowell of Harvard tried to persuade the humorist to deliver the Lowell Institute Foundation lectures. There would be eight, all told, with the topics to be of his own choosing. He gracefully declined. The next month the Royal Society of Canada, from which he had resigned for economic reasons, awarded Leacock the Lorne Pierce medal, in recognition of his great contribution "to the growing reputation of Canadian letters."

At the end of May Principal A. E. Morgan presided at his last McGill Convocation. His resignation had been requested by the board of governors, the same gentlemen who had hailed him on his appointment two years ago as a man of incomparable sterling qualities. His dollar value had apparently been a different matter. Immediately this situation became known, *The McGill Daily* announced a movement on the part of some students to put forward Leacock's name as the next vice-chancellor. The movement died a-borning. Other sources suggested R. B. Bennett, but this idea, too, was dismissed in short order. Eventually the distinguished American Lewis Williams Douglas received the call. Because of the pressure of family business in the United States, Douglas departed with less than twenty-four months service.

It is said that this train of events caused Stephen Leacock to remark: "McGill has established a new two-year course, leading to the degree of ex-principal."

But a sadder parting of the ways took place at Old Brewery Bay in the early summer of 1937. The occasion was the marriage of Barbara Ulrichsen to Donald Nimmo, which meant the end of a decade of dedicated service to her uncle, though she would continue her active interest in him. But Leacock entered into the spirit of things, even building a new trellis outside the house for the occasion. On the day he efficiently stage-managed the ceremony so as to take full advantage of the lovely lakeside setting.

Later in the summer the London publisher of *The Home University Library of Modern Knowledge* wrote to Leacock:

> The index and bibliography have safely arrived in the chocolate box tied together with a pipe-cleaner, which by the odor we approve of both the chocolate and the tobacco. But the office would have appreciated it if you had left a little of each in!

Thus the humorist had shipped the last of the manuscript for *Humor and Humanity*, on which he had been laboring lovingly in between his many other undertakings. The book, of some two hundred and fifty pages, came out in time for Christmas.

The term "introduction" in the subtitle supplied the key to Leacock's intentions. Here was his statement, however simplistic in form, of the root causes and various shapes of humor. Once more he thwacked away at the sublime nature of humor, claiming that the essence of it is human kindliness. However hotly arguable this pronunciamento may have been, the author continued to cling to the theory. "The development of humor was not always and exclusively of a refining character," he admitted, but both the nature and practice of it had kept pace with the general advancement of mankind:

> ... humor goes upon its way, moving from lower to higher forms, from cruelty to horseplay, from horseplay to wit, from wit to the higher "humor of character," and beyond that to its highest stage as humor of life itself. Here tears and laughter are joined, and our little life, incongruous and vain, is rounded with a smile.

Scholastic lint-pickers have missed the real purpose of this modest Leacock work. Since he planned it as a primer-type survey, the author once again assumed the raiment of the pedagogue, talking to his students in homey generalities. His two best chapters, on light verse and humorous poetry, were based on the exemplary teaching method of detecting broad patterns and furnishing illustrative specimens.

Humor and Humanity must be accepted as a very personal document and not anything more than that. Anyone making an academic analysis of it in the hope of finding an explanation of Leacock's own comic devices is bound to be either disappointed or misled.

The most realistic and concise conclusions regarding those devices and Leacock's general approach have been supplied by J. B.

Priestley: "The best of Leacock lies somewhere between—though at a slight angle from—the amiable nonsense of characteristic English humor (e.g., Wodehouse) and the hard-hitting wit and almost vindictive satire of much American humor." It is the "satirical humor of a very shrewd but essentially good-natured and eupeptic man, anything but an angry reformer." Further, Priestley finds that "the Canadian is often a baffled man because he feels different from his British kindred and his American neighbors, sharply refuses to be lumped together with either of them, yet cannot make plain this difference."

As for the humorist himself at this stage, there had been some soul-searching about the probability of his declining powers in the field of funny work. He had even broached the question in a note to René du Roure. Yet, with all his serious writing, he still managed to maintain a flow of light articles to his magazine contacts, meanwhile inflicting migraine on an agent who despaired at the increase of his client's direct dealings with editors and publishers.

Searching for a reason for his prevailing lack of sparkle, and not finding it, he invented one. Admitted in March 1938 to the Royal Victoria Hospital, Montreal, for prostatic surgery (not cancer of the throat as has been erroneously recorded elsewhere), the professor blamed everything on the surgeon, Dr. David W. Mackenzie. Chief of the department of urology, Mackenzie had ordered his famous patient to remain in hospital for a while, if only to relax. In a pencilled missive written in bed, Leacock told a close friend:

> You see, I cry more easily now. David Mackenzie (the best doctor in the world; I wish he could operate on all my friends) has removed my sense of humor,—he said it was inflated and must come out. I said that that might leave me a little too sentimental and he said, yes, but it would do me no harm.

Typically, his convalescence was put to effective use. He gave himself over to preparing the only book he would publish in that year; which may cause the reader to wonder whether maybe Dr. Mackenzie's scalpel had nicked the risible nerve centre. For the chuckles in *Model Memoirs* were widely spaced. Although it was something of an "in" joke—it dealt with some identifiable characters—"The Dissolution of Our Dinner Club" might be regarded as one of the saving graces of the collection. A less felicitous exercise, "All is not Lost!" embodied the latest in a long string of snide references to the fourth estate.

From his earliest days as a public figure, Leacock seemed determinedly set upon some kind of a collision course with the gentlemen of the press. Fortunately for him, they did not respond in kind as a body. In *Frenzied Fiction* and *Moonbeams* either newspapers as an institution or the men who worked on them were among the objects of his condescension. In *My Discovery of England* he resented the pressure of interviews and those who conducted them. A pointed piece in *Short Circuits* spoke petulantly of a news report and, by implication, damned the reporter:

> There! That's the way he does it, as all of us who deal with him are only too well aware. And am I resentful? I should say not. Didn't he say that there was "a capacity audience" when really there were only sixty-eight people; didn't he "punctuate the lecture with applause," and "animate it with keen attention"? . . . What more can a lecturer want?

A conjectural cause of Leacock's attitude is that he took his cue from Charles Dickens, who was affronted by what he called the Rowdy Press of America. In *Martin Chuzzlewit*, for instance, Dickens had plenty to say about their journalistic methods, forgetting that the yellow press had its birth in his native England. Leacock followed suit, though not to the same extent, in viewpoint and performance. As has been noted in Chapter XII—in the incident with the Richmond *News-Leader* reporter—the Canadian humorist concluded that it would be more to his satisfaction if he took matters into his own hands.

On the eve of his tour of the Canadian West, Stephen Leacock mailed a document to every newspaper editor west of the Great Lakes. In it he regretted that "my available time and strength will not permit me to give the Press personal interviews of question-and-answer." Therefore, he enclosed "ample material" on which to base a personal interview. The material, filling eight foolscap pages, covered the itinerary, a biography, notes on the Leacock literary output, copy of an article on U.S. presidential elections, and another in praise of the Canadian West.

At the first stop, in Fort William, the reporters met him anyway. But, wrote Leacock smugly, "I had the interview all ready and merely handed it over. It is far better to write one's own interviews."

And so it went, right across the country.

Shortly after the conclusion of the trip, Leacock went to Watertown, N.Y., to deliver a lecture under the auspices of the Jefferson Country College Women's Club. Frederick H. Kimball, (no relation of Leacock's niece Elizabeth) who was then a young reporter on and today city editor of the Watertown *Times,* has a Leacock manuscript to bear out his story.

Sent to interview the noted visitor, Kimball met him at the train. Leacock told the newspaperman that he did not feel like being interviewed "just now," as he had to finish a murder mystery he had brought with him. He told Kimball to come to the hotel later. The young man returned too soon. "Give me ten minutes," the humorist said, and with that took some sheets of hotel stationery and scribbled what he thought of Mark Twain, Charles Dickens, Watertown itself ("I like it all except its name. Personally, I prefer plain soda with mine."), John Stuart Mill, Washington Irving, U.S.-Canadian relations, and the state of American humor.

Before leaving Kimball asked: "What do Canadians think of the new King George VI?"

"No, not a word about that," Leacock retorted. "You know, the king is a good friend of mine."

In Buffalo, N.Y., another young reporter was assigned to talk to Leacock. The Buffalo *Times* sent Richard Hanser along since he was well acquainted with and admired the humorist's work.

What I chiefly remember is that the interview was painful. Leacock did not act as I had expected a famous humorist to do. He seemed rather heavy and quite vain. He did what no other person I have ever interviewed, before or since, has done: when I took down a remark of his, he would get up and peer at my notes to see that I had it right. This rather put me off and, I must say, made me dislike him.

Also in the thirties, Stanley Handman, of *The Montreal Star,* attended a luncheon meeting at which Leacock was the guest speaker. After the address, the reporter went up to the professor and asked if he could borrow the text of the speech. Leacock agreed readily, warning Handman to be sure to return it.

Back at the office the city editor asked the reporter if the talk had been funny. "No," came the reply, "it's about the gold standard." The city editor snapped, "Then give it three short paras."

When, eventually, Handman took back the text, Leacock remarked: "Your paper didn't think much of my address. Give me the text. I'll show you how to deal properly with an important thing like this."

Ten days later, every newsstand in the city displayed a pamphlet, being Leacock's speech verbatim, and priced at twenty-five cents.

Leacock's disdain for newspapers evidently extended to the *New York Times,* to which for many years he had been a regular contributor and which had always been considerate of him.

In the latter days of 1938 a lady in Brooklyn wrote a flattering letter to Leacock in connection with a humorous article which had appeared in the Sunday magazine of the *Times.* Without delay the humorist sent an acknowledgement in which he deplored at length his treatment by the *Times;* said they always ruthlessly changed his captions, and truncated his material, and that he had been most distressed by the way the *Times* had altered the flavor of his work.

But there were more important matters being reported in the newspapers as 1939 dawned. Hitler had now occupied Austria and the Sudetenland. It appeared only a matter of months before the rest of Czechoslovakia would be doomed. The increasingly bellicose Nazi hysteria dampened the hopes which had been sparked by the signing of the Munich Agreement the previous September. The shadows of war lengthened.

Depressed by what he believed to be the inevitability of a global conflict, Leacock confided to a dinner companion at the club that "the problems of the world are multiplying so fast, it now seems impossible to cope with sinister forces."

And now, no longer with Barbara to take orders and to keep order, he cut another tie with the past. He vacated the comfortable Montreal residence which held so many memories. He moved into the historic old Windsor Hotel. But Leacock could not bring himself to part with his Cotes des Neiges property. That would have constituted a final break, so he rented it. The Windsor would adequately fulfil his city needs during the winter months. Strategically located, it was after all only a short walk to the University Club.

XIX

Three Score and Ten

After he had quit his Montreal house, Leacock's centre of gravity shifted to the shores of Lake Couchiching. Henceforward he would spend the greater part of the year at Old Brewery Bay. By no means, however, did this presage a plan to vegetate. Agile and alert, still swearing like a football coach, the humorist blocked out an agenda for 1939 which included at least one book and the continuation of a successful series of syndicated articles on the foibles of mankind. Lecturing was notably absent from the schedule.

An enticing opportunity to add to his string of honorary degrees reluctantly had to be turned down, since it involved delivering an address. Boston University expressed a wish to confer on Leacock an honorary Doctor of Humanities. It was explained to him that on this occasion he would be expected to address a gathering of alumni. But, once and for all, he had promised himself that he would not lay himself open to the "dismal experience" of speaking in public ever again.

Explaining his inability to participate in "such an honorable and agreeable" affair, Leacock put the blame on his "extremely uncertain" state of health, referring to his "serious operation of last year." In fact, for his years, his health was good, his operation not "serious." These were pretexts to conceal the real reason, which was that

223

he wanted to clear the decks for more writing in order to replenish the domestic treasury. Non-essential interruptions would not be brooked. It had become clear to all in his immediate circle that Leacock had convinced himself that his inner resources were far from being exhausted.

In the twenties the professor, with an amused tolerance, used to make fun of the popular Emile Coué formula, "Day by day, in every way, I am getting better and better." Fifteen years later, consciously or not, he was applying the same psychotherapy to himself. In any case, whatever the cause, he now appeared to have gained a new lease on life.

This fresh impetus was encouraged by the announcement of the impending visit to Canada in the early summer of King George VI and Queen Elizabeth. The at once emotional and pragmatic humorist read into the coming event political implications of great potential significance. In a note to René du Roure, Leacock wrote of his forebodings concerning the European scene. Parenthetically he observed: "And you've seen about our Royal Family coming to this continent—and going to the U.S.A.? Interesting!" The wholehearted reception which was given to the British monarch and his consort would later be counted as an important factor in cementing the Allied cause.

Enchanted by the whole conception of the tour, Leacock put on paper his joy about it. Strangely—since he sought publication of everything he was then writing—this exultant essay remained tucked away in his files, only to come to light in 1959. Then, when Queen Elizabeth II and Prince Philip were about to sail for Canada, it was published for the first time: the trustees of the Stephen Leacock Memorial Home released the manuscript to the Canadian press.

The short article says a lot about Leacock, his pride in the British monarchy, his conviction that the 1939 visit would mean "the inauguration of Their Majesties in the hearts of the plain people of Canada. This is the end of the false starts, the mistaken ambitions, the idle aspirations that for a century and a half led elsewhere and nowhere. This union is now and forever." Canadian as he had shown himself to be, here the unabashed Hampshire lad disclosed his true feeling for home and Empire. So far as he was concerned, "behind the visit of the King and Queen is a meaning unsurpassed in a thousand years of monarchy."

The fact that he wrote this and then did not submit it to his agent is interesting evidence that perhaps Leacock had second thoughts about being caught in public with his real sentiments showing.

But the royal couple did not obtain exclusive possession of the newspaper columns. They may have been the cynosure of all eyes south of the border, but the *New York Times,* on July 10, 1939, still was able to spare front-page space for an item under the heading "Leacock Braves Storm." The setting was Lake Couchiching, whipped into a choppy state by high winds. A young canoeist lost his balance and fell overboard. The small craft was blown beyond his reach. From the shore Stephen Leacock spotted the boy's apparent plight, launched the motorboat and headed to make the rescue. (He probably never learned that the youth could swim with the ease of an Indian, for indeed he was part Indian!)

The humanist as a hero was a new role for Leacock and, as was to be expected, he made light of it:

> Why, the first thing you know, they'll make a lifeboat station out of me. ... You may quote me as saying that in the future I will rescue no one, not even a woman.

He was less than light-hearted over a domestic problem of long standing. Charlie Leacock had borrowed the sum of $500 on an endorsement of his older brother Stephen. After a considerable passage of time, during which there had been no sign of repayment, there began a correspondence (though Charlie lived in Sutton, only a few miles away) which grew increasingly bitter. Stephen laid down the law on the methods to be adopted for repayment, meanwhile sending his brother an allowance of twenty dollars a month.

The pair crossed pens with a vengeance:

> Stephen to Charles: "Get control of yourself."
> Charles to Stephen: "Miserable man! I know you for what you are."

Finally, a telegram arrived from Charles: "Will deposit to your credit not wishing to be under any obligation to a person with your lack of business knowledge."

This particular family spat continued fitfully until Stephen's death. But in his will the humorist left the brother his three boats and all his fishing tackle.

In fighting trim, Leacock next took on the Ontario government.

Someone had been stealing his chickens and he did not propose to put up with it. A matter of such gravity was obviously not a case for the local police: the honor of the province was at stake, so he took his complaint right up to the office of the Premier. The chicken thefts ceased, but there is no indication that the provincial cabinet took credit for it. His chickens were important to Leacock. He maintained a daybook record of the egg laying of his hens and of the price he got for eggs over and above those for his own personal use. Perhaps it was the economist in him, or perhaps the farmer; but careful note was kept in a series of notebooks of the melons, strawberries, beets, peas, beans, tomatoes, and cabbages that the garden produced for his "home-grown" table. Even the trout or bass that were caught were duly recorded.

Another Ontario government department fell prey to his stubbornness. Leacock felt that it was time to have on hand a supply of wine from the Leacock family vineyards in Madeira. He ordered a case from the Ontario Liquor Control Board. The board replied that they would have to import it specially, that a single case was insufficient to handle economically, but that they would consider ten cases. Leacock curtly cancelled his demand. This did not mean that he had given up. He arranged with some friends who carried weight in such quarters to pester both the Ontario agency and the Quebec Liquor Commission. In the long run he talked the OLCB into sending him two cases.

It must be noted that although he brought fame to the town Leacock was never popular in Orillia. Perhaps his *Sunshine Sketches* still smarted; perhaps it was small-town jealousy of a famous figure overshadowing the town; or perhaps Leacock's hedonistic life-style offended the strait-laced natives.

Over the years there had been several occasions when his premises, closed for the winter months, had been broken into by thieves. Now, in July 1939, some person or persons had invaded his barn and relieved Leacock of a few of his farm tools. This roused him to send a letter to the editor of Orillia's *Packet-Times*, with a copy to the Associated Press in New York:

> Sir,
>   If I (or anybody in my employ acting for me) come upon any person who has obviously and evidently broken into closed premises and is obviously and evidently stealing or about to steal, am I (or my agent) en-

NOTED PROFESSORS TO LEAVE McGILL

Stephen Leacock and Dr. Martin Among 13 Who Are Retiring

Thirteen retirements, involving more than 200 years of service, were announced at McGill University today. Those retiring include Dr. Charles F. Martin, senior dean and internationally-known head of the medical faculty, four chairmen of

---

"I have plenty to say about the Governors of McGill putting me out of the university. But I have all eternity to say it in. I shall shout it down to them."
—"Stephen Leacock."

---

departments, the secretary of the university, the r e g i s t r a r at Macdonald College and other members of the teaching staff.

One professor alone accounted for 50 years of service. Dr. Nevil Norton Evans joined the staff at

Dr. C. F. Martin Stephen Leacock

McGill in 1886 and is this session celebrating the 50th anniversary of his teaching career at McGill.

Stephen L e a c o c k, humorist, writer and authority on political economy, is among those retiring.

13 RETIRING.

Dead

COL. W. W. BURLAND

COL. W.W. BURLAND DIES IN HOSPITAL

Former C.O. of Victoria Rifles Had Notable Military Career

Col. W. Watt Burland, D.S.O., a former commanding officer of the Victoria Rifles of Canada and an outstanding Canadian soldier with a brilliant record of five years service in the Great War, died last night at the western division of the General Hospital. He was taken ill during the week-end and brought to the hospital on Monday.

One of the original officers of the 14th battalion to leave Montreal in September, 1914, Col. Burland commanded the unit through eight months of heavy fighting in 1915. Later he served as commandant of

ACTION PROMISED IN DAVID ELECTION

Defeated Candidate Asserts Provincial Secretary Will Never Take Seat

Hermann Barrette, the St. Jerome lawyer who was defeated by Hon. Athanase David, Provincial Secretary, in the one vote provincial election in Terrebonne county Monday, declared today: "David will never take his seat in the Legislature."

He made this assertion pacing furiously up and down the floor of his law offices in St. Jerome this morning, while preparing a legal attack against the Provincial Secretary which he promised to bring before the Superior Court at St. Jerome tomorrow.

FIGHT BEGINNING

"The fight has just begun," the fusion candidate declared, "we will fight to the end. And I can guarantee you that David won't have his seat when the House opens. We won't let the county of Terrebonne be represented by one vote."

Mr. Barrette glared at the reporter.

"You went to school, eh?" he asked.

"Well," he went on hotly, "so did I. And when I went to school zero meant nothing. I am absolutely clear on that point. The law provides that when two or more candidates are equal on the votes they received—the returning officer has the right to vote, otherwise he has not. Both candidates in this election received nothing, zero, nothing. That means no votes."

Mr. Barrette said that his court brief is almost completed and will be filed in St. Jerome tomorrow morning "for sure." He refused to divulge the nature of the proceedings.

PROCEEDINGS NEW

"I can assure you of this," he said, "that it is something that has never been tried in the province of Quebec or even in the Dominion before."

Swinging back again to what hap-

Children'

POI

THE people wh
vided with a
the care of speci
coming generou
Memorial Hospi
Star Office or to
Children's Mem
Additional

H. H. Rumsey .....
Geo. E. Gravel .....
Anonymous ....
Olive Hosmer .....
Kenneth D. Young .
K. G. Blackader ...
Mrs. John Allan ...
Gertrude A. Smith .
Mrs. T. M. Hutchison
Miss M. H. Ball ...
Miss M. M. Turnor .
Mrs. A. R. McMaster
Mrs. E. Wyatt Johns
Mrs. John L. Garland
Mrs. H. Vass ......
Ethelwynn B. Clark
Mrs. H. Bronfman .
Miss Davidson .....
Paul Pratt ....
Mrs. A. L. Bennett .
D. W. M. McKenzie
Mrs. Jas. Park ....
Edwin Lloyd........
Gordon Earl Josefo .
Dr. Marin Barbeau .
Albert C. White ...
E. Lachapelle ......
Muriel Goulet .....
Mrs. M. Cully .....
Miss Olive Hosmer .
G. W. T. Nicholson .
Mrs. Walter M. Stew
Anonymous ....
Hugh Mackay, K.C.
John Gordon Robert:
Jenkins Bros. Limite:
Mrs. W. R. Miller .
Anonymous ....
Lady Roddick......
Betty Wilson ......

(45, 46) In June 1935, Leacock learned that he was to be retired from McGill. He was enraged by the news. (Above–note box). He never forgave the man he held responsible, Dr. Arthur Eustace Morgan (right), principal and vice-chancellor of McGill, 1935-37. (*Above, courtesy of the* Montreal *Star; Right, Photograph by Arnott Rogers Batten, Ltd., courtesy of McGill University Archives*)

(48) Leacock's niece and chatelaine, Barbara Ulrichson, on the day she received her M.A. in 1935. (*Photograph courtesy of Barbara Nimmo*)

(47) Bill Gentleman, custodian of the Arts building and friend and confidant of Leacock, receiving an Honorary B.A. from the Students' Society on his retirement in 1944. (*Courtesy of the Montreal* Star)

(49, 50) When his niece was married to Donald Nimmo in the summer of 1937, Leacock gave the wedding reception at Old Brewery Bay. Leacock (left) calls the guests in for refreshments. (Right) Leacock appears at the left of the reception scene with his niece, the new Barbara Nimmo, in the centre. (*Photographs courtesy of Barbara Nimmo*)

(51) Leacock in the garden at Old Brewery Bay in 1939.
(Courtesy of the Public Archives of Canada)

(52) Leacock's favorite haunt, the University Club of Montreal.

(53) The "Leacock corner" in the Reading Room of the University Club today. *(Photographs by Louis Jaques, by permission of the Council of the University Club of Montreal)*

(54) A general view of the graveyard of the Church of St. George the Martyr, Jackson's Point, on Lake Simcoe, Ontario. Leacock's grave is hidden under the umbrella elm in the centre. *(Courtesy of Orillia Public Library)*

(55) Stephen Leacock's grave. *(Photograph by James Pauk, courtesy of Orillia Public Library)*

(56) Edwin Holgate painted this portrait of Stephen Leacock in 1943. It now hangs in the National Gallery of Canada. (*Courtesy of the National Gallery of Canada*)

titled to open fire upon such a person with small shot aimed at the legs, or must I first challenge such a person, ask him if he has a revolver, and how many others are with him, and would he care for a wrestle on the grass?

The American wire service did not carry the story, but the Orillia paper printed the letter. If there were any replies, Leacock failed to put them in his files.

And so the summer went on. David Spielman, a Montrealer now of Chicago, who attended McGill with Stephen, Jr., spent the holidays with his classmate at Old Brewery Bay. As a healthy young man would, he remembers the mealtimes, with their "always stimulating, if not intellectual conversations." At dinner the soups were a specialty. Leacock himself made certain that infinite care was taken over this part of the repast. "The trouble was, the soups were so good, they tended to spoil the rest of the meal," says Spielman.

One lunchtime, according to George Leacock, Stephen flew into a rage when the cook produced a tureen of tinned consommé of beef. With a garden full of choice tomatoes, this was the limit. The host removed the bowl from the table, poured the contents out of the window, and ordered everybody into the garden to gather fresh tomatoes. He himself calmly sat and waited until proper soup was prepared and served.

As the 1939 summer progressed people everywhere were glued to their radios to learn of Hitler's latest moves. Something was about to burst in Europe. Late in August the Nazi-Soviet pact of non-aggression was revealed to a stunned world. Poland was invaded a week later. World War II had begun. On September 3, two days after the attack on Poland, Britain and France declared war on Germany. On September 10 Canada took the same step.

Now that the conflagration he had feared was a fact, Leacock lost no time in adding his voice to the chorus of condemnation of the Nazis. He had already been at work on a fifty-page appeal called *All Right, Mr. Roosevelt,* which was to form part of the Oxford University Press series, *Pamphlets on World Affairs.* The booklet was published in October and the earnestness underlying the light banter won attention in both countries. Leacock threw out a challenge to the United States for a better understanding of prevailing conditions in Europe. Indeed, much of the book was a call for help:

> If any of the McGruders of Mississippi—they were Highlanders, weren't they, originally?—want to come over and join the Royal Highlanders of

Toronto, we've a tartan and a sporran and a jorum (one forgets these
Highland terms) for each of them. Let them all come. Perhaps they can
bring the Virginia Robinsons and Randolphs with them, or "round heads"
from Connecticut stamped with the image of the Ironsides; or the Low-
ells or the Cabots from Boston,—but, no, I forgot, they don't talk to
anybody—or to nobody that they'd meet in Europe.

Leacock's message prayed for sympathetic comprehension of the
world's tragedy and stressed the need for all who could boast moral
courage and sincerity to do battle against intolerance on behalf of
ethical principles and freedom of conscience.

From the beginning the war stirred an intense patriotism in Leacock. As he had done during the 1914–18 struggle, once more he
took a personal pride in those of his past students who had rallied
to the colors. There were many of these and some were in high
places. His one-time teaching colleague, now a leading European
financier, Sir Edward Peacock wrote from London at this stage: "Do
you know that you and I taught six of the chief Canadian generals
at Upper Canada College?" To which Leacock replied: "Take
three and give me three. I prefer to keep my staff as a unit."

During the first critical months of the war, the Canadian Government, with considerable foresight, set up a committee to begin looking into the problems of demobilization and rehabilitation, with the
accent on the future role of universities. This committee must have
found Leacock's new book, *Too Much College*, of considerable
interest. Certainly it furnished much food for thought for everyone.
Eventually it ran into fifteen editions.

In *Too Much College* much of his personal bitterness was still
in evidence. At the outset he reminded all his readers that this was
one of several volumes he had published "since I was retired as useless." He even signed himself with his full list of honorary degrees.

But despite this occasional sour note, and despite all its comical
interludes and surface chaffing, *Too Much College* fairly summed
up Leacock's philosophy on higher education in the modern world.
While he seemed to be recommending more concentrated education and, therefore, less time to be spent at it, he emphasized that

. . . in the wider sense, what I want to advocate is not to make education
shorter, but to make it much longer, indeed to make it last as long as life
itself. What I find wrong is the stark division now existing between the
years of formal education and entry into the world of life. . . . All that is

best in education can only be acquired by spontaneous interest; this gained, it lasts and goes on. . . . Real education should mean a wonderful beginning, a marvellous initiation, a thorough "smattering" and life will carry it on.

In view of what he had written in previous books about a classical education and the feeble professors who dwelt "out of the world" reading Greek and Latin, it was odd to discover Leacock arguing for Latin as a basis for a sound education. He likened it to the ballast in the hold of a ship, "down in the dark and unseen, which governs every graceful dip and dive of the flag at the masthead and guarantees against disaster."

A chapter on "Has Economics Gone to Seed?" attacked economic theorists and their methods, mostly the latter:

When the world is in danger of collapse from the dilemma of wealth and want, the college economists can shed no light—or only a multitude of crosslights that will not focus to a single beam—in place of a lighthouse, wreckers' signals, or at best, fireworks, elaborate and meaningless.

Then, as though to prove he was playing no favorites, this:

Take enough of that mystification and muddle, combine it with the continental air of the United States, buttress it up on the side with the history of dead opinion and dress it, as the chefs say, with sliced history and green geography, and out of it you can make a doctor's degree in economics. I have one myself.

One economist for whom the veteran professor held a distinct admiration now occupied the position of principal and vice-chancellor of McGill University. F. Cyril James, it will be recalled, had been one of the small group of young men at the London School of Economics who had conspired with Leacock in 1921 to write letters to the editor about a Leacock speech. From humble East London beginnings, James had won scholarship after scholarship, eventually distinguishing himself as an economics professor at the University of Pennsylvania, before his appointment to the McGill post in 1939.

When Leacock heard of the appointment, he telephoned Dr. James to ask him to dinner at the University Club—"for old times sake and to meet a couple of people you'll like." When James arrived he was introduced to René du Roure and the Province of Quebec's Chief Justice Greenshields, as lively a pair of *bons vivants* as could be found this side of Paris.

Inevitably the host steered the conversation round to the subject of his involuntary retirement from McGill.

"Had you been in Dr. Morgan's place," Leacock asked James, "would you have done the same thing to me?"

Equivocally, the principal answered: "I'd have to think very carefully in view of a friendship."

The speculative question deserved the evasive answer.

The dinner, in a private room, went on into the early moring hours in great conviviality.

Leacock could stick it out with the best of them, even though he was approaching his seventieth birthday. On that day, December 30, 1939, there appeared in the *New York Times* a reflective essay from his pen entitled "Three Score and Ten." It considered "the business of growing old." He confessed that the experience could only be described as "not so good." But he would try to "laugh it off in prose," and he did. Possibly the laughter seemed more than tinged with a sense of sorrow as he reflected on his life. He was still under the impression that his birthplace had been the Isle of Wight; otherwise this was an accurate, though cinematic, scenario of his life story—"Such is my picture, the cavalcade all the way down from the clouds of the morning to the mists of the evening."

"Presently," he went on, "I shall be introduced as 'this venerable old gentleman' and the axe will fall when they raise me to the degree of 'grand old man.' That means on our continent anyone with snow-white hair who has kept out of jail till eighty. That's the last and worst they can do to you."

Although the axe had yet to fall, Leacock agreed to a suggestion from Fred Taylor, a McGill graduate who had made a name for himself in the art world, that he should sit for his portrait.

"I can't pay for it," Leacock told Taylor, "but I think you would have at least a good expectation that McGill, or the University Club, or etc., might buy it after I'm dead. If not, you could paint in another face and try again."

When the work had got under way, the professor phoned the artist one day to tell him that he had been in contact with a family whose sons had developed chicken pox. Leacock thoughtfully proposed a postponement of the next sitting in case Taylor's own two sons might become infected. "Anyway, if I did come with spots, you'd have to paint 'em out."

The portraitist has some sharp recollection of those sittings:

He did almost all the talking and I was hard put to get the information I needed as he roared, ranted and walked about, seldom passing momentarily through the pose I wanted to represent. I gradually concluded that he was imbued with, or possessed, a decidedly mean streak and/or small streak and that he was narrowly intolerant in respect of certain subjects, people and events, in spite of his high stature in general and a great number of particulars and his pretty broad humanism. He was human, but the areas of his foibles were such as to disappoint me in him. Possibly I saw too much of the trees and not enough of the woods. If so, it was mainly because of a series of revelations or the accumulation of his statements and opinions.

The most important of these revelations concerned an incident which Leacock had amusingly referred to in *My Discovery of England*. The humorist had been in the full flood of his lecture in a Midlands' city when the chairman touched his elbow, explained that a man had collapsed at the back of the hall, and asked Leacock to sit down until the man was carried out.

Repeating the tale to Taylor, Leacock remarked: "I sat there hoping, *praying* that the man would die."

At this, Taylor expressed considerable surprise.

"My fortune would have been made!" exclaimed Leacock. "Think of the headlines: MAN DIES LAUGHING AT LEACOCK!"

Today the artist states that he was and remains convinced that the humorist, incredible as it seems, really wished that the man had died. "I concluded he was in deadly earnest."

Taylor describes what happened when the painting was completed:

I turned the easel around. I don't know how long it was, though it was certainly half a minute which seemed like half an hour, for even ten seconds in a silent studio, with a man looking at a finished portrait of himself for the first time, is a very long time. I, of course, looked at him as he looked at the portrait. The color rose from his collar and suffused his whole head up to his hair, he grasped the arms of the chair and his expression might have meant anything. I was pretty worried: I couldn't tell what he was thinking. Suddenly he raised his hands, pounded them down on the arms of the chair and surged to his feet, paying me probably the greatest compliment a portrait painter can receive. "My God, Taylor," he roared. "That's exactly how I feel."

But Mrs. Barbara Nimmo remembers how disgruntled her uncle became every time the portrait was mentioned. She says he hated it.

Had the artist really got under his skin? Taylor's painting, brutally faithful, now hangs in the Leacock Room of McGill's McLennan Library.

However haggard Leacock may have looked at this time, certainly he lacked neither spirit nor energy. As with his sixtieth birthday, so his seventieth was marked by the publication of another anthology, *Laugh Parade*. A little later in 1940 *Our British Empire* appeared —a loving, if cursory, treatment of a favorite theme. It was still Empire to Leacock, known to everybody else as the British Commonwealth of Nations.

As usual, the author airily dismissed his inclination to work with haste in broad theories unsupported by detailed study:

> In dealing with the mass of statistical material that goes with the making of such a volume as the present, it is unavoidable that errors and misprints will find their way in. For these I apologise beforehand. For instance, in Chapter III I stated that the number of hogs in the world is 200,000,000. I now believe this is wrong. There seems to be more than that. Reviewers, whose one idea of reviewing is to mop up misprints, will add more hogs.

Leacock gave full play to his feeling for romantic history in *Our British Empire*, not to mention his Anglo-Saxon prejudices. As though still standing before a classroom of freshman, he produced a book which was both a color presentation and an exercise in political science. He set its tone in the beginning: "I write this book in the hope that it may be of service in the present hour. It is a presentation of the British Empire, not for the pageant of its history but for its worth to the world. The Empire is united not by force but by goodwill. It means co-operation, not compulsion. In it we live as free men. . . ."

"In the present hour," which coincided with the German invasion of Norway and the end of the "phony" war, the popularity of *Our British Empire* was assured.

It was now the week of McGill University's 1940 Convocation. Stephen Leacock, Jr., was a member of the graduating class. For the specific purpose of seeing his son receive his Bachelor of Arts degree, the father came down from Orillia. But when the ceremony took place the celebrated parent was not in the audience.

Leslie Roberts, prominent Canadian journalist and broadcaster, for whose book *Canada's War at Sea* Leacock wrote a lengthy preface, is the authority for what occurred:

> At the very time the graduation exercises were taking place at McGill, Stephen Leacock was seated in the University Club. A fellow member approached him and asked why he was not attending Convocation. "Oh, to hell with it," Leacock is said to have replied. "If I went, some co-ed would whisper to her swain about the funny old man with the straw hat and shabby clothes; and the swain would retort that the funny old man was Stephen Leacock and that he was probably drunk."

However sad and inexplicable the episode—no one has been prepared to venture a conjecture—a few months afterwards an event occurred which was to bring lasting sorrow to the humorist. René du Roure died suddenly aged sixty. Ten years his senior, Leacock had cherished his close companionship with the dapper head of the university's French department. In the course of a deeply moving tribute printed in *The McGill News*, Leacock wrote:

> When war came he tried in vain to offer his services to his country, or alternately, to Canada. But there was nothing that he could do; he no longer possessed the physical vitality to carry the courage of his mind. . . . Then came the collapse of France and for René that meant the collapse of life itself. Principal James has finely said that René du Roure died, as a patriot, of a broken heart. We may add to this the thought that his death has not been in vain. In these days of broken alliance and waning trust the memory of René du Roure will serve to keep alive for us our old-time faith in the spirit of France.

Fortunately, a pressing commitment prevented Leacock from becoming too moody over this end to a fruitful and convivial friendship. Samuel Bronfman, founder and president of Distillers Corporation—Seagram's Ltd., considered the time fitting for the publication of a concise history of Canada, which his firm would distribute as a patriotic gesture. He wanted Leacock to write it.

A New York publisher's agent, acting as adviser to Bronfman, got in touch with the humorist by wire: "Have no idea what your fee would be, but must have some idea of costs to present to the president of Distillers. I thought something between $3,000 and $5,000. Please wire me." Leacock replied promptly: "I had something like $5,000 in mind." And that was the agreed figure. Had Leacock got his way—he wanted the right to publish it commercially after Distillers had made their free distribution—his purse would have been infinitely fatter. Over the years Distillers have given away something in the vicinity of 160,00 copies.

Leacock was in his element writing, on commission, the story of Canada. The text flowed smoothly, with a well-rounded symmetry. For once he knew his stuff without having to bother much with research, and worked skilfully at illumining facts with lively allusions. For their part, the sponsors went out of their way to ensure a handsome book. Famous Canadian artists were commissioned by Seagram to do thirty-one full-page illustrations. Among these contributors were F. H. Varley, C. W. Jeffreys, A. Sherriff Scott and H. R. Perrigard.

While *Canada, The Foundations of Its Future* was in production, a rumor gained currency to the effect that there had been strong words between Leacock and Bronfman, who had accused the author of anti-Semitism on the basis of one sentence in the text, which was angrily excised. Samuel Bronfman vigorously denies that this ever happened. "Over a sherry in my office," he assured this biographer, "the professor, whom I'd never met before, and I agreed that we could do without a questionable adjective he had applied to Newfoundlanders, a slighting reference to Winnipeg (after all, my hometown!), and two quite unnecessary remarks about some prominent politicians. It was all very amicable."

The preparatory period of *Canada, The Foundations of Its Future* produced an amusing incident, however, as vouched for by F. John L. Evans, Q.C., a leading member of the Ontario Bar. Mr. Evans' cottage was adjacent to Stephen Leacock's home at Old Brewery Bay. Evans had known Leacock since boyhood.

It was a cold, miserable summer's day in 1941, "just one of those days that was only good for drinking whisky," Mr. Evans recalls. The humorist, Evans and his wife were seated before a blazing fire in Leacock's house swapping yarns when the housekeeper announced the arrival of three people from Montreal. They were the general manager of Distillers Corporation, the New York publishing adviser and a secretary. They came bearing proof copies of the new book for Leacock's final editing.

Evans' on-the-spot account continues:

They were ushered in and with no delay were asked what they would like to drink. The inquiry was perhaps unnecessary for, of course, they said, "Rye, thank you." The whisky cabinet was always kept in the hallway just inside the front door of the residence and also adjacent to the Doctor's study and near the living room, where it was always easily accessible. The Doctor called, "Johnny," from the hallway and, on my reaching him, he enquired quietly if I had any Seagram's at my cottage as he had only Walker's, a distillery company whose stock he held in his portfolio. I told him I would be back in a minute. My cottage was quite a distance away so, rain or no rain, I ran to the Doctor's bottle dump (no small pile!), quickly found a V.O. bottle, handed it to the housekeeper in the kitchen to wash and she helped me decant into it the Walker's brand of rye. Placing it on the sideboard, the Doctor came and brought it to his guests who poured their drinks, drank several and, in time, departed. When they left I told Dr. Leacock that his guests had been drinking Walker's out of the V.O. bottle. The Doctor's face wrinkled up as he chuckled over the incident and, rather surprisingly, commended me for my ingenuity. Jones, the hired man, brought in more logs for the fire and we never did get to the trout stream that day.

Samuel Bronfman heard this story for the first time in 1969 when discussing the *Canada* book with this biographer.

He threw up his hands and exclaimed, "What desecration!"

XX

"Give Me My Stick . . ."

With the Canadian history for the House of Seagram off his hands, Leacock, at seventy-one, turned his attention to Hollywood again. He remembered the film *David Copperfield*, which David O. Selznick (of *Gone With the Wind* fame) had produced in 1935. The humorist instructed his agent to get in touch with the Selznick organization, which specialized in literary adaptations, with a view to selling them a cinematic treatment (not yet written) of *Pickwick Papers*. Evidently Selznick's passion for Charles Dickens had subsided, since negotiations over the Pickwick idea never even began. Unabashed, Leacock nudged his agent into another approach to the motion-picture world.

His friend and admirer Robert Benchley had done some work for Walt Disney, why shouldn't Leacock do the same? This project, too, came to a dead end very quickly. Meanwhile, a movie opportunity which presented itself was brushed off. A U.S. film distributor offered Leacock the job of doing English subtitles for Sacha Guitry's French production *They Were Nine Bachelors*. The humorist gave no reason for turning this down.

Later in the year, however, a bright prospect opened with a suggestion from Thomas B. Costain, whom Leacock had known years before in Toronto as editor of *Maclean's* magazine. Now, as an

237

editor of the distinguished publishing house of Doubleday, Costain had two things on his mind. In August he wrote urging Leacock to undertake his autobiography, reckoning that it well might become a Book-of-the-Month Club selection and "sell some 700,000 copies." Leacock begged off. He was still reluctant to face such a project.

Leacock then heard from Costain about another scheme. Doubleday had begun publishing a series of books on famous American ports. "We now want to take it beyond the bounds of the United States and naturally our first thought was of Quebec, the most colorful of all ports on the American continent." No Montrealer could possibly tolerate such a statement, least of all Leacock. He promptly impressed Costain with arguments why Montreal would be a much superior subject for the Doubleday series.

Leacock called his book *Montreal, Seaport and City*. After paying tribute in his preface to all who had helped him, including Mrs. Shaw "for her research work in the library," Leacock concluded: "Acknowledging all these debts, I feel also that I owe a good deal of this book to my own industry and effort." Indeed, he did. His pride in the book knew no bounds. He had been in his element writing it. His love for the city and for Canadian history in general shone through even its most critical passages.

The narrative abounded in accounts of high adventure, heroism, great achievements and defeats; there was even a paragraph stressing the fact that for many years there wasn't even one brewery in the city. And French Canada would forever be grateful to him for his defence of its native tongue. He spoke out against the derogatory description of French Canadian speech as patois, pointing to its value in preserving ancestral words and pronunciations.

Much of *Montreal, Seaport and City* had been composed at his country retreat, where he complained of being "short in library facilities." The book, nonetheless, was not short on facts. He himself brimmed over with facts on the subject, and on the rare occasions when uncertainty stalked him, an appeal to knowledgeable friends swiftly produced the desired information. There were, for example, missing details about the railway tunnel which had been bored under Mount Royal. He wrote to Dean Ernest Brown of McGill's Engineering faculty:

It was bored from both ends, wasn't it?
It met with a very small error, didn't it?
What else did it do?

Thus, typically, Leacock endowed the tunnel itself with movement, implying that it was alive and had a will of its own.

Recent research, however, has undermined one of Leacock's claims in this book—that the University Club was situated in the very centre of Hochelaga, said to be the original site of Montreal. Today scholars have concluded that the Indian village on the University Club site was not the one visited by explorer Jacques Cartier, and that the real Hochelaga has yet to be located.

With this informative and colorful volume launched, Leacock remained in the peaceful surroundings of Lake Couchiching, content to let national politics go their noisy way. After the sweeping 1940 victory of Mackenzie King's Liberals two years before, the humorist had mused: "There are only two Conservatives left, and one of them is in England." The latter referred to the former Canadian Prime Minister Bennett. In a huff he had gone to settle in the United Kingdom, where he was elevated to the peerage as Viscount Bennett.

The parliamentary squabbling in Ottawa may have ceased to stir him, but Leacock's concern about the possible danger to the democratic process after the war remained constant. Accordingly, he chose this moment in 1942 to produce his testament of faith in democracy, *Our Heritage of Liberty*. Obviously aware of its limited public appeal in the present circumstances, Leacock expressed to his publishers his willingness to waive royalties on the first five hundred copies of the book. For a change, money didn't count. Above all, he wanted to be on record. Once again he announced his conviction that only the democratic system could have brought about the social and economic progress of the last hundred years. It was good, straightforward advocacy in the field of political science.

In the sphere of humor, too, Leacock demonstrated a liveliness which had been missing for far too long. While spasmodically considering the autobiography (which he felt should not be published until the war's end), Leacock had gathered up thirty of his latest pieces to make a volume which he called *My Remarkable Uncle*. In this he recaptured the sure touch of his most effective writing days. Variety and quality went hand in hand in these refreshing pages.

As we have already seen, it took Leacock half a century to put his remarkable uncle down on paper. Fascinated in his boyhood by this Edward Philip Leacock, the nephew had since kept in touch with his uncle's outrageous behavior; somehow the unmitigated avuncular gall was made acceptable by an ineluctable charm. Yet, as literary material, Stephen Leacock ignored him until, in World War II, the *Reader's Digest* sparked in the humorist the idea for a profile of E.P.

The relish with which Leacock wrote about his father's brother recalled the child's entrancement with a man who clearly knew how to do things in style. In later years the nephew entertained some reservations about the dashing, if dubious, political and commercial accomplishments of E.P. In fact, Leacock dismissed him as a humbug. When, however, his uncle, penniless, left the country to tuck himself away in an English monastery, distance lent enchantment and he became fair literary game. Now the nephew could safely talk about "the unbeatable quality of his spirit, the mark, we like to think just now, of the British race."

Wisely, the humorist recognized that his relative's "character was so exceptional that it needs nothing but plain narration. It was so exaggerated already that you couldn't exaggerate it." Thus, with very little embellishment, the title sketch of the book was destined to become one of the most delightful tales of the entire Leacock corpus.

According to Leacock, E.P. never contemplated a crooked deal in his life; "all his grand schemes were as open as sunlight—and as empty." But here were some of his ambiguous activities:

He was president of a bank (that never opened), head of a brewery (for brewing the Red River) and, above all, secretary-treasurer of the Winnipeg, Hudson Bay and Arctic Ocean Railway that had a charter authorizing it to build a road to the Arctic Ocean, when it got ready. They had no track, but they printed stationery and passes, and in return "E.P." received passes all over North America.

Stephen Leacock's father, Peter (who died, aged ninety-two, in Nova Scotia in 1940) shared some of his brother's qualities. Before

he went to pieces, he had been charmingly capable of giving pleasure and of dreaming dreams. He simply lacked the energy and
unabashed ostentation of E.P. Mrs. Nimmo has written that even
her Uncle Stephen "reminded me to some small degree of old E. P.
Leacock. . . . Not that he was the likeable humbug 'E.P.' was, but
he always saw the best in things about him and not the worst, the
possibility of what they might be and not what they really were."

Some of the succeeding pieces in *My Remarkable Uncle* were of
an equally high order. "The Mathematics of the Lost Chord" was
as good as anything he had ever written in his moments of youthful
imaginativeness. In consoling musicians who were trying to find the
Great Amen, Leacock proved that a search might ultimately yield
something; at any rate, it could not possibly take more than ten
million years. At the other end of the scale, "The Transit of Venus,"
more sentimental than amusing, showed what the author could do
when he tackled the short story form seriously. Exercises in nostalgia
abounded—memories of the farm, of Upper Canada College, of
various Christmas festivities. "War-time Santa Claus" contained a
paragraph which represented the humorist at the top of his form:

> I once asked a Christmas Eve group of children if they believed in Santa
> Claus. The very smallest ones answered without hesitation, "Why, of
> course!" The older ones shook their heads. The little girls smiled sadly
> but said nothing. One future scientist asserted boldly, "I know who it is";
> and a little make-strong with his eye on gain said: "I believe in it all; I
> can believe in anything." That boy, I realized, would one day be a bishop.

Pleased with the critical reception of his new book, Leacock
required little persuading to sit for another portrait. A group of
friends approached him at the beginning of 1943 to suggest that
Edwin Holgate, the distinguished Canadian artist, should paint him.
Leacock retorted: "Well, when do we start?" Holgate's experience
differed a good deal from that of Fred Taylor.

"We were rarely serious," Holgate writes. "Many times my wife
came out on the *soupente* of the studio to ask what the hubbub was
about. Leacock would be mopping his eyes from laughter. I made
no attempt to paint him as a funny man. He impressed me as being
a philosopher with a great good humor. But first, a philosopher. He
plied me with questions as if he were a small boy—and listened to
the answers with an attention they did not deserve."

The portrait, an excellent likeness, hangs in Canada's National Gallery.

Following the sittings, which took place on Saturdays and Sundays, Leacock went back to Old Brewery Bay with a docket of notes for a couple of books and several articles for periodicals. At seventy-three, agile and full of ideas, he set himself to carry out a task simply to satisfy his own vanity. He had written about the meaning and technique of humor; now he felt like writing a book about writing. It didn't take him long to do it and he named it *How to Write*.

In a letter to McGill's librarian, Dr. Lomer, Leacock said:

> This book *How to Write* is like a favorite child to me because I wrote it purely to suit myself, with no eye on editors, or sales, or the public. If that means that it fails, then it is a favorite all the more, as the feeble child always is to the fond parent.
>
> So what more fitting book to present to the unbiassed mind of a Librarian.

There have been better books on the subject, but at least the author avoided pedantry, rather providing a beginner's course, marked by simple advice and accompanied by some amusing allusions. Yet, according to Lomer, eventually *How to Write* became a school reference text in South Africa and was later translated into Braille.

With this little conceit out of the way and with his eye ever on possible royalties, Leacock made another selection of his latest magazine pieces. He published them in 1943, as *Happy Stories*, and most of them were. Again there were touches of the earlier perceptive, light-hearted Leacock. He reintroduced his remarkable uncle briefly but to expectedly good effect. He revived Mariposa. And there were several sketches which he had tossed off hastily for a Canadian Victory Loan appeal.

Editors' rejection slips had played a relatively minor part in the course of the humorist's career, to the point that he could handle such situations with more tolerance than most authors. However, no sooner had *Happy Stories* come on the market than he received a refusal.

Leacock wrote a semi-serious article on "How to Abolish Poverty" and sent it along to Harry C. Clarke, editor of *Maclean's* magazine. Clarke didn't like it and returned the manuscript. Acknowledging its receipt, Leacock replied: "Too bad. Poverty is harder to abolish than we thought."

Other articles poured from his pen on all manner of topics throughout the summer. He even wrote copy for an American airline advertisement—a thousand words at a dollar per word. At the same time he completed work on *Canada at Sea*, due for publication the following year. Once more his knowledge of and love for the theme stood him in good stead, allowing him to get away with little or no research. The pages of the short history were enlivened by sprightly descriptions of marine exploration and naval encounters.

Deeds of derring-do had never failed to excite Leacock since the days in Porchester when his mother had filled him with stories of *H.M.S. Victory* and of the Crimea. With equal avidity he followed closely the progress of World War II, especially the actions in which a Canadian corps was now engaged in Italy. Petty hardships on the home front were largely ignored, even when alcoholic beverages were in short supply. Anyway, the stock at Old Brewery Bay seldom ran low.

During the autumn months of 1943 Leacock concentrated on two major projects—his autobiography, and another collection of articles for a book which was to be entitled *Last Leaves*. If there was some vague foreboding in the title, there was even more of a presentiment in the way he dubbed it "Ba's book." Barbara Nimmo, who with her family continued to enjoy many happy days at the Leacock home, was charged with the eventual publication of *Last Leaves*. Yet, despite such precautions, Leacock thought only of the immediate postwar period for the completion and publication of the autobiography.

The only indication that he was feeling out of sorts in the fall of 1943 found its way into a letter to his friend of radio days, Joe McDougall. As a kind of sideline, Leacock had been whipping out material for a booklet of twenty-five thousand words, all of which were directed to the defence of the free enterprise system in Canada. The ageing professor had read into the social and economic findings and recommendations of Oxford University's Lord Beveridge portents of what he considered to be grave significance. To him the social security provisions and other trappings of a welfare state held the odor of socialism. In his short *While There Is Time: The Case against Social Catastrophe* Leacock took a final pot shot against any extreme form of government interference with individual effort.

McDougall had been asked to prepare a work along similar lines and asked Stephen Leacock for guidance. He received it in the form of an encouraging note to which was attached a précis of the approach to be taken, with a chapter-by-chapter breakdown of the subject matter.

But the telltale sentence in the covering note ran: "Sorry to say am not well enough for interview or talk."

Nearing the close of 1943 Leacock really felt off-color, and looked it. Finally he took to bed with an attack of influenza. Early in the new year Gladstone Murray, whose notable career had been practically launched by Leacock, received a scrawl from the patient at Old Brewery Bay:

> ... getting better & hope soon to be out of the woods—as an aftermath of flu something went wrong with my swallowing—I believe (and please God) it is clearing up now. ...

The condition did not clear up. It grew steadily worse. In the first week of February Leacock scribbled another line to Gladstone Murray:

> At the present I am a very sick man. With good fortune I may pass a present corner and go on for a good time yet, even for years. But at the present I find it very hard.

His physician's diagnosis was confirmed by a specialist. Leacock had cancer of the throat. They moved him into the Western Hospital in Toronto. When Mrs. Shaw learned of this in Montreal, she went to Toronto and took up residence nearby to be of what help she could.

Despite the constant pain, Leacock maintained an amazing outward cheerfulness, and went on writing propped up in his hospital bed. Speech came hesitatingly and with obvious effort. Yet fourteen days after he entered hospital, he looked up at his radiologist with a grin, after an x-ray had been taken, and said: "Did I behave pretty well? Was I a good boy?"

A few hours later, Stephen Leacock died. It was March 28, 1944. He was in his seventy-fifth year.

"Give me my stick," he had written in "Three Score and Ten," "I'm going out on No Man's Land. I'll face it."

Following cremation in Toronto, as he had stipulated, he was buried on a blustery March day in the family plot of the lovely churchyard of St. George's at Sibbald's Point. The simple Anglican service was read by the Most Reverend Derwyn Owen, Primate of All Canada. Among the mourners at the snow-carpeted graveside were representatives of McGill University, the University of Toronto, and Upper Canada College.

With the rising crescendo of the war occupying most people's thoughts and monopolizing newspaper space, the press of the world nonetheless found time and room to pay tribute to the Canadian humorist. Of the thousands of editorial comments, perhaps that of the *Christian Science Monitor* sounded the note which best caught the feeling of his multitude of readers:

> On the train this morning we saw a man chuckling as he might not have done if Stephen Leacock had not just passed on. His passing had caused the newspapers to reprint some of the humorist's remarks. . . . It is all that a man can ask that his fellows should be unable to remember him without a smile, that laughter should be the ultimate expression of their love.

The College Times, the UCC newspaper which he had edited forty-seven years earlier, published an obituary which recalled some amusing stories about the school's famous Old Boy:

> Again and again it happened that some unknown man well on in middle life accosted him with a beaming face. "You don't remember me. You licked me at U.C.C. . . ." Upon this they shook hands with a warmth and heartiness as if Leacock were a long lost companion. Sometimes Leacock anticipated the greeting. As soon as the stranger grasped his hand and said, "Do you remember me?" he broke in to say, "Why, let me see, surely I licked you at U.C.C. . . ." In such a case the man's delight was beyond all bounds. Professor Leacock was proud of the fact that "I have licked, I believe, two generals in the Canadian army, three cabinet ministers, and more colonels and mayors than I care to count. Indeed all the boys that I have licked seem to be doing well."

The writer in *The College Times* also remembered that Leacock thought the greatest nuisance of all to the schoolmaster was the parent who does his boy's homework:

Whenever he found himself correcting exercises that had obviously been done for the boys, he used to say to them, "Robert, tell your father that he *must* use the ablative after *pro*." "Yes, sir," replied the boy. "And William, you tell your grandmother that her use of the dative simply won't do. She's getting along nicely and I'm well satisfied with the way she's working, but I cannot have her using the dative right and left on every occasion. Tell her it won't do." "Yes, sir," said little William.

Considering the intensity of his literary labors over the years, the Leacock estate amounted to relatively little—some fifty thousand dollars in securities, his Old Brewery Bay property, his town house. Rumor had it that he had lost heavily in the stock market crash, but this was not so. His small holdings had been widely and safely spread. But he had achieved his principal aim—to set up a trust fund for his son. This ran well over a hundred thousand dollars. In his will he remembered all his faithful help at the farm, as well as his closest relatives and friends. All his manuscripts immediately "findable" were consigned to McGill University. The copyright on all his unpublished material was left to his niece, Barbara Nimmo.

In the ensuing months Mrs. Nimmo gave her full attention to the preparation of the contents for *Last Leaves*, which was published in the following year. Much of the mixture by the old brewmaster was infused with the sparkle and taste of the early Leacock. The wartime pieces showed him waving his prejudices proudly, damning the Japanese and Germans with great fervor, and citing the British race as virtually the only hope for civilization. While there was hardly a timeless quality about these topical outbursts, a muted and more reflective Leacock recalled the virtues of Izaak Walton, extolled the value of taking walks (but not with women!) looked to the future of urban living, or worried about the state of education. In his advice "To Every Child" he wrote:

> Try to buy happiness, by the quart or by the yard, and you never find it. Motion it away from you while you turn to Duty, and you will find it waiting beside your chair. So with Good Will on Earth. Cannons frighten it. Treaties fetter it. *The Spirit brings it.*

A different spirit manifested itself in the unfinished autobiography, as though he were being forced to talk about himself and his kin against his wishes. *The Boy I Left Behind Me* (a title which his son thinks Stephen Leacock would have disliked) found the humorist at times cantankerous, discursive and inaccurate. Only four chapters were completed at his death and Leacock only deals with the first years of his life. What the final document would have been like, assuming he had adhered to the rambling pattern, one hesitates to think. Among other certainties, it would have been wearyingly repetitive.

In the absence of his own personal summing up, it is left to those of us who knew the man as well as his writing to venture some conclusions, and let others surmise to their heart's content. In making judgments, it is imperative to be mindful of Keats's observation that "A man's life of any worth is a continual allegory, and very few eyes can see the mystery of his life. . . ."

In Stephen Leacock's case pertinacity surmounted early adversity and subsequent personal sorrow. He fought to "get above the average," ultimately surpassing his fondest expectation. He felt what all geneticists know, that all men are not born equal, and that his own case was one proof. Yet there were moments, as he confessed in his closing days, when "back I slip to such crazy ideas as that all men are equal. . . ."

Stephen Leacock's Victorian background shaped him for life. Anticipating future biographers, he readily admitted this in the first paragraph of *The Boy I Left Behind Me*:

> I was born in Victorian England on December thirtieth in 1869, which is exactly the middle year of Queen Victoria's reign. If I were analyzed by one of those scientific French biographers who take full account of the time, the place, the circumstances, or by the new school of psychologists who study "behavior," I imagine much could be made of this. As expressed in a plain sense, I am certain I have never got over it.

Much has to be made of this. It colored his whole field of thought, in and out of academic life. He was slow to change, frequently opposing change because he believed firmly that the new standards fell short of the old values (though he was even to question some of the latter). He could never fully, however much he may have tried, come to terms with such obvious developments as the emancipation of women or the welfare state or the new economics, or the dominance of science.

If Mark Twain was right and the secret of humor itself is not joy but sorrow, Leacock's life story is the perfect illustration. The bright facade which so effectively masked the melancholy was not maintained without courage.

When Leacock entered the second half of his life span as both an established academic and an established humorist, he faced what was indeed a moment of truth. The problem which then presented itself echoed John Heywood's much-battered challenge: "Would ye both eat your cake and have your cake?" There was no doubt in Leacock's mind. Thenceforward he pursued two disparate objectives—the prestige of an academic economist and the fame and fortune of a wit. In the process, inevitably his undisputed gifts were spread thin. In both spheres material success came his way; divided loyalties denied him complete supremacy in either.

Literary surgeons have sliced him up and laid him out in pieces for investigation—as a satirist, an economist, a parodist, an historian, a public performer, an ironist, a political scientist, a burlesque artist, a tippler, a fisherman, a politician, a gardener, a parent, an administrator, a sailor, an actor, even as a potential novelist. At no one time did he ever begin to be any one of these, exclusively.

But some of us are sure where his true happiness lay. The power to touch the risible nerve of millions should have been spiritually as well as financially rewarding. His own fulfilment, however, had less to do with millions than with thousands. It was implicit in his lovely description of a true university—"the shaded caravanserai in a long and weary pilgrimage."

Thirty-seven days before Stephen Leacock died, he kept a promise to McGill's graduating class of 1944. He had written the last of some two dozen annual messages to the young men and women in their final college year. A covering letter, in uncommonly legible penmanship, explained that the state of his health at first had forced him to aim at writing not more than a couple of sentences—"but I found that, like all professors, I couldn't be brief if I tried."

Penned under the most distressing physical conditions, and at a time when war raged in all parts of the globe, the message constituted a plea to the younger generation to try to make a better world "in the best traditions of honor, courage and decency."

They were in a position to do so, he argued, for they had been equipped and trained and inspired by their university experience. Nor had his fatal illness dulled his sense of humor:

A college is a queer place, full of freak characters and odd activities, with alternating aspects of drowsy inefficiency and alert effectiveness; a queer place, but it gets there just the same. If all the world did its work as well as the college does, then the world, in the words of the old song, "would do very well then." You are a product of the college: see to it that what you do justifies what the college has done. You carry away a parchment—keep it. In the time being its utility is small although even now you can use a McGill degree as constructive evidence of mental sanity, barring any direct evidence to the contrary; and even now you will find that your degree is accepted practically everywhere as absolving you from any test of illiteracy except as a mere matter of form.

In the first eagerness of life's struggle the college seems left behind and but little thought of; but as the years pass and the foreground of life loses its color and its interest in favor of the deeper background, your memory of college will rise before your mind in an outline as deep and firm as that of some ageing picture which a garish illumination confuses and a softened light revives.

Here, at death's door, Stephen Leacock spoke with his entire being: the man whose highest art was not to amuse, or to teach in the ordinary sense of the word, but whose great historical sense and earthy humanity were employed to awaken the natural curiosity of young minds and to propel them into channels of independent thought.

This was Stephen Leacock's most enduring contribution.

McGill's Leacock

A decade after the death of Stephen Leacock, Dr. Richard Pennington, the then librarian of McGill University wrote:

> Whether we like it or not—and we do—the name of Leacock is inseparably connected in the minds of many with McGill. The first inquiry of the American pilgrim is always for our Leacock shrine; and their astonishment at not finding it just about equals our embarrassment at not having one.

With the passage of still another decade the McGill authorities at last did something about the oversight. The university commemorated the professor-humorist in concrete terms. A large extension to the Old Arts building in which he taught was named the Stephen Leacock Building, and a Leacock Room in the central library was established.

By so designating the new structure on the campus, as the then Principal and Vice-Chancellor Dr. H. Rocke Robertson put it, McGill was perpetuating the name of "the scholar who for thirty-five years, from 1901 to 1936, was a beloved teacher in the social sciences, who won world-wide renown as a man of letters, and who brought great honor to the university."

The eight-storey building, which is devoted to the humanities and

251

social sciences, was dedicated on October 7, 1965, by His Excellency Major-General Georges P. Vanier, Governor-General of Canada.

The Leacock Room—the "shrine" as Dr. Pennington called it—is located in the rare-books section of the university's McLennan Library. The oak-panelled room, which contains the desk the humorist used in his Arts building office, has ceiling-high bookshelves on two sides. On these are displayed many original manuscripts (including *Arcadian Adventures with the Idle Rich*) and, among other papers and books, eighty-one Leacock first editions (plus articles in nearly two hundred periodicals) which were the gift of Norman H. Friedman of Montreal, a former student and friend of the professor.

On the wall facing the books hangs the portrait of Leacock in old age painted by Fred Taylor—more gnarled than jovial, though a fine piece of character portraiture.

In recent years a number of McGill graduates have been evidencing concern over the division of Leacock treasures now existing between the university and the Stephen Leacock Memorial Home at Orillia (see Appendix II). They have expressed the feeling that everything of a literary nature relating to the distinguished professor-writer should be brought under one roof at the college which he served for so long. An informal committee has been set up to look into the possibility of effecting this desirable end.

On November 12, 1969, the Canadian Government marked the centenary of the humorist's birth by issuing a special six-cent postage stamp. With the active co-operation of the Canadian Post Office Department, the Graduates' Society of McGill University mailed in a "first-day cover" to some sixty thousand graduates all over the world a biographical brochure along with selected quotations from Leacock's humorous works.

One former honors student and close friend of the great man remarked on the occasion of this stamp issue: "Wouldn't Stephen Leacock have loved it if he knew that twenty-two million Canadians were licking his backside!"

Orillia's Leacock

On July 5, 1958, Stephen Leacock's estate at Old Brewery Bay near Orillia, Ontario (the Mariposa of *Sunshine Sketches of a Little Town*), was declared by the Canadian Government to be a national historic site. Thenceforth it has been known as the Stephen Leacock Memorial Home.

A few years earlier the rambling, nineteen-room frame house and thirty-two acres of pleasant lakeside grounds had been sold by the humorist's son, Stephen, Jr., to a private purchaser. The property was later bought from the latter by the citizens of Orillia, who had conducted a fund-raising campaign over many months in order to acquire and restore the premises as a Leacock shrine and tourist attraction. The civic bylaw establishing it as such was subsequently confirmed by an act of the Ontario legislature.

The home is maintained and operated by a board of eight members, who are elected annually. Since its inauguration the home has been supervised during the summer months by Dr. Ralph L. Curry, professor of English at Georgetown College, Kentucky. With a small staff to assist him, Dr. Curry has sorted and catalogued the contents of a dozen large packing cases of Leacock's private papers, amounting to about twenty thousand items. He is also the author of the first biography of Stephen Leacock.

The main house, which is open to the public from June until mid-September for a small admission fee, contains a display of memorabilia ranging from original manuscripts to personal letters, from photographs to cancelled cheques, and from accounts books of the farm to personal mementoes. Guides conduct tours through the house and grounds.

The original memorial committee, which was largely responsible for bringing these plans to fruition, was renamed the Stephen Leacock Associates. The organization has drawn its membership from Leacock fans throughout Canada, the United States and the United Kingdom.

The Associates continue to supervise the annual award of the Leacock Medal for Humor, struck in 1947, which is presented at a dinner held in Orillia in early June for the best book of humor by a Canadian author.

As well as being represented on the Stephen Leacock Memorial Home Board, the Associates maintain an educational committee which works to provide scholarships and awards for student writing, creative or research, humorous or scholarly, in fields related to Leacock and to Canadian humorous literature.

In May 1970, the government of Ontario, through the Stephen Leacock Centennial Committee, arranged a commemoration ceremony at Swanmore, Hampshire, at which time a plaque was placed on the cottage in which Stephen Leacock was born one hundred years before.

In July, 1970, a mountain in the Yukon's Saint Elias range was named after the Canadian humorist. Rising 10,200 feet, Mount Leacock looms over an arm of the Kashawulsh Glacier, worlds away from the gentle landscapes of Swanmore and Orillia.

Sunshine Sketches of a Little Town

Considered to be Canada's most valuable literary manuscript, the handwritten original of *Sunshine Sketches of a Little Town* was presented to the Stephen Leacock Memorial Home twenty-two years after the author's death in 1944.

Throughout this period the manuscript had been in the possession of Mrs. Donald Nimmo, of Bloomfield Hills, Michigan, niece of the humorist and executrix of his estate. Fully aware of its great value in the literary market and of the fact that various institutions in the United States were ready to bid for it, Mrs. Nimmo accepted a much lower figure than the market value when she was assured that *Sunshine Sketches* would be certain of a home in Orillia, Ontario, the town which was the inspiration for the book.

In 1966 John G. McConnell, president and publisher of *The Montreal Star* and president of the Montreal Standard Publishing Company, Ltd., bought the manuscript for the sum of $20,000 and presented it to the Stephen Leacock Memorial Home.

It was in 1912 that Sir Hugh Graham (later Lord Atholstan), founder and then publisher of *The Montreal Star*, commissioned Leacock to write a series of articles, "to be typically Canadian," which were to become the famous *Sunshine Sketches*. These appeared every Saturday in *The Star* from February 17 to June 22 of

255

that year. They were then incorporated into a book which has generally been accepted as one of the most Canadian ever written.

A second-impression copy of *Sunshine Sketches* of special interest is now owned by Mrs. Peter M. McIntyre, of Westmount, Quebec. This was presented to her father, Colonel J. J. Creelman, who had been a pupil of the humorist at Upper Canada College. The two subsequently became "bosom pals."

Affixed to the frontispiece of this autographed copy was a document written in Leacock's hand detailing the "plans and ideas" and "the beginning (the Genesis) of the book."

In 1953 *Sunshine Sketches* was adapted for radio by Mavor Moore, Canadian producer and writer, and presented by the Canadian Broadcasting Corporation. The following year this musical comedy version was produced on CBC television. In 1956 Moore's full-length stage adaptation toured the country. It has been revived a number of times.

It was stipulated in the purchase of the manuscript that if the Stephen Leacock Memorial Home ever should be terminated, the manuscript will be presented to McGill University.

Articles Lost and Found

Almost all Leacock's humorous books are collections of articles, essays and sketches which had been published previously in periodicals and newspapers. Many of these have had to be treated separately in this volume in the interest of chronology.

For the convenience of the reader these pieces are listed below together with (on the right) the titles of the books in which they eventually appeared. In the Index, of course, they appear under the titles of the respective books.

"All is not Lost"	*Model Memoirs*
"Back from the Land"	*Frenzied Fiction*
"Boarding House Geometry: Definitions and Axioms"	*Literary Lapses*
"Boy who Came Back, The"	*Hohenzollerns in America, The*
"Buggam Grange: A Good Old Ghost Story"	*Winsome Winnie*
"Butler of the Old School, A"	*Wet Wit and Dry Humor*
"Cast Up by the Sea"	*Over the Footlights*
"Come and See Our Town"	*Dry Pickwick, The*
"Confessions of a Soda Fiend"	*Wet Wit and Dry Humor*
"Curie, Madame Marie (radium)"	*Winnowed Wisdom*
"Darwinian theory"	*Winnowed Wisdom*
"Dead Man's Gold"	*Over the Footlights*

"Raft, The"	*Over the Footlights*
"Ram Spudd: The New World Singer"	*Moonbeams from the Larger Lunacy*
"Recent Advances in Science"	*Winnowed Wisdom*
"Restoration of Whiskers, The"	*Garden of Folly, The*
"Rival Churches, The"	*Arcadian Adventures with the Idle Rich*
"Rutherford, Sir Ernest (the atom)"	*Winnowed Wisdom*
"Shakespeare, William"	*Winnowed Wisdom*
"Short Circuits in Literature"	*Short Circuits*
"Side Lights on the Superman: An Interview with General Bernhardi"	*Moonbeams from the Larger Lunacy*
"Soul Call, The"	*Over the Footlights*
"Split in the Cabinet, The, or The Fate of England"	*Winsome Winnie*
"Stamp Album World"	*Short Circuits*
"Story of the Professor, The Gold Fish and the Policeman"	*Too Much College*
Straits Settlements, The (verse)	*Over the Footlights*
"This Strenuous Age"	*Frenzied Fiction*
"Three Score and Ten"	*Last Leaves*
"To Every Child"	*Last Leaves*
"Transit of Venus, The"	*My Remarkable Uncle*
"War Sacrifices of Mr. Spugg"	*Hohenzollerns in America, The*
"War-time Santa Claus"	*My Remarkable Uncle*
"White House Without In, The"	*Further Foolishness*
"Who do You Think? or, The Mixed-up Murder Mystery"	*Winsome Winnie*
"Yahi-Bahi Oriental Society, The"	*Arcadian Adventures with the Idle Rich*

One article was never published. In March 1944, Leacock wrote an article entitled "World Co-operation After War." The manuscript is now preserved in a case on an Upper Canada College wall.

The article begins:

> I believe that a post-war world of great happiness is within the reach of mankind provided always that mankind can make the moral effort of such a reach. This would be based on one of the oldest and most beautiful ideals of humanity, peace on earth; good will towards man.

Above the shaky signature of a man writing from a hospital bed the discussion of the world's future hopes ends:

> All these things will depend for success not on the letter but the spirit. In the long run there is only that.

One week later Stephen Leacock died.

Notes on Chapters

NOTE: Unless otherwise indicated, page numbers of Leacock's humorous works cited below refer to reprints in the McClelland and Stewart New Canadian Library series.

Chapter I

Page

1   "It is the wont . . ."—*Charles Dickens*, by Stephen Leacock. Doubleday, Doran, New York, 1933.

1   "I always feel . . ."—*The Boy I Left Behind Me*, by Stephen Leacock. Doubleday, New York, 1946, p. 67. (Hereinafter referred to as *The Boy*.)

1–2   Leacock's family background—*The Boy*.

2   E. P. Leacock—*My Remarkable Uncle*, p. 14.

2–5   Agnes Emma Butler's family background—Letters to the author from Miss Catherine Butler, Victoria, B.C.; conversation with Brig. H. D. G. Butler, Bury Lodge, Hambledon, Hants, England; Agnes (Butler) Leacock's brief diary at Stephen Leacock Memorial Home, Old Brewery Bay, Orillia, Ont.; and *The Boy*.

3   Leacock on cricket—*The Boy*, p. 15.

3   "hit-and-miss player"—"Stephen Leacock," by Pelham Edgar, *Queen's Quarterly*, LIII (May, 1946). (Hereinafter referred to as Pelham Edgar.)

3   Marriage—certified copy of an entry of marriage issued by General Register Office, Somerset House, London, June 11, 1969.

3   Agnes Leacock as watercolorist—letter to the author from Mrs.

Donald Nimmo, Bloomfield Hills, Mich., Leacock's niece.

4   Marriage settlement—in files at Stephen Leacock Memorial Home (hereinafter referred to as Memorial Home).

4   Maritzburg episode—Agnes Butler's diary; also *The Boy*, p. 18.

5   Stephen's birth and father's occupation—certified copy of an entry of birth issued by General Register Office, Somerset House, London, June 17, 1969.

6   Confusion re birthplace—*The Boy*, p. 10.

6   Shoreham-by-the-Sea—*The Boy*, p. 21.

6   Kansas adventure—*The Boy*, p. 21.

6   "Simple people, like . . ."—*My Remarkable Uncle*, p. 16.

7   Tim Butler's V.C.—letter to the author from Miss Catherine Butler.

7   Priory Church—from "A Short History of the Priory Church of S. Mary in the Close", available at the church, Porchester, Hants.

7–8   *Chesapeake* affair—*The Boy*, pp. 32–35; also, conversation with present millowners, Wickham, Hants.

7   Return to Porchester—*The Boy*, pp. 31–32.

8–9   Leacock farm near Sutton, Ont.—*The Boy*, chapter, "Life on the Old Farm."

9   "Who wouldn't be?"—*My Remarkable Uncle*, p. 120.

9   *S.S. Sarmatian*—*The Boy*, pp. 50–51.

9   Sea shanties—*My Remarkable Uncle*, pp. 165–66.

Chapter II

11   Old Tommy—*The Boy*, p. 62.

11–12   Farm description—*The Boy*, pp. 53–63.

13   "Perhaps the old farm . . ."—*My Remarkable Uncle*, p. 24.

13   School Section No. 3—*The Boy*, pp. 65–71.

13   Children's reading—*The Boy*, p. 81.

13–14   "When I was a boy . . ."—Report in *The Gazette*, Montreal, May 27, 1925, of Leacock address to the Canadian Historical Association.

13   "Tom Sawyer . . ."—"What I Read as a Child," *The Library and Its Contents*, ed. Harriet P. Sawyer. Classics of American Librarianship, 1925, pp. 143–44.

14   E.P.—*My Remarkable Uncle*, p. 14.

15–16   "Memories of Christmas"—*My Remarkable Uncle*, p. 106.

16   "Hoodoo McFiggin's . . ."—*Literary Lapses*, p. 76.

16   "Showing off"—letter to the author from Mrs. Agnes Robinson, New York City

16   "Cease to be gentlemen . . ."—*The Boy*, p. 72.

16   "Social life . . ."—*The Boy*, p. 81.

17   Mr. Park—*The Boy*, pp. 74–78.

17–18   Dr. Noble tribute—*The McGill News*, autumn issue, 1931.

18   Leacock brothers at UCC—*The Roll of Pupils at Upper Canada*

College; January 1830, to June 1916. Kingston, Ont., 1917, p. 365.

18   "A school for gentlemen"—*My Remarkable Uncle*, p. 24.

19   Scarlatina—*Stephen Leacock, Humorist and Humanist*, by Ralph L. Curry. Doubleday, New York, 1959, p. 34. (Hereinafter referred to as Curry biography.)

19   School record—School report, 1882, in Memorial Home files.

19   Mrs. Leacock's move to Toronto—Curry biography, p. 36.

20   "The rotten place . . ."—*The Boy*, p. 101.

20   "We grow tired of . . ."—Author's conversation with Dr. G. P. Grant, McMaster University, Hamilton, Ont.

20   ". . . this new integument . . ."—*The Boy*, p. 125.

20   Fifth form prizes—UCC *College Times*, November 4, 1886. Leacock was editor of the paper during this period.

21   Election comment—editorial in *College Times*, January 27, 1887.

21   Comment on literature—editorial in *College Times*, December 2, 1887.

21   Signed verse—*College Times*, June 9, 1887.

21   Matriculation—Leacock won the University Honors at matriculation competition. In the school hall his name appears on the honors list to the right of the front platform, while his name appears in the list of head boys flanking the platform on the other side.

22   Father's "brutality"—*The Boy*, p. 100.

22   Father's departure—episode at the railway station as related by Stephen's brother, George.

22–23   Father's estate settlement—*The Surviving Trustee of the will of T. M. Leacock deceased with the children of W. P. Leacock deceased*, and other documents in the files of the Memorial Home.

23   "Got rid of the rotten . . ."—*The Boy*, p. 101.

23   University of Toronto exam results—University of Toronto Class and Prize Lists, 1888.

Chapter III

25   . . . grudgingly conceded . . .—*The Boy*, p. 151.

26   "Easy and agreeable . . ."—*The Boy*, p. 162.

26   "My education . . ." *The Boy*, p. 154.

26   Strathroy Collegiate—*The Boy*, p. 156.

26   Incident with principal—*The Boy*, p. 159–

26   "The need for human kindliness . . ."—*The Boy*, p. 160.

26–27   Arthur W. Currie—*The Boy*, p. 160.

27   Language specialist—*The Boy*, p. 163.

27   Harry Park—*The Boy*, p. 165.

28   "Dull as ditchwater . . ."—*The Boy*, p. 167.

28   "A couple of glasses . . ."—*The Boy*, p. 173.

28   School trustees—*The Boy*, p. 181.

28   Junior master—*The Boy*, p. 181.

29   Leacock and women—Dr. G. P. Grant in conversation with the author.
29   *The Varsity*—Vol. X, 1890.
30   "Above the average"—Curry biography, p. 173.
30   "A job with a blind wall . . ."—*My Remarkable Uncle*, p. 50.
30   John Stuart Mill—*My Remarkable Uncle*, p. 50.
31   Sentimental fiction—Pelham Edgar.
31   UCC staff troubles—Pelham Edgar, pp. 174–77.
31–32 Salary letter—S. Boy Millen, O.B.E., Montreal, in conversation with the author.
32   Parkin anecdote—Curry biography, pp. 64–65.
33   Beatrix Hamilton—Curry biography, pp. 65–66.
34   Marriage—certificate No. 13050, Bureau of Records and Statistics, City of New York.
35   University of Chicago comment—letter to the author from Dr. Jacob Viner, Princeton, N.Y.
35   Oral exam—*Record of Work, Stephen Butler Leacock*, University of Chicago.
35   Doctor on ship—*Leacock's Montreal*, ed. John Culliton. McClelland & Stewart, Ltd., Toronto, 1963, Preface, p. vii.
35   "In a moment of false . . ."—preface to the original edition of *Sunshine Sketches of a Little Town.*

Chapter IV

37   Prof. Mavor—Curry biography, pp. 59–60.
38   McGill appointment—"The Flight of College Time," *McGill Fortnightly Review*, I (November 21, 1925), p. 3.
38   Arts '02 gesture—*The McGill News*, autumn issue, 1936.
38   Old McGillian—George E. Cole, Winnipeg, Man.
38–39 Turn-of-century Montreal—*Leacock's Montreal*, p. 216.
39   Second honeymoon—Curry biography, p. 70.
39   Arts' enrolment—figures furnished by Colin McDougall, registrar, McGill University.
39   "McGill doesn't have to . . ."—*Leacock's Montreal*, p. 303.
39   Murray G. Brooks' diary—letter to the author from Mrs. John Ellis Gilbert, Easthampton, Mass.
40   "Over a prescribed ground . . ."—*My Discovery of England*, p. 82.
40–41 Three students incident—George S. Currie, McGill '11, Montreal, in conversation with the author.
41   *Elements of Political Science*, by Stephen Leacock. Houghton Mifflin, New York, 1906—Curry biography, p. 72.
41   "Leacock's abilities . . ."—Leacock's letters to Principal Peterson concerning Bryn Mawr and request for salary increase in McGill Archives.
42   Leave of absence—McGill University board of governors' minutes, 1905.

42   "He let it be known . . ."—Dr. Flux' letters to Principal Peterson concerning Leacock in McGill Archives.

42   Associate professor—board of governors' minutes, 1906.

43   Rutherford–Mrs. Leacock—as told to the author by W. E. Gladstone Murray.

43   Dean Johnson—*The McGill News*, summer issue, 1943.

43–44   Goldfish story—*Too Much College*. Dodd, Mead. New York, 1939, p. 221–23.

44   "In the Spring of 1907 . . ."—Correspondence between Governor-General Earl Grey, Stephen Leacock and Principal Peterson in McGill Archives.

44   Cecil Rhodes Trust—H. A. Innes in *Canadian Journal of Economics*, X (May, 1944), pp. 216–17.

45   Leave of absence—McGill board of governors' minutes, 1907.

45   Departs on tour—Curry biography, pp. 73–74.

46   "When I state that these . . ."—*Canada*, Aug. 23, 1911. Also, *Sunshine Sketches*, preface, p. xv.

46   Letter to sister—Miss Grace Crooks on "A Taste of Humor," *Canadian Library Journal*, May–June 1969, p. 223.

46   Later letter to sister—Miss Grace Crooks, p. 224.

47   Letter to mother—in files at Memorial Home.

47   "To take charge"—McGill board of governors' resolutions book, March 23, 1908.

47   Appointed chairman—board of governors' resolutions book, 1933.

47   University Club—archives of the University Club of Montreal.

47   Mausoleum Club—Stephen Leacock in conversation with the author, 1927.

48   Orillia property—Orillia, N.S., book 2, Registry Office, Simcoe County, Ont., p. 346

48   Old Brewery Bay address—Mrs. Barbara Nimmo's preface in *Last Leaves*. Dodd, Mead. New York, 1945.

48   Vegetables anecdote—letter to the author from Mrs. Eleanor Cruickshank, McGill '10, Toronto, Ont.

49   "Literary files"—as told to the author by B. K. Sandwell, 1947.

49   Manuscript rejection—holograph note in autographed first edition copy inscribed (December 12, 1934) to his friend Norman H. Friedman, in Friedman collection, Leacock Room, McLennan Library, McGill University.

50   Negotiations with Gazette Printing Co.—correspondence in Memorial Home files.

50   John Lane episode—letter to the author from S. R. Norris Hodgins, M.A. '29, Ottawa, Ont.

51   C. Harold Hale letter—This letter (March 25, 1910, in Memorial Home files) was typed, an unusual procedure for Leacock, who rarely used a typewriter.

52   *Harper's* letter—in Memorial Home files.

Chapter V

53   "I did not permanently..."—*How to Write*. Dodd, Mead. New York, 1943. Preface, p. v.

53   Leacock's economics—letter to the author from Dr. Jacob Viner.

54   Imperial Federation exam—A. Sydney Bruneau, Q.C., McGill '17, Montreal, in conversation with the author.

54   "Tut, tut..."—Bruneau.

54   Classroom humor—Bruneau.

54   *Novels in Nutshells*—series, ten in number, began in *Saturday Night, December* 10, 1910.

56–57   "Awful formulas" in literature—correspondence between the author and Dr. Alexander Cowie, professor emeritus, Wesleyan University, Middletown, Conn.

57   Montreal residence—Leacock occupied his Cote des Neiges house from 1911 until 1940. It was sold shortly after his death in 1944, and demolished in the 1950s when construction on the new Montreal General Hospital began.

57   Sleeping outdoors—as told to the author by Miss Grace Reynolds, Point Claire, P.Que., who served as secretary to Leacock from 1924 to 1927.

57   The professor was heading...—as told to the author by W. E. Gladstone Murray, 1961.

57   *The Martlet*—McGill undergraduate publication ran from October 1908 until May 1911. W. E. Gladstone Murray was its last editor.

58   *The McGill Daily* founding—W. E. Gladstone Murray in conversation with the author, 1961.

58   G. K. Chesterton—article by W. E. Gladstone Murray in *The Telegram*, Toronto, August 8, 1950.

58   "One of the prizes..."—*Sunshine Sketches*, Preface, p. xiv.

58   Academic estate—*Sunshine Sketches*, Preface, p. xiv.

59   He was in the fight...—the author in conversation with R. H. Babbage, Chambly, P.Que., political reporter at the time.

59   Dr. Hemmeon anecdote—S. Boyd Millen recollection.

59   Fleet Street character—R. H. Babbage recollection.

60   Reciprocity address—letter to the author from Hon. Leslie M. Frost, former premier of Ontario, and friend of Leacock.

60   Leacock and cabinet post—Hon. Mr. Frost.

60   "One of the most brilliant..."—Dr. Eugene A. Forsey, Ottawa, author and economist, former Leacock student and colleague, in a CBC broadcast June 11, 1958.

60–61   "I failed entirely..."—*Leacock's Montreal*, Preface, p. xiii.

61   Origin of *Sunshine Sketches*—article by B. K. Sandwell in *Saturday Night*, Toronto, September 1952.

61–62   Leacock letter—photographic copy in Orillia Public Library, Orillia, Ont.

62   How sketches evolved—B. K. Sandwell, *Saturday Night.*

62   Early Mariposa—*John Ramsay of Kildalton,* by Freda Ramsay. Peter Martin Associates, Toronto, 1969. Diary entry dated Beaverton, Wednesday, August 24, 1870.

62   "Anything so ridiculously . . ."—*Sunshine Sketches,* Preface, pp. xv–xvi.

63   "The great Canadian novelist"—Stephen L. Leacock, the humorist's son, in a CBC broadcast, December 30, 1969, commemorating the centenary of Dr. Leacock's birth.

63   "About seventy or eighty . . ."—*Sunshine Sketches,* Preface, p. xvi.

63   *Varsity* book review—letter to the author from Dr. Douglas Bush, Cambridge, Mass., formerly of Harvard University, et al.

64   Young patient—described in a CBC broadcast by Herbert Stewart, of Orillia. Script supplied to the author by Harry J. Boyle, vice-chairman, Canadian Radio and Television Commission, Ottawa, and perennial "Mayor of Mariposa."

64   Principal Peterson—Edgar A. Collard's chapter in *McGill: The Story of a University,* edited by Hugh MacLennan. George Allen & Unwin, Ltd., London, 1960, p. 82.

65   Lotus Club—"Q.R." in *The Montreal Star,* February 2, 1923. University Club move—archives of the University Club of Montreal.

66   Paris sketches—"Parisian Pastimes" in *Behind the Beyond,* pp. 66–102

66   Literary revenues—in Memorial Home files.

67   There he would head . . .—Mrs. Nimmo's preface, *Last Leaves.*

67   Chicago German friends—as told to the author by A. Sydney Bruneau, Q.C

Chapter VI

69   McGill campus, 1914—*The McGill Daily,* Vols. II and III.

70   Professor du Roure—Mrs. Clifford Powell, Westmount, P.Que., his one-time secretary; Mrs. Donald Nimmo; the McGill archives.

70   The big city—*Leacock's Montreal,* p. 226.

70   G.B.S. quotation—Sidney Brooks on "Mark Twain in England," *Harper's Weekly,* LI (July 20, 1907).

71   Plutoria Avenue—*Arcadian Adventures with the Idle Rich,* p. 1.

71   "I mix a good deal . . ."—*Literary Lapses,* p. 17.

71   "The rich in Montreal . . ."—*Leacock's Montreal,* pp. 234–35.

71–72 *McGill Daily* quotation—Vol. 3, 1914.

72   Leading Presbyterian churches—St. Andrew's and St. Paul's churches.

72   "When a thing is funny . . ."—George Bernard Shaw's *John Bull's Other Island,* Act. II

72   Adcock Brown—*The Glory that was Grub Street.* The Musson Book Company, Ltd., Toronto.

72–73   "The Great Fight"—*Leacock's Montreal*, p. 226.
73   Members of a family—*The McGill Daily*, February 1914.
74   du Roure at war—Leacock tribute, *Old McGill*, 1941.
74   McGill regiment—*The McGill Daily* special war contingent supplement, March, 1915.
74–75   Knight errantry—letter to the author from W. G. Cuttle, Hudson Heights, P.Que.
75   Belgian Relief Fund—*The McGill Daily, December*, 1914.
75   Mayor of Nantes—*My Discovery of the West*. John Lane, The Bodley Head, London, 1937, p. 25.
75   Chairman's remarks—*My Discovery of England*, p. 157.
76   Birth of son—Curry biography, p. 121.
76–77   Letter to mother—in Memorial Home files
77   Mrs. Leacock's character—information drawn from numerous sources, but particularly from Mrs. H. M. Little, Montreal; Miss Grace Reynolds, Pointe Claire, P.Que.; Mrs. Nimmo and Mrs. Edward B. Savage, Montreal.

Chapter VII

79   Co-ed enrolment—Colin McDougall, registrar, McGill University.
80   All-female college—*Old McGill*, 1931.
80   "There is no use pretending..."—*My Discovery of England*, pp. 90–91.
80   Practical alternatives—*My Discovery of England*, p. 91.
80–81   "College education for girls..."—"Woman's Level" in *Last Leaves*.
81   "Either angels or..."—address to Women's Art Society, Montreal, 1934.
81   "Women are not humorous..."—*Humor and Humanity*. Thornton Butterworth, Ltd., London, 1937, p. 143.
81   "A witty woman..."—George Meredith in *Diana of the Crossways*, 1885.
81   "Are witty women..."—*Last Leaves*, p. 6.
81   "Many of our so-called..."—*Humor: Its Theory and Technique*, John Lane, The Bodley Head, London, 1935, p. 222.
81   "Noxious atmosphere"—*Humor: Its Theory and Technique*, pp. 266–67.
82   Basil Macdonald Hastings—correspondence in Memorial Home files.
82   Spiritualism lecture—*The Montreal Star*, February 20, 1920.
82   "Q" staged—information supplied by editor and staff of *The Stage*, London.
83   Century Publishing Co.—letter in Memorial Home files.
83   London Theatre Co.—letter in Memorial Home files.
83   American agent—letter in Memorial Home files.
83   V. C. Clinton-Baddeley—correspondence in Memorial Home files.
83   *Behind the Beyond* staged—information supplied by editor and staff of *The Stage*, London.

85   "A friend of mine . . ."—*Further Foolishness*, pp. 150–51.

86   Primary condition of humor—*Further Foolishness*, p. 158.

86   "Let Us Learn Russian"—article in the Toronto *Daily Star*, September 23, 1916

86–87   O. Henry—*The New Republic*, IX (December 2, 1916), pp. 120–22; also, Curry biography, p. 111; also, *Wet Wit and Dry Humor*, Dodd, Mead, New York, 1931, pp. 188–89

87   *Essays and Literary Studies*. John Lane, The Bodley Head, London, 1916.

87   Professor Lafleur—Information supplied by H. G. Lafleur, Q.C., Montreal, nephew.

87   "Ordinary people . . ."—*Further Foolishness*, pp. 163–64.

88   J. B. Priestley—Editor's Introduction, *The Bodley Head Leacock*. The Bodley Head, London, 1957, p. 10.

89   Canadian *Punch*—letter in Memorial Home files.

89   "A rather ingenious mixture . . ."—*Further Foolishness*, pp. 156–57.

Chapter VIII

91   "The greatest British . . ."—*The Road Past Vimy, the Canadian Corps 1914–1918*, by D. J. Goodspeed. Macmillan, Toronto, 1969.

91–92   "George Grossmith . . ."—*Further Foolishness*, p. 161.

92–93   Canada, 1917—*Canada's First Century*, by Donald Creighton. Macmillan, Toronto, 1970, pp. 148–54.

93   "You just jot down . . ."—*Frenzied Fiction*, Introduction, p. ix.

94   "It appears that . . ."—*Frenzied Fiction*, pp. 123–24.

94   "If a farmer . . ."—*Frenzied Fiction*, p. 126.

94–95   "Spirit World"—*Frenzied Fiction*, p. 43.

95   "Very dreadful . . ."—*Frenzied Fiction*, p. 110.

96   One young man—as told to the author by A. Gordon Nairn, Oakville, Ont

96   His flask—*Last Leaves*, Mrs. Nimmo's preface.

97   Leacock fined—letter in Memorial Home files.

97   House-building story—*Laugh with Leacock*, p. 99.

98   du Roure story—Mrs. Clifford Powell in conversation with the author.

98   Death of Peterson—Edgar A. Collard in *McGill: The Story of a University*, p. 96.

99   Auckland Geddes—McGill archives.

99–100   Sir Arthur Currie—David L. Thompson in *McGill: The Story of a University*, p. 100.

100   Leaning for advice—Mrs. H. P. McMurray, secretary to McGill Principals Currie, Morgan, Douglas, James, in conversation with the author.

100   Columbia University—letter to the author from John B. Johnson, Short Hills, N.J.

101   Six articles—the *New York Times*: August 31, 1919, IV, 1; September 7, 1919, IV, 7; September 14, 1919, IV, 7; September 21, 1919, II, 4; October 2, 1919, IX, 2; and October 5, 1919, X, 10.
102   Benchley tribute—*Laugh with Leacock*, p. vi.

Chapter IX

103   Lachrymose missive—"Letters to the New Rulers of the World" in *The Garden of Folly*. John Lane, The Bodley Head, London, 1924.
104   Conservative politics—*The McGill News*, summer issue, 1936.
105   *The Unsolved Riddle of Social Justice*. John Lane, The Bodley Head, London, 1920.
105   "With perfect citizens . . ."—*Unsolved Riddle*, p. 113.
106   *The Hohenzollerns in America*. John Lane, the Bodley Head, London, 1919.
106   "To avoid all error . . ."—*Hohenzollerns*, p. 218.
106   Treaty of Utrecht story—told to the author by Hon. Harry P. MacKeen, Q.C., Halifax, N.S.
106   Letter to publisher—Curry biography, p. 137.
107   "Of all the tastes . . ."—Sir Compton Mackenzie's *My Life and Times, Octave Eight, 1939–1946*. Clarke, Irwin & Company, Ltd., Toronto, 1969.
108   Life on "farm"—*Last Leaves*, Mrs. Nimmo's preface.
108–9   Paddling of ducks—Prof. Ralph L. Curry in conversation with the author.
109   Quotations on prohibition—"Letters to the New Rulers of the World" in *The Garden of Folly*.
110   Mark Twain house—letter to the author from Prof. A. C. Cowie, Wesleyan University.
110–11 A twelve-year-old boy—letters to the author from Colin G. Jameson, Eaton's Ranch, Wolf, Wyoming.
111   McGill Political Economy Club—founded by Professors Leacock and Hemmeon in 1913.
111   Course in French—information from Judge R. G. M. Gammell, Montreal
111   Henry Seidel Canby—*The Reader's Encyclopedia of American Literature*, ed. Max J. Herzberg. Thomas Y. Crowell Co., New York, 1962, p. 761.
111–12 John Lane letter—written from New York, November 4, 1921, in files of Memorial Home.
112   Copyright Act—Curry biography, pp. 145–46.
112   Canadian Authors Association—Curry biography, p. 147.
113   Currie anecdote—Leacock's "Some Anecdotes of McGill" in *The McGill News*, summer issue, 1943.
113–14 Currie conversation—told to author by Col. Wilfrid Bovey, 1926.

Chapter X

Chapter XI

129   Mother of Parliaments—*My Discovery of England*, p. 63.

130   "He, before Winston ..."—John Culliton in *The McGill News*, summer issue, 1944.

130   Hemmeon story—told to the author by S. Boyd Millen.

130   St. Lawrence waterway—told to the author by Wallace W. Goforth.

130–31 The enquirer—William Gentleman, janitor, Arts building, retired 1944.

131   Burlesque plays—letter to his American agent, October 1922, in Memorial Home files.

131   *Cast Up by the Sea*—dramatized by V. C. Clinton-Baddeley.

132   Dramatic rights—letter to his American publishers, April 1923, in Memorial Home files.

133   Lacrosse team—V. C. Wansborough in *The McGill News*, winter issue, 1955.

134   *College Days*. John Lane, The Bodley Head, London, 1923.

135   "The Oldest Living Graduate"—first appeared in *Old McGill*, undergraduate annual, 1922.

135   "A member of Leacock's ..."—Jean Martineau, Q.C., Montreal.

135   *Stephen Leacock*, by Peter McArthur, *Makers of Canadian Literature* series. Ryerson Press, Toronto, 1923.

135   Norworth-Bayes episode—letters to the author from Bruce Evans, South Casco, Maine

136–37 Fairbanks-Pickford—story from a number of first-hand sources.

137   Peter McArthur background—Dr. Alec Lucas' introduction in *The Best of Peter McArthur*. Clarke, Irwin & Company, Ltd., Toronto, 1967.

138   Letter to agent—letter to American agent, October 1924, in Memorial Home files.

138   1923 income—Curry biography, p. 161.

Chapter XII

140   Golf accident—letter to the author from Frank Lloyd, Carmel, Calif.

140   Rejection slip—letter from editor, *College Comics*, January 1925, in Memorial Home files.

140   "How I ..." series—letter to American agent, 1925, in Memorial Home files.

140   Famous Players-Lasky—letter of instruction to agent, March 1925, in Memorial Home files.

140   *The Garden of Folly*, John Lane, The Bodley Head, 1924.

141   "The growth of ..."—"The Restoration of Whiskers" in *The Garden of Folly*

141   Export Club—*The Gazette*, Montreal, December 17, 1924.

142   Smith College—letter to author from Mrs. Robert V. Boname, Rye, N.Y

142   Texts—Memorial Home files contain numerous specimens of lecture notes and speech outlines.

142–44 Richmond, Va., incident—letter to author from John Archer Carter, Charlotte, N.C.

144–46 University of Chicago fund drive—copy of Leacock letter sent to author by Eddie N. Williams, vice-president for public affairs, University of Chicago

146–47 McGill *Fortnightly Review*—Leacock articles in *Old McGill*, 1925, and *The McGill Daily*, October 25, 1925; also letter to the author from T. F. M. Newton, Ottawa

147–48 Mrs. Leacock's illness and death—letters to author from Mrs. Marie Monsarrat, Bath, Somerset; *The Gazette*, December 14, 1925; *The McGill Daily*, December 15, 1925.

148   Currie cable—in Memorial Home files.

149   "The real adoring . . ."—*Last Leaves*, p. 4.

Chapter XIII

151   Chapter title—Viola speech, *Twelfth Night*, II, iv, 112.

151   "When Trix died . . ."—remarks to author by Miss Grace Reynolds.

151   Cancer donation—McGill board of governors' minutes, 1926.

151   Cancer quacks—New York Cancer Committee luncheon, June, 1935.

152   "So began a . . ."—Dr. Goldbloom's *Small Patients*, p. 210.

152   Liverpool consultant—Mrs. Monsarrat, Bath, Somerset.

152   New York specialist—correspondence between Dr. Goldbloom and Leacock in Leacock Room and Memorial Home files.

152   Dr. O. Schloss—letter, April 1926, in Memorial Home files.

152   "Sheer brilliance . . ."—*Small Patients*, p. 210.

152   "One morning when . . ."—*Small Patients*, p. 210.

153   Secretarial duties—the author in conversation with Miss Grace Reynolds.

153   *Winnowed Wisdom*, John Lane, The Bodley Head, London, 1926.

153–4   *The Laundry Problem* complaints—as told to the author by Mrs. Nimmo.

154   Average Man, Average Woman—Preface, *Winnowed Wisdom*.

155   "A fad of mine."—Leacock letter to his publishers in Memorial Home files.

155   "Perpetual half-smile"—*Small Patients*, p. 210.

156   French summer school—letter to the author from Dr. Alan Leslie, Los Angeles, Calif.

156–57 "Had he concentrated . . ."—from Dr. Eugene Forsey's CBC broadcast.

157   *Behind the Beyond*, play—opened in London's West End December 31, 1926, closed March 12, 1927.

157   Encyclopaedia Britannica—Curry biography, p. 178.

157   Two cents a word—Leacock letter to T. H. Matthews, then registrar, McGill University, April 12, 1938, loaned to the author by Mr. Matthews.

157–58   Horatio Bottomley—letter, February 28, 1928, to Leacock, in Memorial Home files.

158–59   European trip—told to the author by Miss Grace Reynolds.

158   "On Literature"—*The Times*, London, July 1, 1927, p. 21.

159   "Squeeze it out"—letter from Dodd, Mead, 1928, in Memorial Home files.

159   "If this book . . ."—*Short Circuits*, p. 218.

159   Radio and movies—*Short Circuits*, pp. 93–111.

160   Books for juvenile—*Short Circuits*, pp. 199–203.

160   "The moral of all . . ."—*Short Circuits*, pp. 202–3.

160–61   Golf—*Short Circuits*, p. 38.

161   "Let us say there . . ."—*Short Circuits*, p. 41.

162   New house—Curry biography, pp. 188–90.

163   Barbara Ulrichsen (Mrs. Donald Nimmo)—author in conversation with Mrs. Nimmo and others

Chapter XIV

165   Lecture memorandum—dated October 7, 1928. Leacock distributed the one-page memorandum from his McGill office.

166   Japanese ambassador—as told to the author by Judge R. G. M. Gammell, Montreal.

166   December 7, 1941—as told to the author by D. Lorne Gales, executive director, Graduates' Society of McGill University.

166–67   UCC centenary dinner—UCC *College Times*.

167–68   *The Iron Man and the Tin Woman and Other Futurities*. John Lane, The Bodley Head, London, 1929.

167   Twenty per cent terms—letter from Dodd, Mead, September 6, 1929, Memorial Home files.

168   Literary revenue—in Memorial Home files.

169   Leacock on Depression—John Culliton's Introduction, *Leacock's Montreal*, p. xii.

169   Sir Herbert Holt—as told to the author by H. Carl Goldenberg, Q.C., Montreal.

169–70   *Economic Prosperity in the British Empire*. Constable & Co., Ltd., London, 1930. Macmillan of Canada originally published this under the title of *Economic Integration of the British Empire*.

170   "None of the Dominions . . ."—*Economic Prosperity*, p. 243.

170   Editorially praised—*The Montreal Star*, April 10, 1930.

170   "It bristles with . . ."—*Times Literary Suplement*, 1930, p. 723.

170   Orillia Board of Trade—Curry biography, p. 201.

170–71   Eskimos—the author in conversation with Dr. Leacock, 1927.

171   July campaign—told to the author by John Culliton.

172   *The Leacock Book*. John Lane, The Bodley Head, London, 1930.

172   "A moment ago . . ."—*Laugh with Leacock*, Preface, pp. iv–v. The preface was unsigned.

173   Chic Sale—Curry biography, p. 287; additional information from Mrs. H. M. Little, Montreal.

174   *Wet Wit and Dry Humor*. Dodd, Mead, New York, 1931.

174   "A Butler of the Old School"—*Wet Wit and Dry Humor*, pp. 74–75.

174   Dinner party—told to the author by H. Carl Goldenberg.

174–75 "Confessions of a Soda Fiend"—*Wet Wit and Dry Humor*, pp. 8–92.

Chapter XV

177   Tolstoy on wrinkles—*War and Peace*, Vol. 1 of Penguin Classics edition, p. 176.

177–78 *Back to Prosperity*. Macmillan, Toronto, 1932.

178   Liberal organ—the Toronto *Daily Star*.

178–79 Mrs. H. T. Shaw—background supplied by numerous sources, but principally by Mrs. Nimmo, Mrs. H. M. Little, Dr. Ralph L. Curry, Mrs. Elizabeth Kimball, David Cassils.

178   René du Roure telegram—the author in conversation with David Spielman.

179   *Mark Twain*. Dodd, Mead, New York, 1932.

179   *Lahontan's Voyages*. Graphic Publishers, Ottawa, 1932.

179   Not a cent—holograph note in Friedman copy, Leacock Room, McLennan Library, McGill.

179–80 *The Dry Pickwick*. John Lane, The Bodley Head, 1932.

180   "It would be tedious . . ."—*Mark Twain*, p. 85.

181   Reverence for rank—*Mark Twain at Large*, by Arthur L. Scott. Copp Clark, Toronto, 1969, p. 295.

181   Royal Society—*The Montreal Star*, May 30, 1932.

181–82 Evangelist incident—as told to the author by R. Lyman Williams, Montreal.

182-83 *Stephen Leacock's Plan*. Macmillan, Toronto, 1933.

183   FDR Brains Trust—Papers and Proceedings of the Canadian Political Science Association, V (1933), p. 21.

183   Gold standard incident—Graham F. Towers in CBC broadcast, December 30, 1969, and subsequent letter to the author.

184   Strange oversight—McGill board of governors' minutes, 1933.

184–85 Second-hand bookstore—the author in conversation with Louis Melzack, and Melzack CBC broadcast December 30, 1969.

185–86 Anthology incident—correspondence between the author and Norris Hodgins, Ottawa, Ont.

186–87 *Charles Dickens: His Life and Work*. Peter Davies, London, 1933.

186   "In him was . . ."—*Charles Dickens*, p. 184.

186   "In all the records . . ."—*Charles Dickens*, p. 185.

187   "The best of Dickens . . ."—Prof. G. W. Latham, department of English, McGill University.

187–89 Tribute to Currie—the Montreal *Herald*, December 1, 1933.

189–90 Letter to mother—dated December 7, 1933, in Leacock Room, McLennan Library, McGill.

190 Mother's death—*The Globe*, Toronto, January 30, 1934.

Chapter XVI

191 Newman biography—letter in Memorial Home files.

191 ". . . a religious man . . ."—*Lincoln Frees the Slaves.* Peter Davies. London, 1935, p. 84.

192 "The red man . . ."—*Lincoln*, p. 12.

192–93 Inscription in Mrs. Shaw's copy—Leacock Room, McLennan Library, McGill.

193 "Mr. Shaw never . . ."—letter to the author from F. John L. Evans, Q.C., Hamilton, Ont.

193–94 French luncheon club—as told to the author by Mrs. H. M. Little, Montreal.

194–95 Radio experiment—in conversation with Joseph E. McDougall, Montreal, who kindly supplied extensive documentation.

194 "The clever man's need . . ."—*H. G. Wells: His Turbulent Life and Times*, by Lovat Dickson. Macmillan, London, 1969.

195 Mark Twain Medal—*The Montreal Star*, December 7, 1934; *The Gazette*, Montreal, January 15, 1935.

195–96 Club anniversary—as told to author by A. Sydney Bruneau, Q.C., Montreal.

196 Confidential pamphlet—printed January, 1935.

196 "I know where . . ."—*The McGill News*, spring issue, 1935.

196 "Very naturally . . ."—*The McGill News*, spring issue, 1935.

196 "This socialism . . ."—*The McGill News*, spring issue, 1935.

197 Bank of Canada—as told to the author by S. Boyd Millen, Montreal.

197 R. B. Bennett—letter to Leacock, July 12, 1935, in Memorial Home files.

198 Pierce incident—as described to the author by Hon. Sydney D. Pierce, Ottawa.

199 Retirement action—McGill board of governors' minutes, June, 1935.

199–200 Retirement reaction—as described to the author by David Macfarlane, for forty years the McGill "beat" reporter on *The Montreal Star*

200 Morgan letter—dated November 13, 1935, in Memorial Home files.

200 Sir Edward Beatty—letter dated December 14, 1935, in Curry biography, pp. 248–49.

200 "A cold fish"—Mrs. H. P. McMurray, Montreal.

201 "Rid the university . . ."—letter to the author from Mrs. Rena Patenaude, Victoria, B.C.

201 Pension—McGill board of governors' minutes, June, 1935.

201–2 Private Fitzharris—letter in McGill archives.

Chapter XVII

203   "The piece, while . . ."—*College Comics*, May, 1935, letter.
203   *Vogue* rejection—letter, June, 1936, in Memorial Home files.
203   Dental bills—in Memorial Home files.
203   Obtuse friend—letter signed "Andy" in possession of the author.
203–4   Mrs. R. B. Hamilton—correspondence between Leacock and "Granny" in Memorial Home files.
203–4   "A mixture of . . ."—*Around Toronto*, by John Richmond and Bruce West. Doubleday Canada, Ltd., Toronto, 1969.
204   Louis Kon—correspondence between Kon and Leacock in files of Leacock Room, McLennan Library, McGill.
205   "I am giving up . . ."—copy of mimeographed anouncement in Leacock Room, McGill.
205   "I dropped into . . ."—letter to the author from Professor Sheffield, Toronto.
205–7   *Humor: Its Theory and Technique*. John Lane, The Bodley Head, 1935.
206   *Star* review—*The Montreal Star*, October 22, 1935, signed "D.M.L."
206   Arch absurdist—letter to the author from Mrs. John Cumming, Albany, N.Y
206   "Generally speaking . . ."—S. J. Perelman in the *New York Times Magazine*, January 26, 1969, p. 76.
207   "The wholesale theories . . ."—Jesse Bier in *The Rise and Fall of American Humor*. Holt, Rinehart and Winston, New York, 1968.
207   "In this, if what the . . ."—*Humor: Its Theory and Technique*, pp. 287–88
207–8   *The Greatest Pages of American Humor*. Doubleday & Co., Inc., 1936.
208   Robert Van Gelder—the *New York Times*, March 20 ,1936.
208   *Hellements of Hickonomics*, Dodd, Mead, New York, 1936.
208   *Poetry* magazine—"The Poet as a Funny Man," by John Wheelwright, L (July 1937), p. 211.
209   "I wish you would . . ."—Leacock letter, 1936, to Dr. Gerhard Lomer, librarian, McGill University, in files of Leacock Room, McGill.
209–10 Farewell dinner—*The Gazette*, Montreal, and *The Montreal Star*, May 5, 1936; *The McGill News*, summer issue, 1936.
210   Three weeks later—Report of Convocation, McGill Archives.
210   Citation, LL.D.—McGill Archives.
210   *Times* editorial—the *New York Times*, December 21, 1935.
211   UBC offer—the Toronto *Daily Star*, December 11, 1937; correspondence in Memorial Home files.
211   Proposed tour—correspondence in Memorial Home files.
211   U.K. proposal—*The Daily Express*, London, August, 1937.

211   "Thank you, Mother England . . ."—*Funny Pieces*. John Lane, The Bodley Head, London, 1937, pp. 326–28.

211   "I still believe . . ."—note from Sir Edward Beatty, November 12, 1935, in Memorial Home files.

212   "If I'm too . . ."—in advance notes sent by Leacock to newspaper editors in western Canada, in Memorial Home files.

212   Newspaper series—as told to author by A. J. West, executive editor, *The Montreal Star*, 1946

212   Tour's purpose—*The Montreal Star*, November 10, 1936.

212   "Stephen Junior . . ."—in advance notes sent to western editors.

Chapter XVIII

213   "State of quasi-semi . . ."—phrase used by Sir Edward Beatty in note to Leacock, June 1936, in files of Leacock Room, McGill.

213   Prevailing attitude—*The Montreal Star*, March 6, 1937.

214   "I struck also . . ."—*The McGill News*, winter issue, 1936.

214   Letters from West—Mrs. Nimmo's preface in *Lost Leaves*, and correspondence in files of Memorial Home.

215   *My Discovery of the West*. Thomas Allen, Toronto, 1937.

215–16 *Funny Pieces: A Book of Random Sketches*. John Lane, The Bodley Head, London, 1937

216   "His class?"—*Funny Pieces*, p. 281.

216   *Here are my Lectures*. Dodd, Mead, New York, 1937.

216   Canadian critic—*The Montreal Star*, November 27, 1937, unsigned.

216–17 Investment firm—Johnson, Ring & Co., Toronto.

217   *Other People's Money*—files of Royal Trust, Montreal.

217   Lowell Institute—letter from President Lowell to Leacock, March 9, 1937, in Memorial Home files.

217   Lorne Pierce Medal—Royal Society of Canada, Proceedings and Transactions, XXXI (1937), p. 40.

217   A movement on the part . . .—*The McGill Daily*, October 1937.

217   Ulrichsen-Nimmo wedding—Curry biography, pp. 289–90.

217   Later in the summer—letter to Leacock from Thornton Butterworth, Ltd., London, July 1937.

218   *Humor and Humanity*. Thornton Butterworth, Ltd., London, 1937.

218   Human kindliness—*Humor and Humanity*, Preface, p. 9.

218–19 "The best of Leacock . . ."—J. B. Priestley's introduction, *The Bodley Head Leacock*, 1957.

219   "You see, I . . ."—letter to Mrs. Drinkwater, written in Royal Victoria Hospital, April 5, 1938, in Leacock Room, McGill.

219   *Model Memoirs*. Dodd, Mead & Co., New York, 1938.

220   Newspapers—*Frenzied Fiction*, p. 128.

220   Newspapers—*Moonbeams from the Larger Lunacy*, p. 124.

220   Newspapers—*My Discovery of England*, pp. 28–34.

220   Newspapers—*Short Circuits*, p. 55, p. 167.
220   Newspapers—advance document to Western editors in Leacock Room, McGill.
221   Newspapers—letter to author from Frederick H. Kimball, Watertown, N.Y.
221   Newspapers—letter to author from Richard Hanser, Larchmont, N.Y.
221–22 Newspapers—Stanley Handman, Montreal, in conversation with the author.
222   Newspapers—re the *New York Times*, letter to the author from George F. Bray, Brooklyn, N.Y.

Chapter XIX

223   Boston University—letter, April 14, 1939, in Memorial Home files.
223   Leacock reply—letter, April 19, 1939, in Memorial Home files.
224   "And you've seen . . ."—letter, May 4, 1939, in Leacock Room files, McGill.
224–25 Royal visit article—*The Montreal Star*, February 28, 1959.
225   "Leacock Braves . . ."—*New York Times*, July 10, 1939.
225   "Why, the first . . ."—the Toronto *Daily Star*, July 13, 1939.
225   He was less than light-hearted—correspondence between Stephen and Charlie Leacock in Memorial Home files.
226   Chicken thefts—letters in Memorial Home files.
226   Madeira wine—letters in Memorial Home files.
226–27 Letter to the editor—in Orillia Public Library.
227   Summer at Old Brewery Bay—the author in conversation with David Spielman, Montreal and Chicago.
227   *All Right, Mr. Roosevelt.* Oxford University Press, Toronto, 1939.
227–28 "If any of the . . ."—*All Right, Mr. Roosevelt*, p. 5.
228   "Do you know that . . ."—letter from Sir Edward Peacock in Memorial Home files.
228–29 *Too Much College.* John Lane, The Bodley Head, London, 1940.
228   ". . . in the wider sense . . ."—*Too Much College*, p. 7.
229   "When the world . . ."—*Too Much College*, p. 144.
229   "Take enough . . ."—*Too Much College*, p. 144.
229–30 Leacock dinner—as told to the author by Dr. F. Cyril James.
230–32 Taylor portrait—the author in conversation and correspondence with Frederick B. Taylor, A.R.C.A., San Miguel de Allende, Mexico; also Taylor's account in *The McGill News*, summer issue, 1950.
232   *Our British Empire.* Dodd, Mead, New York, 1940.
232   "In dealing with . . ."—*Our British Empire*, Preface, p. 2.
232–33 Convocation, 1940—as told to the author by Leslie Roberts, Montreal.
233   René du Roure tribute—*The McGill News*, spring issue, 1941; also *Old McGill*, 1941.

233   "Have no idea what . . ."—letter from agent in Memorial Home files.
233   *Canada: The Foundations of Its Future.* "A private and limited edition," Montreal, 1941.
234   Rumor denied—as told to the author by Samuel Bronfman.
234–35 Old Brewery Bay visit—in conversation and correspondence with F. John L. Evans, Q.C., Hamilton, Ont.
235   He threw up his hands—the author in conversation with Samuel Bronfman.

Chapter XX

237   Selznick—letter re *Pickwick Papers*, January 1941, in Memorial Home files.
237   Disney—letter to Disney studios in Memorial Home files.
237   Sacha Guitry—letter to Leacock re subtitles in Memorial Home files.
237–38 Costain—Leacock-Costain correspondence, December 1941, in Memorial Home files.
238–39 *Montreal, Seaport and City.* Doubleday, Doran, 1942; revised edition re-entitled *Leacock's Montreal*, edited with an introduction by John Culliton, McClelland & Stewart, Ltd., Toronto, 1963.
238–39 Mount Royal tunnel—Copy of letter, May 10, 1942, supplied by Mrs. C. J. Warrington, Ottawa, Ont., Dean Brown's daughter.
239   Hochelaga—*The Montreal Star*, December 3, 1969.
239   "There are only . . ."—*The McGill News*, summer issue, 1941.
239   *Our Heritage of Liberty.* John Lane, The Bodley Head, London, 1942.
239   Autobiography—correspondence with Dodd, Mead in Memorial Home files.
240   "The unbeatable quality . . ."—*My Remarkable Uncle*, pp. 19–20.
240   "Character was so . . ."—*My Remarkable Uncle*, p. 14.
240   "He was president . . ."—*My Remarkable Uncle*, p. 16.
241   "Reminded me . . ."—Mrs. Nimmo's preface, *Last Leaves*, p. 19.
241   "I once asked a Christmas . . ."—*My Remarkable Uncle*, p. 116.
241–42 Holgate portrait—correspondence between the author and Edwin Holgate, Morin Heights, P.Que.
242   *How to Write.* John Lane, The Bodley Head, London, 1943.
242   Lomer letter—from Leacock to Lomer, January 11, 1943, in Leacock Room, McGill.
242   South African order—Dr. Lomer, *Stephen Leacock*, McGill, 1936, p. 33.
242   *Happy Stories.* John Lane, The Bodley Head, London, 1943.
242–43 "Poverty" piece—Leacock letter, September 23, 1943, to Clarke, and final acknowledgement, October 2, 1943, in Memorial Home files.
243   Advertisement copy—for Pan American Airways.
243   *Last Leaves.* Dodd, Mead, New York, 1945.

243   The only indication—letter loaned to author by Joseph McDougall, Montreal.

244   Gladstone Murray letters—Curry biography, p. 330.

244   Mrs. Shaw—as told to the author by Mrs. H. M. Little, Montreal.

244   "Did I behave . . ."—*The Telegram*, Toronto, April 11, 1944.

245   "Give me my . . ."—*My Remarkable Uncle*, p. 179.

245   Burial—*The Telegram*, Toronto, April 1, 1944.

245   Tribute—*Christian Science Monitor*, March 30, 1944.

245   Tribute—*College Times*, Upper Canada College, Toronto.

246   Trust and will—Curry biography, pp. 340–41.

246   Izaak Walton—*Last Leaves*, p. 20.

246   On walking—*Last Leaves*, p. 21.

246   "Try to buy . . ."—*Last Leaves*, p. 107.

246–47 *The Boy I Left Behind Me*. Doubleday, New York, 1947.

247   "A man's life . . ."—letter to George and Georgina Keats, February 14–May 3, 1819

247   "I was born . . ."—*The Boy*, p. 9.

248   "Would ye both . . ."—John Heywood's *Proverbs* (1564), Pt. II, Ch. 7.

248   Covering letter—February 19, 1944, *The McGill News*, summer issue, 1944.

249   Message to graduating class—*The McGill News*, summer issue, 1944.

Bibliography

Benchley, Robert. *The Benchley Roundup*. New York: Harper and Bros., 1954.

Bergson, Henri. *Laughter*. New York: The Macmillan Co., 1911.

Bier, Jesse. *The Rise and Fall of American Humor*. New York: Holt, Rinehart & Winston, Inc., 1968.

Booth, Wayne C. *The Rhetoric of Fiction*. Chicago: University of Chicago Press, 1961.

Cameron, Donald. *Faces of Leacock*. Toronto: Ryerson Press, 1967.

Careless, J. M. S., with R. Craig Brown, eds. *The Canadians, 1867–1967 (Part One)*. Toronto: Macmillan Company of Canada, 1968.

Collier's Encyclopedia. New York: Crowell-Collier Publishing Co., 1963.

Culliton, John, ed. *Leacock's Montreal*. Toronto: McClelland & Stewart, Ltd., revised edition, 1963

Curry, Ralph L. *Stephen Leacock: Humorist and Humanist*. New York: Doubleday & Company, Inc., 1959.

Davies, Robertson. *On Stephen Leacock*, in *Our Living Tradition*. Toronto: University of Toronto Press, 1957.

Dickson, Lovat. *H. G. Wells: His Turbulent Life and Times*. Toronto: Macmillan of Canada, 1969.

Dodgson, Charles L. *The Annotated Alice: Alice's Adventures in Wonderland and Through the Looking Glass*. New York: Clarkson N. Potter, Inc., 1960.

Dunne, Finley Peter. *Mr. Dooley at his Best*. New York: Charles Scribner's Sons, 1938.

Frye, Northrop. *Anatomy of Criticism*. Princeton, N.J.: Princeton University Press, 1957.

Goldbloom, Dr. Alton. *Small Patients: The Autobiography of a Children's Doctor*. Toronto: Longmans, Green & Co., Ltd., 1959.

Hackett, Alice Payne. *70 Years of Best Sellers, 1895–1965*. New York: The R. R. Bowker Company, 1967.

Kimball, Elizabeth. *The Man in the Panama Hat: Reminiscences of My Uncle, Stephen Leacock*. Toronto, Montreal: McClelland and Stewart Ltd., 1970.

Klinck, Carl F., ed. *Literary History of Canada*. Toronto: University of Toronto Press, 1965.

Lucas, Alec, ed. *The Best of Peter McArthur*. Toronto: Clarke, Irwin and Company, Ltd., 1967.

McArthur, Peter. *Stephen Leacock*. Toronto: Ryerson Press, 1923.

MacDonald, Dwight, ed. *Parodies: An Anthology from Chaucer to Beerbohm—and After*. New York: Random House, Inc., 1960.

McGill News, The, publication of the Graduates' Society of McGill University, issues from 1919–69.

MacLennan, Hugh, ed. *McGill: The Story of a University*. London: George Allen & Unwin, Ltd., 1960

Partridge, Eric. *The "Shaggy Dog" Story: Its Origin, Development and Nature*. London: Faber & Faber, Ltd., 1953.

Priestley, J. B., ed. *The Bodley Head Leacock*. London: The Bodley Head, 1957.

Scott, Arthur L. *Mark Twain at Large*. Chicago: Henry Regnery, 1969.

White, E. B., and Katherine S., eds. *A Subtreasurery of American Humor*. New York: Random House, Inc., 1941.

Acknowledgements

I wish to thank the following for their kind interest and helpfulness during the preparation of this book:

Dr. H. Rocke Robertson, former principal and vice-chancellor, McGill University; Dr. F. Cyril James, principal emeritus, McGill University; M. C. Lapointe, librarian, *The Montreal Star*; J. G. McClelland, president, McClelland and Stewart, Toronto; Fred Taylor, San Miguel de Allende, Mexico; Samuel and Gerald Bronfman, Montreal; Dr. Ira M. Freeman, Boundbrook, New Jersey; Mrs. H. M. Little, Montreal; Miss Dita Vadron, producer, Canadian Broadcasting Corporation, Toronto; R. V. Rosewarne and Miss L. A. Wraight, National Library, Ottawa.

Hon. Leslie M. Frost, Lindsay, Ont.; Dr. D. W. Sparling, Montreal; Prof. Carl F. Wells, University of Michigan; Miss Grace Crooks, chairman, The Stephen Leacock Associates, Orillia, Ont.; D. Lorne Gales, executive director, the Graduates' Society of McGill University; Joseph Sedgwick, Q.C., Toronto; Eddie N. Williams, vice-president for public affairs, the University of Chicago; Prof. Alexander Cowie, Wesleyan University, Middletown, Conn.; Douglas M. Moseley, president, Canada Wide Feature Service, Ltd., Montreal; Norris Hodgins, Ottawa; H. Carl Goldenberg, Q.C., Montreal; Mrs. S. Waxman, *Saturday Night*, Toronto; Agnes A. Robinson, New York City; S. Boyd Millen, O.B.E., Montreal; Frank Paluka, head of special collections, University of Iowa.

Mrs. Marie Monsarrat, Bath, Somerset, England; Judge R. G. M. Gammell, Montreal; D. H. Rhydwen, *Globe and Mail*, Toronto; Alex Davies, supervisor, information services (English), Canadian Broadcasting Corporation, Montreal; Mrs. John L. Ellis, Southampton, Mass.; Miss Marilyn Lewis, librarian,

Punch, London, England; Mrs. Alton Goldbloom, Montreal; J. A. Russell, Glasgow, Scotland; Dr. Michael Sanders, Boston, Mass.; Miss Catherine Butler, Victoria, B.C.; Mrs. Seton L. Richardson, Montreal; Edwin Holgate, Morin Heights, Quebec; staff of *The Stage,* London, England; T. F. M. Newton, Ottawa; Mrs. Lewis, rare bookroom, McLennan Library, McGill University; David H. Stern, San Diego, Calif.; Mrs. H. G. Stockwell, Montreal; Brig. H. D. G. Butler, Hambledon, Hants, England; F. John L. Evans, Q.C., Hamilton, Ont.; Colin G. Jameson, Wolf, Wyoming.

Andrew Allen, director of alumni relations and administration, the Graduates' Society of McGill University; Miss Helen Wynn, *The Montreal Star;* Dr. Alan Leslie, Los Angeles, Calif.; Louis Jaques, photo editor, *Weekend Magazine,* Montreal; staff of the newspaper section, British Museum, London; Prof. Douglas Bush, Cambridge, Mass.; Mrs. Rena Patenaude, Victoria, B.C.; Joseph E. McDougall, Montreal; T. H. Matthews, Ottawa; Mrs. Robert V. Boname, Rye, N.Y.; Hon. Sydney D. Pierce, Ottawa; David Spielman, Chicago, Ill.; Hon. A. D. P. Heeney, Q.C., Ottawa; Dr. G. P. Grant, McMaster University, Hamilton, Ont.; George S. Currie, Montreal.

Abel Green, editor, *Variety,* New York; David B. Macfarlane, Montreal; John B. Johnson, Short Hills, N.J.; Henri G. Lafleur, Q.C., Montreal; A. Gordon Nairn, Oakville, Ont.; Colin McDougall, registrar, McGill University; Miss F. Samwell, *Queen's Quarterly,* Kingston, Ont.; A. Sydney Bruneau, Q.C., Montreal; Mrs. George Openhym, Wellsville, N.Y.; Stephen Franklin, Stephen Leacock Centennial Committee, Toronto; Henry S. Hamilton, Q.C., Hamilton, Ont.; Richard Apted, director, historical branch, Department of Public Records and Archives, Toronto; Michael McCormick, Montreal; Jack Holton, secretary, board of governors, McGill University.

Dr. Jacob Viner, Princeton, N.J.; Miss Kathleen Jenkins, Montreal; Miss Elizabeth B. McNab, director, McGill Fund Council, Montreal; Miss Eleanor Cruickshank, Toronto; W. G. Cuttle, Hudson Heights, Que.; Eugene F. Forsey, Ottawa; R. A. Sargent, Vancouver, B.C.; Frank Lloyd, Carmel, Calif.; Mrs. Elizabeth Kimball, Toronto; Bruce Evans, South Casco, Maine; Graham F. Towers, Ottawa; Mrs. Edward B. Savage, Montreal; John Archer Carter, Charlotte, N.C.; Stanley Handman, *The Montreal Star;* Mrs. John Cumming, Albany, N.Y.; Harry Shaw, Winnipeg, Man.; Prof. Edward F. Sheffield University of Toronto; Fred H. Kimball, Watertown, N.Y.; Lester Chan, Hong Kong; Mrs. Clifford Powell, Montreal; Bruce N. Jones, associate director, McGill Fund Council; J. C. L. Andreassen, university archivist, McGill University, and staff of the Archives; C. G. Greenshields, Q.C., Montreal; Richard Hanser, Larchmont, N.Y.; Louis Melzack, Montreal; George F. Bray, Brooklyn, N.Y.; Mrs. C. J. Warrington, Ottawa.

Principal Patrick T. Johnson, Howard F. A. Lacey and Harold A. D. Roberts, Upper Canada College, Toronto; Miss Grace Reynolds, Pointe Claire, Que.; Miss Alison Cole, McLennan Library, McGill University; J. Michael McGean, secretary of the college, Dartmouth College, Hanover, N.H.; Miss Maysie S. McSporran, Montreal; Dr. E. Thorburn Cleveland, Montreal; Mrs. Rosemary Eakins, Oxford University; Fred V. Stone, Montreal; Edward Wellen, New Rochelle, N.Y., Edgar A. Collard, editor emeritus, *The Gazette*, Montreal.

Philip D. Jones, University of Chicago Press; Stuart M. Kaminsky, University of Chicago; R. Lyman Williams, Montreal; John F. Barry, Jr., associate editor, *Brown Alumni News*, Brown University, Providence, R.I.; Stanley Triggs, curator, Notman Archives, McCord Museum, McGill University; David A. Cassils, Montreal; Mrs. D. Lorne Gales, Montreal; Dr. Brian Little, Cleveland, Ohio; Alexander Brailow, Keuka Park, N.Y.; Robert Lapalme, Montreal; Queries Editor, *The New York Times Book Review*; Raleigh Parkin, Montreal; Jean Martineau, Q.C., Montreal; Jean-Pierre Rénaud, Paris, France

Hon. Harry P. MacKeen, Q.C., Halifax, N.S.; Harry J. Boyle, Ottawa, Ont.; Pierre Gascon, editor, *Perspectives*, Montreal; Mrs. Lena Newman, Montreal; Ernest Haller, Washington, D.C.; Mrs. Agnes Coffey, Montreal; R. H. Babbage, Chambly, P.Que.; John Brown, Sydney, Australia.

I am particularly grateful to the management of *The Montreal Star* for making it possible for me to concentrate on this biography, and to Douglas M. Gibson, my Doubleday editor, for his patience and wise counsel.

D.M.L.

INDEX

Compiled by Marjorie C. Legate

In "Index: There is no Index" (*My Remarkable Uncle*), Stephen Leacock wrote: "Authors themselves would prefer not to have any. Having none would save trouble and compel reviewers to read the whole book instead of just the Index." Obviously, his biographer disagrees.